# THE DEVIL TO PAY

# THE DEVIL

## A MOBSTER'S ROAD TO PERDITION

# TO PAY

## SEAN SCOTT HICKS

BLACK
STONE
PUBLISHING

First edition: 2024
ISBN 979-8-8748-1050-4
Biography & Autobiography / Personal Memoirs

Version 1

Blackstone Publishing
31 Mistletoe Rd.
Ashland, OR 97520

www.BlackstonePublishing.com

*To Henry Simons for showing me how to be an honorable man
and get through some of the toughest and darkest times in my life.
You were a true guiding light and are in my memories daily.
I will love you always and forever.*

# CONTENTS

# PROLOGUE

Maybe I know only one thing in this loathsome, deteriorating, shit-bucket world—or I know just one thing for sure: the truth, in whatever self-comforting manifestation it's viewed, does not set you free. Or at least not like I've heard it said, and definitely not like I've said it myself to others countless times.

With my breath soaked with whiskey and hands dripping blood, I stood countless times in back rooms, dank cellars, and warehouses, and as I beat and tortured men to confess their secrets to me, I lied to the poor bastards, tricked them. Contrary to what I told them, the truth does not rescue you or make you whole again. There's nothing restorative about it. Telling the truth doesn't suddenly let you surge above the encumbrance of lies, secrets, and lesions of your heart.

The gospels I have learned hold me down like concertina wire in a cold and dark cell. It's a place where the truth is not something to lay eyes on or consider. It is the niche where malevolence waits, where it blows its hot breath—every rancid puff—into your mouth and nose until you choke and cannot abscond from it. Thus, it consumes you. This is what I know. The only fucking thing!

I was well aware of this the day I drove into Boston for a job that would lead me into darkness. At eighteen years old, I knew my life's calling would always take me to the putrid places where evil waits. And still I went, though unprepared for the upcoming moment when the devil himself would crawl from his hiding place. And I was surely not prepared for when he would charge at me like a rabid dog, biting and dragging me down into his cold, black abyss . . .

# ONE

## REDHEADED BASTARD

*"And whosoever was not found written in the*
*book of life was cast into the lake of fire."*
                                    —*Revelation 20:15*

I was unceremoniously flung into this world on the night of September 10, 1971. Evicted—mewling, bawling, shocked by light, gravity, and cacophonous sounds—from an earlier place of warmth and rhythmic beats that had comforted me in an ethereal darkness. I arrived tainted in blood, torn from between quivering legs; the umbilical cord, which had kept me alive inside my mother's toxic womb, was tightly wound around my tiny neck, trying to take me out.

Shit only got worse from there. Before I even took my first breath, some stranger slapped me. I cried, and he slapped me again. The maternity nurses at the South Shore Hospital in Weymouth, Massachusetts, then deposited me into the crux of dear old Mom's arms. Maybe things would have turned out differently if I hadn't been abandoned atop that dreadful bosom. I would have preferred if that sonofabitch had just kept slapping me.

My mother spoke little of her past, reserving those recollections to punctuate her shit-faced, drug-induced rants. However, if you care to put any stock into her version of events, Constance Elaine Hicks was born in the coal-mining town of Fairmont, West Virginia, on September 28, 1939. The family homestead was a three-room tar-paper shack with no running water or electricity. A torrential onslaught of booze combined with a drought of self-control and morals often brought her father's groping hands to her body, usually late at night. Her tears, in her own words, would streak the coal dust transferred onto her cheeks from her father's face during these moments of disgusting closeness. Her insecure mother, for whatever reason, chose not to see or prevent the abuse. This horrendous display of parenting continued habitually until my mother finally fled at age fourteen.

Over the next ten years, my mother found herself in a whirlwind of different men and different beds, bouncing from one part of the country to another. You could find her rubbing elbows with the likes of astronauts and artists, national heroes, mobsters, pimps, and tricks. She walked among giants and lay down with scum. Selling her body from flophouse to flophouse, she managed to support a constant flow of narcotics in her bloodstream. She stuck needles into her arms, powder up her nose, and cocks into every hole she had.

In autumn of 1970, Constance Elaine Hicks gave her nose and veins a break to breathe in the icy, acrid New England air of Marshfield, Massachusetts. She had fucked and sucked her way to spawning two daughters, Heather and Valentina Tomasetti, and was pregnant with her third child, although she didn't know it yet. At the time, she was dating William "Red" Baker and was the mistress of William R. Winter Jr., fucking him on the days he wasn't sticking it in his wife.

Red was a fixer for the Winter Hill Gang at the historic Suffolk Downs racetrack in Revere, Massachusetts—as well as other racetracks along the East Coast. The gang would purchase horses and have them lose their first several races, making these horses eligible for handicap races, where Red and his cohorts would profit from the fixed comebacks. It was Red's job to ensure that the selected horses lost by any means necessary. He would inject the animals with custom cocktails, fracture cannon bones with a hammer, and intimidate or corrupt the jockeys.

Constance's other lover, Bill, was one of four siblings born into a family of German Irish descent. Bill was the older brother of Howie T. Winter, the man who would go on to cofound and eventually lead the country's most powerful Irish American mob: the Winter Hill Gang.

Howie T. Winter and James "Buddy" McLean built a criminal empire from blueprints drafted decades prior by Frankie Wallace. Wallace was the architect of the infamous Gustin Gang back in the mid-1910s. His gang had patrolled the cobbled streets of South Boston, hijacking delivery trucks, holding up company payroll, and robbing banks and jewelry stores. Due to the gang's political control, they remained largely unaffected by law enforcement and hardly served any jail time. On January 17, 1920, the Volstead Act brought federal charges nationwide for the manufacturing, selling, and distributing of alcoholic beverages. What was meant to cleanse American society of vice instead opened the floodgates for the criminally ambitious Irish American Gustin Gang, among others.

The Gustin Gang unsuccessfully operated a fleet of rumrunners before reverting back to their specialty of hijacking and confiscating rival shipments. They soon owned all the bootleg liquor and the speakeasies the booze was consumed in; the gang owned Boston.

It was also at this time that they stole a shipment of illicit beer from the North End Italian mob. In an attempt to settle the ensuing dispute, Frankie Wallace and "Dodo" Walsh agreed to a sit-down with Joey Lombardi and Filippo Buccola, leaders of the Italian Mafia. On December 22, 1931, on their way into the C.K. Importing Company in Boston's North End, two members of the Lombardi gang, Caruso and Cangemi, shot and killed the two Irish Americans. A scramble for power followed.

Amidst the internal Italian territorial struggles, Filippo Buccola made a treaty with the Rhode Island Italian mob, and the two families stepped up together into the void created by the chaos. The New England crime family was created. They voted Buccola into power, and he assumed control of organized crime activity in Boston and the surrounding areas. Buccola's reign of terror lasted twenty-two years until he retired in 1952, passing his crown to Raymond L. S. Patriarca. The Italian monopoly lasted another three years until, in 1955, Buddy McLean and Bernie McLaughlin split from the Patriarcas and started what would become rival gangs: the Charlestown Mob and the Winter Hill Gang.

Each of these new gangs were named for the territory they controlled: the Charlestown Mob controlling neighborhoods east of the

River Charles, and Winter Hill running the once blue-collared and infamous Winter Hill neighborhood of Somerville, Massachusetts, just
northwest of Boston. Tensions between the two gangs festered as each
faction gained more power and spotted new opportunities beyond their
own proverbial boundaries.

The Boston Irish Gang War started in 1961 over pussy and ended six
years later with bullets to the head. To this day, I haven't figured out which
is deadlier. In 1965, during this violent dispute, Buddy McLean, founder
of the Winter Hill Gang, was shot and killed, leaving the reins to his co-
founder and right-hand man, Howie Winter. Two years later, in 1967,
Howie finally ended the war by killing the last of the Charlestown mobsters.

When the dust settled, only the Winter Hill Gang remained.

Among the mobsters now at Howie's disposal were Johnny Martorano, Kevin Weeks, Joseph McDonald, Patrick Nee, Toby Rust, Joe
Simpson, and Dave Breen, as well as the psychopaths Stephen Flemmi
and James J. "Whitey" Bulger.

Now, if you want any more history on Irish American organized
crime, do me a favor and fuck off—look it up yourself.


Constance was working in one of the organization's strip clubs, the
Naked Eye, when Bill Winter knocked her up. To the outside world, Bill
was an outstanding citizen: an air corps veteran donning starch-pressed
shirts and Windsor-knotted ties. He was happily married to his wife,
Helen, and was in no way associated with the criminal activities of his
younger brother.

Needless to say, my mother's existence was a disgrace to the Winter
family. So, they decided to hide the liability close to the vest, where they
could keep tabs on her unpredictability, "giving" her a job at Casabrini's
Bar. My mother was a hostess working the second late-night shift. It
was one of her first jobs that required her tits to be covered. On paper,
a patsy owned the bar, so that the government minded their own fucking business when it came to audits, raids, and forfeitures. However, it
was actually Henry Simons and several of his connected associates who
held the keys to the door.

Henry, known as Hank, was a Polish Jew born on March 15, 1933, in Boston, Massachusetts. His parents, Emmanuel and Anna Simons— the only members (along with one of Anna's sisters) of their respective families who managed to narrowly escape the impending labor camp atrocities of World War II—had immigrated to the US from the city of Kraków, Poland, a year before Hank was born. In the beginning, the family was "too poor to afford the ink to print him a middle name," so he never had one. In his adolescence, he shined shoes and swept the floors at the J&A Cigar Company in West Roxbury, Massachusetts. By the early 1940s, his father had saved enough money to start a construction company of his own, which a teenage Hank was obligated to join in adherence to strict European values.

Having come from good, hardworking stock, Hank put in as many as eighty hours a week. He was a no-nonsense young man. If the sun was up, he was making money. Whether on a construction site or by wheeling and dealing with a close-knit crew of childhood friends, who were fast becoming junior mobsters, Hank was laying a foundation for his future.

And in no time, his future came in the form of Mary McDonald, a thin-waisted, big-breasted, blue-eyed Irish bombshell from South Boston. Due to an early consummation and unplanned pregnancy, both families insisted that the two lovebirds wed immediately. Deborah Simons was born in 1954. Because of Mary's hot temper, the marriage was rocky right from the honeymoon, but Hank's familial piety compelled him to forge ahead through the next decade, spoiling his little girl, Deborah, like any loving father would.

In his quest for a legacy namesake, Hank and Mary tried year after year to conceive a son—to no avail. Arguments ensued: Mary accused Hank of "shooting blanks." Hank accused Mary of having a "barren fucking wasteland between her legs." The marriage ended not long after when Hank caught Mary fucking a local cop.

By the time he employed my mother, Hank, along with others in his circle, was a silent partner in Casabrini's Bar, H&S Custom Home Improvements, and a few rental cottages on the South Shore, right there on the ocean.

Casabrini's was a seven-thousand-square-foot nightclub with two separate dining rooms, each with its own fifty-foot oak bar top running the length of the rear wall, separating patrons from the wall of stolen liquor bottles. The second floor was reserved for functions, private meetings, and card games.

Hank was able to find humanity where none existed, even in Constance Elaine Hicks. As her pregnancy developed, Hank reappropriated her workload to the task of nannying his daughter, Deborah.

Several months later, my mother showed up late for work. Her distended belly hung out over her waist, life growing inside a cesspit of poison, and she was hiding the truth behind a pair of oversized Jackie-O sunglasses.

Right away Hank knew where the obsidian-black eyes and caked-on makeup—concealing the bruising of her broken nose—had come from. No doubt in a drunken confession, my mother told her boyfriend, Red, that the baby wasn't his. Seven months of truth and rage poured from her like water, inciting not an argument from Red but a vicious beating.

Before Hank left to go deal with Red, he made my mother a promise. The promise would prove to be the greatest act of kindness ever shown to her and me and all of us. Hank promised Constance that he would look after her and take care of her unborn baby, the son he could never have, as if it were his own.

Before I was even born, Henry Simons was my pops.

"Hammering" Hank walked out into the hot, sticky night. His iconic twenty-four-ounce ball-peen hammer hung comfortably in the loop sewn into the left interior breast of his sport coat as he made his way to the rundown tenement doubling as a brothel where Red and my mother had been staying. The hickory-handled persuader was swift and punctual when sending Red a message—as easy as if it were pounding in a nail.

By the time my mother left work that night, Red was hospitalized with broken ribs and a fractured elbow. His shattered jaw was missing a handful of teeth. Upon his release from the hospital, he fled to Florida, never to be seen in Boston again . . . or so I was told.

I was born two months later, and although I was first dropped into my mother's arms, I was in Hank's soon after, so it wasn't all bad. Within four months they were married. They had two more children, Laura and Emanuel, within the two years after that. (It seems the curse of infertility had been Mary McDonald's the whole time.) Hank kept his word, and I was treated as his first son.

The first several years were a blur, but I recall a few piercing stabs with absolute clarity. Just before my fifth birthday, Hank took us down to Florida for the first time. He had bought my mother a brand-new '76 Ford Country Squire station wagon: light green with the stripe of wood paneling running down the side. We piled into the back of the wagon for the trip, everyone except Hank. Instead, he drove a big truck that had its bed covered with a rolled-down green military canvas. I cried and wailed and begged Pops to let me ride in the cab with him instead of in the car behind, but he didn't cave. I threw a tantrum the entire twenty-two-hour trip.

Pops pulled the truck and its contents into a rusty steel building inside a fenced area in Deerfield Beach, Florida, and was met by a small group of men riding motorcycles. Hank climbed out of the cab, flipped the truck's keys to one of the men, and walked back to us. He made my mother climb into the passenger seat and took over as driver.

One of the bikers, Vinnie, wore a leather vest and had a long goatee. He split off from his compatriots and led us to the house we were staying in.

The following day was my big day: five years old. It was always my mother's routine not to go overboard for any of her children's birthdays, but this year was different. It was the first year ever that my birthday celebration was being handled by my pops. Hank was taking me deep-sea fishing.

My mother opposed the whole thing because it was an overnight trip and she would have to watch my siblings alone while we were gone, but that didn't sway Hank. Mom was cooking us macaroni and cheese to take on the boat when she and Hank got into an argument over the addition of sliced hot dogs into the pot.

My mother refused, but Hank insisted, "It's what my son wants. It's his birthday, for chrissakes. Put the fucking hot dogs in."

She did, and I puked them into the moonlit water later that night. We made sure to never tell her. It was our secret.

Early the next morning, the horizon enthroned the first sunlight. We had been fishing all night with little success. We sat in silence next to one another, Pops and me. For several long minutes, we watched the line twitch, listening to the gulls screech overhead and the waves slap against the hull.

Pops quickly deposited me onto his lap when the line went taut, and my fishing rod doubled upon itself in protest. Secure against him, his strong hand over mine, we enthusiastically pumped the reel's handle. As we continued to struggle with the beast, a few of the other guys on the trip gathered around to watch the fight. For a moment, the line went slack as an elongated silver head broke through the water before sinking back down and resuming the action.

Me and Pops reeled a few more times, bringing the fish closer, before Toby Rust, my father's friend, plunged a gaff over the side of the boat into the battleground, hooking the curved point just under the fish's gills. He twisted and hauled the kingfish over the gunwale and onto the deck. The fish wriggled and flopped around at our feet, its powerful tail whacked against my tiny legs, knocking me flat on my ass.

Pops threw down the fishing rod, gathered me into his arms, and pressed me tight against his chest, kissing the top of my head as he repeatedly stomped the fish's head. The tail relaxed, and a runny stream of blood flowed from the mangled fish corpse.

Toby, who'd come down to Florida to "visit," came over to my pops and lectured him about how the fish was too big and could have dragged me overboard. My pops just shrugged him off and congratulated me on the catch.

Back at the docks, we measured the giant kingfish. It was forty-two inches and the biggest catch of the day. A few weeks later, the charter company sent me a certificate with my name and measurement of the fish. My pops proudly hung it on the wall of his office for as long as I can remember.

Soon after that first trip, Hank bought a two-story town house on a canal in North Lauderdale that we moved into. Hank made monthly trips to and from Florida in his truck. As we settled into the pseudo-normalcy Hank was providing us, I began primary school. When we weren't in school, me and the neighborhood kids ran around the streets, mostly unsupervised.

Patrick Murphy lived a few houses down and was dumb enough to do just about anything I told him to. And on one occasion, I went a little too far with his gullibility. That day we went up to the bathroom on the second floor, slid open the window, and looked down to the beanbag chair we had placed on the ground to soften his landing.

I handed him a black trash bag and reassured him I'd seen it done before; all he had to do was hold his arms apart and he'd drift down, like a paratrooper, to the landing zone. Easy. Except he missed the bag, hit the ground, and crumpled.

In the act of breaking both legs, his knees were driven into his mouth, mangling it completely. The ensuing catfight between my mother and Patrick's was instantly silenced as soon as Pops got home. Hammer in hand, he pounded on the Murphys' door and then had a talk with Patrick's father. Needless to say, I never hung with Patrick again after his plunge.

Later that year, 1979, Hurricane David demolished the east coast of Florida. Powerful winds ripped the aluminum-framed screen porch right off the back of our home, shattering windows and downing power lines. The torrential rains flooded the streets, putting the entire first floor of our home underwater and literally moving the gators—"lizards," as Hank called them—into the house with us. The neighborhood remained partially underwater for two days until the tide carried the excess back to the Atlantic.

Over the next few weeks at our house, Hank and his construction crew pulled and replaced carpets, walls, and floors—anything that was too far damaged by the storm. In the middle of restorations, while stripping carpet, Hank lost consciousness and collapsed. An ambulance rushed him to the hospital, where they referred him to specialists back in Massachusetts before giving him a diagnosis and treatment. He was shipped up to Boston later that week.

Hank wound up in a private room at the Joslin Diabetes Center in Boston. Amidst the chronobiological beeps of the machines he was hooked up to and the hum of LED lighting, the doctors informed him that he had type 2 diabetes and would have to stabilize his blood-glucose levels with daily injections of insulin. Having had a kidney removed at the age of seven, Hank was warned that he was at a greater risk for complications. His condition would have to be closely and meticulously monitored.

My mother and the rest of us were going to fly up north and pick him up from the hospital—or at least that's what my mother told him. The ultimate betrayal happened a day later when, instead of taking us to Boston to be with Pops, she changed the locks on the house.

Her meal ticket was gone, and she panicked. Faced with uncertainty, my mother refused to show any sympathy for my father. She had no intention of being by his side in the hospital. In her eyes, the second the wheels were up and his plane was in the air, he was as good as dead.

When she bolted the new locks, I lost all respect for my mother. How could she do that to my father? He was the only man that hadn't left or given up on her; he'd protected her, he'd seen through the veil of promiscuity and treated her better than the whore that she was, and she had turned her back on him before he even got off the fucking plane.

Upon hearing what she had done, Hank yelled at her through the phone, "Let me have the children, please. You can have the house, the cars, the bank accounts, all that shit, just send me the children."

Out of spite of his survival, Mom broke up the family when Hank demanded that us kids go back to him. Legally, she couldn't keep Laura or Manny from him, but she sent Heather and Tina back to their biological father and kept me with her.

It wasn't more than a month before the money ran out, the car broke down, and the whoring began. She spread her legs for any low-level gangster and their friends who could supply her with a fix and a bed.

I was a liability and an unnecessary burden, an extra body to shelter and feed. I was told to fold blankets in half for a mattress and hang a bedsheet as a door to section off a part of the room. Once I was out of sight, I was quickly forgotten. The hundred-thread-count curtain did little to stop the lewd uproar from the train of three to five men my mother would "entertain" most nights. After a day or two in one place, the "boyfriend" of hers would recognize the parasitic nature of my mother and would kick the two of us out. My mother blamed me for our evictions.

It took another two years of this revolving door of low-level vermin for my mother to appreciate my worth. When I was seven, she realized her guardianship over me was an asset. I was the ace she palmed when the deck was hot. When it came to Hank, I could be used as a bargaining chip.

In Fort Lauderdale, my mother would drop me off at a twenty-four-hour fishing pier before going off with her current trick. I was babysat by the pier and the strangers that walked its twisted and weathered boards for days at a time until she picked me up, often berating me for being a burden to her.

After two weeks of this, she had had enough and assaulted the pay phone keypad, dialing Hank. She started small: demanding he wire a few thousand to her, and she'd put me on a plane up to Boston. She ran this scam two or three times, saying his first installment barely covered the bills. Not until the blatant act of extortion had run its course did she actually put me on the plane.

I walked out of the automatic sliding doors of Logan Airport and into the strong arms of my father. That night I'd sleep in a real bed, eat a hot meal, and be safe. Although we didn't know it yet, our feelings at that first arrival were a high we'd chase for years to come; with it came the fool's hope that this was the last time my mother would separate us.

She came groveling back into our lives six months later—this time, pleading with my father for asylum from a biker she had robbed. I begged him not to let her in the door.

My words fell on his unconditionally loving and deaf ears.

Throughout the remainder of my mother's life, Pops and I would repeat that same conversation without fluctuation. He would end the argument by saying, "No matter what fucked-up shit she's done, she's still your mother." The truth of the matter was that, through it all, Hank never stopped loving her.

My mother's next breaking point came a few months later. Knowing that I wouldn't leave any other way, she grabbed me by the hand and dragged me away from my father's love and into the night.

The cycle began again as my mother fucked one guy after another. Moving around so often created a lack of uniformity in my formal education. I was always trying to catch up in school. While my classmates were reading and solving arithmetic, I was learning to identify my letters and numbers. When I was ten, my mother took me out of school for the last time. It had become too difficult to enroll me into a new school every time she had a new dick in her. And with that, my formal education ceased.

The first boyfriend of my mother's that I can remember by name was an Italian schmuck called Vinny. He was a bookie making his rounds up and down the Sunshine State, breaking kneecaps when he didn't get paid. He kept my mother and me apart from his wife, Leanne, and his four children by putting us up in his apartment in Coral Springs, right around the corner from the golf course.

A few extramarital blow jobs later, he bought my mother a 1980 chocolate-brown Chrysler New Yorker Fifth Avenue. When he was busy with his family, my mother and I spent our time at the Coral Springs Country Club. Vinny should have known she couldn't be left unsupervised for very long without a cock in her, and within a month, she was spreading her legs for some Egyptian fuck named Abasi Soliman as well.

Abasi was an international shippingmonger, running container ships between Central and North America. Entire forty-foot containers and their contents often disappeared from his arrival manifest and the port yard. He had houses in New Jersey and Florida and a penthouse apartment in Manhattan. Both he and Vinny knew about one another and moved us around like chess pieces to keep their mistress and her woebegone bastard a secret from their wives and kids. She'd stay at Vinny's apartment and fuck him for a few days before we would be forced to leave, and then we'd be cooped up at Abasi's townhome for another round of her whoring.

Not to be outdone by a lowly bookie, Abasi bought her a two-door T-top sports car: a brand-new Chrysler LeBaron. The two men would pass my mother and me off to one another as if we were just dirty money in another one of their business transactions. Both Abasi and Vinny spent their weekends playing the family man, which, once again, left my mother to her own vices.

Cliff Pittard was the Miami assistant police chief and my mother's weekend fuck. He snuck away from his family most weekends and into my mother's bed, which was really Abasi's. The three assholes came and went on punctual rotation for almost a year until the whole shit show went belly-up. It started with a WTVJ news report spotlighting the newly promoted, fired, and disgraced Police Chief Clifford Pittard, who was caught up in what would become known as "Palm Beach County's little Watergate." With so much publicity and notoriety centered on him, I never saw him again.

Vinny and Abasi followed suit soon after, proving the shelf life of a mistress isn't much longer than a loaf of bread's. My mother was a habitual mistress, but she wasn't a home-wrecker. Or rather, the only family she managed to disassemble and disfigure was her own.

Those three men made me think of my pops and how all he wanted was a family. Maggots like them pissed it away like the highballs they constantly threw back. I vowed never to become like them. I was going to be like my pops, except I would know the look of a Siren luring me toward the wreckage.

The only boyfriend of my mother's that I liked was Warner P. Grant. He moved my mom and me from Titusville to Ocala, two and a half hours northwest. He was the first guy that commented on how my mother's parenting was fucking me up, insisting that if she was going to stay with him, I'd have to go back to school.

I remember his garage—rusted wrenches, rotator ratchets, screw-drivers, electric drills, and all the hammers that decorated the walls. One of them reminded me of my father's ball-peen. A tall cherry-red toolbox on wheels was pushed into the back corner. He had every tool imaginable and necessary to fix up the 1978 Ford Ranchero GT that was parked proudly in the middle of the shrine. Warner kept the American muscle car in pristine, museum-quality condition. There wasn't a nick or imperfection in the chocolate-brown paint. A golden band, straight as an arrow, wrapped around the car's bed.

Every time after he drove the car, Warner would tune and tinker with it. He pulled the front wheels up on two black ramps to lift the car a few feet; then he lay down on his creeper and disappeared beneath the car. He rolled around, inspecting the undercarriage, grunting approval to himself. He dropped the car down and popped the hood, propping it open with the metal support bar. He called out the names of various tools and sizes for me to retrieve and hand him. I'd run from one wall to the next or sift through the toolbox and bring him what he asked for. I watched as he leaned way over into the engine compartment with the tool I got him as he adjusted and tuned the throaty carburetor of the big 351 Windsor for the next drive. He would occasionally explain this and that about what he was doing and how each part was integral to the performance of the vehicle.

We stayed with Warner for a little over a year. One whole year of partial and primal normalcy ended with the usual sirens and flashing lights that accompany disastrous change. My mother was too hysterical to tell me what happened, so the police had to: Mr. Grant had suffered a massive heart attack and passed away in his sleep.

His affairs were in order, but they didn't include us. A few weeks later, his ex-wife and grown children showed up at the house and kicked us to the curb. We were back with Hank within the week. I was glad because he'd never leave us like that.

I was thirteen when I was taught how to manufacture crack cocaine—that biker shit. Eugene "Gene" Roberts taught me. He was in the Hells

Angels and rode a Harley and was fucking my mother. Gene wasn't so bad, but he beat my mother.

He began my lesson by showing me how to break open those cockroach traps and combine the contents with baking soda and ammonia in a Pyrex dish. The roach motels used to be made with a concoction of pharmaceutical-grade cocaine and arsenic, or so I was told. Either way, you could probably get fucked up off the stuff. After we finished cooking the solid, glassy narcotic windowpanes, I learned to break them apart and wash the rocks like pots and pans in the sink to remove the excess ammonia. Gene and I each had our own packaging station equipped with a scale and ziplock bags.

One night, in the midst of working, my mother told me to scrape up the residue and crumbs from my chopping plate and bring it to her in the kitchen. She wanted to get high before she made herself a drink. There wasn't much on the ceramic plate in front of me.

I wiped it onto the floor. "Get it yourself," I said.

The Campbell's soup can she snatched up off the counter came down on me like Thor's hammer. The hard palate of my mouth, along with whatever teeth attached to it, were decimated by the impact. Don't stand between a crackhead and their fix, even if it's your own mother. Later in life I would need major reconstructive surgery to repair the damage of that soup can. I've never had a can of Campbell's tomato soup since.

I wasn't terribly unhappy when she married Gene later that year. It meant that I'd be sent back to stay with my pops. These stints with Hank would now run longer and be more consistent—at least until Gene went to prison and Mom stole me back.

# TWO

## THE FAMILY BUSINESS

I liked living with my pops. For a while now, he'd started bringing me along to hang around my "uncles." They were all Hank's childhood friends and associates. A few times a week, we all met up at Toby Rust's place: an aluminum-sided split-level ranch in Holbrook, Massachusetts. It had an oversized garage with a steel roll-up overhead door that was constantly opening and closing for the armada of cargo trucks that trooped in and out every few hours. All business was done downstairs, in the house's basement. There was a functioning bar down there that was fully stocked with top-shelf liquors, card tables, dealing machines, and enough seating for everyone. His wife, Kitty, fed and waited on the guys. I was young, my balls hadn't dropped yet, my feet didn't touch the floor, and my chin barely made it above the table, but as part of the family, I was included in their conversations.

I listened to each uncle talk about their respective businesses and illegal rackets. Uncle Toby talked about the boxcars, tractor trailers, and valuable scores that brought him infamy as the largest "fence" in New England. Uncle Joe Simpson reported on the success of his two chop shops in Quincy and Roxbury. Dave "The Hog" Breen rattled on about his pot fields in Braintree. My pops would say things were running without issues down at the nightclub or construction company. Howie used to sit at the head of the card table until "Fat Tony" Ciulla ratted on him for masterminding the horse rackets. That sent him off to federal prison, leaving a vacancy for James J. "Whitey" Bulger—Uncle Jim—to sit in his place.

Whitey was always joking about his stint in Alcatraz a few years back (he was released in 1965), but he'd get real serious when he brought up what jobs needed to be handled and garbage that needed to be taken out.

He had two crews. More well-known was his notorious Southie crew, the one with Johnny Martorano, Steve Flemmi, and Kevin Weeks; but he also had his South Shore crew, the Quincy guys: my uncles.

He kept the operations separate from one another; in fact, he kept the entire Quincy operation a secret from the Southie guys. That way he didn't have to cut the Southie psychos in on the profits. My pops told me that he was well aware of the operation in Southie, but he and my uncles never bothered getting involved with them because they were "more trouble than they're worth"—the understatement of the century.

I listened to the intricate and complex workings of each facet of the Winter Hill Gang, though I understood little of what was said. I only heard that the family business was running smoothly. But I was just a kid . . . *What the fuck did you expect?*

Amidst the perpetual gin rummy games and an endless flow of Canadian Mist, Uncle Toby would turn to me and, in his guttural voice, say, "Ay, kid, go up in the garage 'n' grab us a bottle of booze 'n' while you're up there, crack a box. Might be somethin' in there for ya."

I took the stairs three at a time. Toby always knew I was coming over and made sure to have something special waiting for me whenever I was asked to grab booze or a deck of cards. I remember the brown cardboard boxes, stacked from floor to ceiling, stuffed with board games (Monopoly and Operation), video game consoles, or Red Sox jerseys. This time, the box was filled with Rawlings baseball mitts, the real leather kind that every kid dreamed of owning.

*Fuck, yeah!*

You can't help but grow up fast when you listen to the intricacies of the world straight from the mouths of those who created it. And after a few years in Uncle Toby's basement, I had uncovered the truth—or at least part of it. The family business wasn't about the baseball gloves or the toys or even the video games; it was about one thing: respect. The money, power, and responsibilities were just by-products, but pretty fucking good ones if you ask me.

I wanted it all. *How could I not?*

I was inducted into their ranks not long after I turned eleven. The bark of a horn put a stop to the card game. I watched Uncle Toby check his wristwatch, throw back what was left in his highball, turn toward me, and say, "C'mon kid, got a job for ya."

I was glued to the large man's heels as he walked into the garage. I helped him pull the chain that opened one of the roll-up garage doors, and like clockwork, a large white unmarked box truck was idling outside, waiting to enter.

Uncle Toby guided the truck as the driver backed it in. The driver, who I only knew as Irish Mike, hopped out of the cab and raised the cargo bay door. Front to back, floor to ceiling, were cases of hijacked Canadian Mist whiskey. Uncle Toby placed one of his reassuring meat-hook-sized hands on my shoulder, gave it a gentle squeeze, nodded toward the haul, and said, "I'll give you half a C-note if this fuckin' thing's empty in a half hour."

*You shittin' me?* Of course I would. Back then, fifty bucks was nothing short of a fortune to an eleven-year-old kid. He instructed me where the boxes would go and told me to come find him when I was done.

Looking to Irish Mike, Toby said, "Let's knock back a few," and the two mobsters went back into the main house, leaving me hard at work with a smile. The cases of liquor were heavy as fuck, but I was too excited to even notice the weight. I could have moved the boxes if they were two hundred pounds apiece. My shirt clung with sweat to my body, and my little arms hung lifeless at my sides as I returned to the basement less than a half hour later.

"Done already?" Toby grunted, looking surprised. I nodded. He produced a wad of bills from his pocket and peeled a fifty off the roll. "Kid's quick . . . a hard worker," he said, smiling toward my pops. "Here," he continued, extending the payment to me. "Got plenty of jobs for a good worker, kid. Keep that shit up 'n' I'll keep findin' more for you ta do."

He kept his word. There was plenty of work. If it moved through New England by land, air, or sea, Uncle Toby knew about it. He had eyes and ears everywhere, and the scores were going down quicker than a three-dollar hooker.

At every seaport, freighters are required to hand over a comprehensive manifest detailing the contents of every container as well as the final destination where the goods are headed. And if that wasn't convenient enough, it's fucking color-coordinated. So, from Connecticut to Maine, Toby had a network of loyal dock and warehouse workers.

In exchange for a good tip-off, any worker could end their week with a few extra hundred dollars in his or her pocket. It was simple. If the customs officer wasn't the one to pass on a copy of the cargo plan, then the next guy down the line, the longshoreman, would send word of what he had just unloaded. If it wasn't the stevedore, it was the security guard working the yard's gate. Toby was getting similar tips out of every railyard, warehouse, and airport.

But if the shipment left the container terminals or airport hangar, then Toby would get his tip-offs from law enforcement. He had a couple cops and troopers deep in his pocket. More than a couple, really; he basically had whole fucking departments and state police barracks in there. They would let him know about any high-dollar shipments that they were supposed to be keeping a watchful eye on, and he would organize a hit just as the law enforcement details were on a coffee or bathroom break or sometimes stuck miles away with a convenient flat tire. Once or twice a week, a different police cruiser would drive up to the house, and I was told to run out with a case of either liquor or cigarettes and throw it in the trunk.

After repeatedly putting the same specific boxes into the same police car trunks, I learned the smoking and drinking habits of half the local law enforcement agencies. I don't recall ever being recompensed by any of those crooked bastards.

That being said, Uncle Toby got most of his information from the truck drivers. After picking up a load, the drivers could give Toby a call, and they'd make a quick couple grand. The plan was always the same: the driver would pull into a "No-Tell Motel" and leave the truck unattended while they got cheap blow jobs from ugly hookers.

Our crew would then hit the truck and bring the haul to Toby's. His only caveat was that the shipment had to be insured—that way no one lost any money. If you weren't in the game, we weren't going to fuck you over; it was one of the codes that Winter Hill stood behind. The code Whitey would eventually go on to destroy. *The no-good fucking rat!*

After two years of off-loading at his home, I was inducted as the lookout into one of those low-level crews that took down anything that held what Toby deemed to be valuable. "Glue your eyes to the street, kid," I was told, "'n' bring some extra hands next time . . . guys you trust." Okay. No problem, I trusted Scott Quinn, my best friend.

Quinny and I stood as sentinels for hundreds of jobs and began recognizing some of the regular drivers. There was Charlotte Charlie, who drove a sixteen-wheeler full of Pall Mall and Camel cigarettes up to Maine. Quinny and I smoked his unfiltered cigarettes as we unloaded them into the garage. Carolina Jack was another regular. He transported furniture north a few times a month. He liked stopping at a strip club named King Arthur's Lounge in Chelsea, Massachusetts, when our crew hit.

One time, Carolina Jack was moving two hundred La-Z-Boy swivel rocker recliners. Full-grain brown leather. For the insurance claim (and to cover up Carolina Jack's role), the guys were told to slash the canvas on the curtain-sided trailer to make it seem as if they needed to look inside first to know what they were stealing.

Over the next couple days, Quinny and I sat at the end of Toby's driveway under a tarpaulin lean-to, selling the things. I painted a cardboard sign, and we had a line of customers around the block.

"Buck 'n' a quarter a chair . . . brand fuckin' new La-Z-Boys, still in the plastic . . . No, we don't deliver, *cash 'n' carry,* now buy one or move on."

The second day we were open for business, a local paddy wagon drove up with an official police logo painted across its side. We loaded a few chairs into the rear, and the cops were able to outfit the station with three nice new comfortable recliners, courtesy of the Winter Hill Gang.

Quinny and I got rid of all two hundred chairs within a week.

Seeing how I was handling the jobs and responsibilities that were given to me, my uncles decided to diversify my portfolio by adding fire insurance salesman, debt collector, and one-way valet to my internship. Résumé filler for my future rap sheet.

When a new business moved to the area, they were told, more often than not, where to purchase supplies; auto shops got their parts from Uncle Joe's junkyard, bars got their liquor from Uncle Toby, et cetera. If a shopkeeper decided to outsource, Jimmy would send Dave "The Hog" Breen to set the matter straight.

And from time to time, The Hog brought me along after work hours in his beat-up Bronco to visit the reluctant business. It was my job to deliver the Winter Hill welcome package: a red gas can, full to the spout, positioned neatly by the front door for the shopkeeper to find in the morning.

Most of them got the message, but on a few occasions, further "communication" was required. The first time I remember was an unwilling and cocksure mechanic who opened an automotive garage within the territory of Uncle Joe's Roxbury chop shop. I overheard my family talking about the guy's lack of cooperation with standard practices. *The fuckin' moron's got more balls than brains*, I remember thinking, knowing the repercussions he'd face for going against us.

That same night The Hog and I returned to the wayward mechanic's garage, armed with enough gasoline to drive to California. Under the streetlamp's dim yellow light that would accompany many of my future crimes, I shimmied my way up the electrical conduit pipe that was bolted to the rear of the building and climbed onto the roof with a crescent wrench slipped through the belt loop of my jeans. Two rows of large skylights bisected the flat roof, allowing natural light to filter in during the daytime. I picked a square of glass that looked down onto a large metal shelving unit and busted the skylight with my wrench.

I climbed to the floor, careful of my footing around the shards of glass and spare parts, and crossed the shop to unlock the door for The Hog.

"Just watch yer feet when you're dumpin' this shit, don't let it splash on ya," The Hog said, handing me one of the gas cans. Ten minutes and a few gallons of high-test later, we were standing back outside. The Hog stuck a cigarette in his mouth, lit it with a match, and handed me the rest of the matchbook.

"Light 'er up," he said, speaking out of the side of his mouth. The fire was beautiful and just and necessary.

Other times Uncle Toby would commission my services by telling me to head over to this or that business and to "let 'em know I sent ya. They got a bag waitin' for me. Grab it 'n' c'mon back." By that point, he didn't even have to look away from his cards to make sure I understood; he knew that whatever he asked of me would get done exactly how he wanted it. There were only two rules to be a successful bagman: (1) don't accept excuses, and (2) *never* leave empty-handed.

That spring I was sent over to the Polish American club to pick up an envelope that contained the vig on a loan Toby had given the owner; the two-point fee amounted to somewhere around $300. As I walked in and found the guy at the far end of the bar, I overheard part of the conversation he was having with another shady-looking Polish mobster.

". . . dime on the Bruins," the owner said as he counted out ten one-hundred-dollar bills and handed them to the bookie. He must have heard me walking up because he spun around before I even opened my mouth. "Who the fuck are you?" he asked, gargling his words as if he had a mouthful of marbles.

"Toby sent me to pick up the envelope you got for 'em."

He looked over to the bookie and said, "You hearin' this shit? Kid's here to collect. They shouldn't be sendin' no kid over 'ere to do a man's business." He returned to me and continued, "I ain't got it, kid. You can tell that prick I'll call 'em later 'n' that I only do business with fuckin' grown-ass men." He concluded with a cordial "Now get the *fuck* out." I watched as he counted out more money for the bookie; this time it was a nickel on the Celtics.

I had never left empty-handed before, and I sure as shit wasn't going to let this asshole be the reason I did for the first time. As he turned his back, I noticed the car keys behind him on the bar. I quickly grabbed them without him noticing and left.

Turns out he drove a big boxy Lincoln Continental that looked as if it had just rolled out of the factory or off a showroom floor. I hopped in, slid the driver's seat forward as far as it would go, cranked over the V8 engine, and, looking through the gap between the dashboard and the top of the steering wheel, drove straight to Joe Simpson's junkyard.

Joe just laughed, shook his head, and clapped his hands together when I told him what had happened and where the car came from. He gave me $500 for the big maroon car. I went back to Toby's, paid off the Polish prick's vig, and still had a couple hundred left over. The dickhead came by later that day, interrupting the card game and yelling at my pops about how I owed him a new goddamn car.

Jimmy calmly got up from the table and went outside to talk to the guy. Flemmi followed. They returned a few minutes later. Jimmy looked at me and said, "Ya did yourself a good job, kid," and smiled and went back to the game. I don't know exactly what they said to the guy outside, but he never missed a payment again. He never interrupted another card game either, nor did he ever get that new car.

From that first payoff from Uncle Joe, I learned the real dough was in clipping cars, and I asked how I could get into a boosting crew. He laughed but took it seriously and decided to try me out. For the next two or three months, me and a couple guys were driven out to the South Shore area, Cape Cod, or Rhode Island and scattered around to find a ride back for ourselves. We always worked out of town so that the car wasn't too hot when you brought it in and also because you shouldn't shit in your own backyard. We didn't steal from our own. And if you got good at it, which took me less than a couple months, you could make two or three trips per day. The trick was to know where and what to look for. The new fledglings always went after the foreign shit, the Mercedes or BMWs or Jaguars, before Joe set them straight. He wanted Cadillacs and Lincolns. Good ol' American steel. Not to mention, when selling scrap metal, heavier is better.

Uncle Joe ran a smooth operation that had been polished through a decade of success. Let's say I pulled an '81 Cadillac Fleetwood Brougham up to the shop at noon. I would hand off the car keys to one of the garage monkeys, and by the time I finished talking and getting paid by Joe, the car had been stripped naked. The wire spoke wheels had been carefully removed and neatly stacked on a hand truck that was being pushed around back; the plush hand-stitched leather seats had been taken out and strategically placed alongside a sea of others to resemble a New England equivalent of the Terracotta Army; the engine had been pulled out and deposited on an engine hoist; exhaust manifolds, windshields, catalytic converters, drive shafts, brakes, rotors, radios, you name it—if it could be resold, it was removed with surgical precision. Seconds later the tines of a forklift carried away the skeleton chassis off to the compactor, and by half past the hour, a once functional eighteen-foot automobile had been crushed into a three-by-three-foot metal cube ready to be sold as scrap. A weekly rotation of semitrucks would come and haul the car cubes up to Canada, where no questions would be asked.

Following success in my tryout, I asked Uncle Joe if he thought I was ready to join a crew and get some constant work.

"Mmm," he grunted, taking a second to think about it before he answered. "Yeah, yeah, all right. Gimme a week or so to find a crew that's lookin' for an extra set of hands, 'n' while ya wait whyn't you run ova to Canton 'n' drum up some business fer the shop?"

For the next seven days, a smile never left my face as I took a hammer and ice pick to every tire, window, and body panel I saw in the affluent suburb.

# THREE

## THE WHALE

Uncle Joe threw me into a crew that reported to a guy known as The Whale. He was a gluttonous fuck in the back end of his forties with the battered face of a bare-knuckle boxer, the kind you bet against safely. I was told The Whale had grown up running in various car theft rings and had the experience, but as far as I could tell, a fucking baboon would have been better suited for his job. He'd gotten too comfortable, too arrogant, too cocky and disrespectful. In some instances, he got physical with the guys he knew wouldn't retaliate in order to impress the turnstile of gutter sluts he had come by the shop. He would deal out open-hand slaps like a dealer pulling cards from a shoe. Witnessing these assaults on underlings pissed me off. One thing I've always hated is a bully.

The Whale spent most days stuffed into his straining office chair with his fat rolls hanging over the arms like melting candle wax. He kept his beady little pig eyes glued to the clock, sweating like a whore in church, waiting until he could hit the strip club and pay for a girl to play with the prick he promised was "down there somewhere." I think he used to fuck my mom, too, when she was in town. Wouldn't surprise me. When he wasn't in his office, which was most often the case, he was up at the Wonderland racetrack in Revere, betting on the greyhound races. The only time you could find him on his feet was when he was impatiently waiting in line to throw his money away on Super High-5 and Pick-6 bets. After every race, his long-shot yellow slips always ended up crushed into a ball and tossed on the ground.

With his degenerate gambling and excessive whoring, he barely managed to run the two-tiered operation; there were six hardworking guys in the garage and another eight that brought in the cars. The guys that boosted cars were all under eighteen. That way, if any of us got pinched, instead of jail time, we'd likely just get a slap on the wrist and be back to work before nightfall. The shop ran twenty-four hours a day, three hundred and sixty-five days a year. It had to; we couldn't have a conga line of stolen vehicles parading into the yard in the daylight. And someone had to be on the grounds to make sure the feds didn't break in and bug the place. With a designated driver waiting to take us back out the second we returned and the extended hours of operation, I was able to pull in six cars a day with ease—three times as many as I had been grabbing without the crew. But the payout was fucked. The Whale's whoring and gambling had gotten him in debt up to where his man-tits met his third chin. To keep himself afloat, he shortchanged us on every car.

Before, I was getting a buck fifty to two hundred per car. Now it was an argument to get seventy-five. I tolerated his bullshit for almost a year. Then one day the cheap fuck cut commissions back to fifty bucks per car. I talked to the other guys: everyone was shorted.

*Fuck that.* I went straight back into the office to ask The Whale why my cut for the day was a few hundred light.

"Where's my fuckin' money?" I asked, tossing the small stack of twenties on top of the race results scattered across his metal desk.

He laced his chubby fingers together, licked his lips, and sighed. "The market's down, kid. Everyone's takin' a short."

"Only thing short is your prick, you fat fuck. I want my money," I said. "Matter of fact, I want straight money for my guys too."

"You don't like it, walk," he said. "There's a line of punks here to the Cape, do what you do. Now get the fuck out! An' don't neva run your cocksucka like that again."

I walked out of the office and was met by the shop crew who'd obviously ear-hustled the heated exchange and were waiting to see if anything happened. It hadn't, but *something* needed to, as everyone felt the same way: we were sick of risking our necks and having our end clipped. By the wide eyes and slacked jaws staring at me, I guessed that I was the first and only one to actually stand up to The Whale.

I brought it up to Joe later that day. "Why do I gotta listen to The Whale? He's a fucking joke. Guy's more interested in getting blow jobs than making money." I filled him in on how The Whale was stealing from the earners, including me.

"Think you can do better?" Joe asked.

"What? Runnin' the shop?" I said. "Fuck yeah."

Joe chuckled from the gut. "Maybe down the road I can see it. For sure."

I may have been a kid age-wise, but I was committing a grown man's crimes and demanded a grown man's pay. "I'm out there earnin' every night. The only thing I see in the future is a dead end," I said. "I'm fuckin' serious, Joe."

Joe did what he always did before getting serious: thrust his hands deep into his front pockets, tilted his head back, and exhaled deeply before leveling his gaze on you and speaking. "All right," Joe said, "then take it from him, no blowback."

*No blowback.* That meant more than just no repercussions. It meant that I had earned Joe's respect and trust and that he believed I could run a crew and do it right—which meant bringing in fucking money. I had a few changes in mind, but first I had to deal with The Whale.

My plan was simple, as any good plan should be. Step one was to get The Whale alone in the junkyard, and step two was to put him out of commission. *Piece of fucking cake.* Organized crime operates on fear, corruption, and violence. The easiest avenue to any one of those pillars is preying on predictability and weakness. I was too young and had no connections at the racetrack, so all I needed to find was a whore that was willing to set him up. No problem. They were a dime a dozen in the South End.

The next morning I walked over to Pug's Pub. It was at the intersection of Magazine and George Street, a block or so up from the junkyard. The place was a haven for some of the regular girls who were depraved and desperate enough to take money from The Whale. The bartender had just finished flipping the stools down off the bar top and was pouring buckets of ice into the wells when I entered. The pub was empty.

"Nobody's 'ere yet . . . usuals'll be in 'round ten," the bartender responded after I asked where the girls were.

"If I can't wait?" I said.

"Then you kin find most dem girls down the shootin' gallery gettin' fixed up for the mornin'," he said. "Blue triple-decker down the next corner."

I knew the place. I had been there once before. About two years back, Hank and I were about to leave the construction shack at a job-site when he got a phone call. I couldn't hear what was said, but he slammed down the phone and diverted our route home to the ramshackle flophouse. Hank parked on the street, left the van running, then went inside. It was raining out. I sat in the passenger seat, watching the wipers struggle to keep rain off the windshield. It was no use—regardless of how quickly they worked, the water always came back. My pops came out a few minutes later, carrying an unconscious woman over his shoulder. He opened the van's side door and threw my mother's limp body into the cargo bay.

The place was worse than I remembered. A real shithole. I had to jump over two of the rotted porch steps to get to the front door. I didn't knock; it wasn't the type of place you had to—you just walk in. There was a seasoned junkie in the kitchen, carefully balancing a needle between his lips as he tightened a belt just above his elbow. I walked by him and went up the stairs.

In the first room off to the right, I found a girl sitting on a dirty mattress propped against the wall. She was swaying back and forth to a song only she heard. I had seen her around the shop before. She was a regular late-night pump-n-dump of The Whale's. She had straw-thin, overbleached hair and ugly purple track marks tracing her translucent skin. A real hard-core street girl. She was perfect. If I was going to beat the living shit out of The Whale and it went south, I needed to be certain the girl that set him up would keep her mouth shut. And she would.

The woman flashed what few teeth she had left in her mouth when I walked in the room. "It's . . . ten for a tug, twenty for a suck, fifty for a fuck," she mumbled, reciting the words a pimp had obviously beat into her. "But I don't do no kids, honey," she slurred once her eyes had eventually focused in on me. "Not for less than a hundred, dat is."

"I'm not tryin' to fuck you, bitch," I said bluntly. "I got a job for you . . . if you're interested." She looked at me in confusion. "You know The Whale?" I asked. She nodded. "And the junkyard he works at?" She nodded again. "All you gotta do is call the shop and tell him you're stoppin' by tonight. And when you're done wit the prick, just bring him out into the yard. That's it," I said.

The Whale had over three hundred pounds on me, so the only way I could take him down was by surprise and if he was incapacitated to some degree. It would be my only chance.

She thought for a moment, or at least I think that's what she was doing. "How much you got?" she asked.

"A C-note for the job," I said. "Anotha fifty for your amnesia."

"How'm I 'posed to get him outside?"

"Don't know 'n' don't give a fuck. You in or out?" I said.

"An' you'll give me a hundred and a half?" she asked.

"Hundred at the gate, fifty when you deliver."

She flashed a broken smile.

I brought in four cars that day. Not great. Two hundred bucks. But I had been sidetracked, working and reworking the plan in my head. For such a simplistic approach, there were a thousand ways it could go down and only one way I wanted it to: quick and easy. I ran through it again.

The shop had two gates. The outer gate was on a rolling track and had a green cloth tacked to it so that anyone outside had trouble seeing in. It was padlocked to a stationary fence at night. To get by the second gate, we would have to be buzzed through. I could find a wrench or pipe anywhere, but a lot was riding on the broad to get us inside and handicap the prick.

*Fuck, was I putting too much faith in the whore?*

The question plagued my concentration until I finally saw her stumble down the street sometime around ten o'clock. She was carrying a liquor bottle by the neck. I couldn't read the label but knew she had already broken the seal by the stench on her breath.

"Hey, baby," she said, putting poisonous emphasis on the *H*. "Got any money for me?"

I still had the envelope with my payment for the day tucked into my front pocket. I took out five twenties and waved them in front of the streetwalker. "Don't fuck this up," I said, placing the bills into her hand.

She greedily eyed the other bills in the envelope, and I knew she'd play her part flawlessly.

We squeezed between the gap in the outer gate and the fence. The padlocked chain had been loosely secured, and I, being a small fifteen-year-old kid, and the girl, being a malnourished dope fiend, ducked under it with ease.

I stood ten feet back, keeping flat against the gate just outside the frame of the CCTV camera aimed at the shop's entrance. The girl frantically assaulted the call button four or five times before we heard a buzz and the door was unlocked. She flung it wide open. Careful to avoid detection, I kept my body pressed up against the gate and sidestepped into the yard.

We split up. I ducked behind one of the junkers near the entrance and made my way around the perimeter of the yard, looking for a weapon. I had told the hooker to entertain The Whale for an hour in order for the alcohol to kick in. She wasn't happy about that, complaining that he always blew his load in less than two minutes and didn't know what to do with the other fifty-eight minutes . . .

She gave in the second I offered to throw in another fifty. Exactly what dear ol' Mom would've done.

I found a tire iron in the trunk of a car near the back of the lot and tested it against the palm of my hand. It had some weight. It would work. I kept to the security camera's blind spots and got into position, crouching in the alcove just beside the shop door, which was covered by a large piece of corrugated sheet metal.

The wait paralleled the torturous silence before a deliberated jury reads their verdict at a murder trial. *Anticipation is a real motherfucker.*

I heard him coming. The Whale struggled to catch his breath directly on the other side of the door as 390 pounds of fat crushed his lungs. He came out first. A soft and lumbering behemoth in the moonlight. Even bigger and more monstrous than I recalled. He wobbled with in-toxication as he neared his demise. He was carrying the last few gulps of liquor in a clear bottle in his swollen right hand. Two steps away now. I held my breath and let the sonofabitch pass. *Fuck it, now or never.*

I sprang from my hiding spot, swinging the tire iron with the fury of God. A terrible crack rang through the yard as I split his forehead wide open. Blood ran down his swollen face and into his eyes. He stag-gered, dropped the liquor bottle, unleashed a growl of rage, and with arms outstretched, he lunged at me. I swung again and again. Each blow opened a sickening gash in his flesh. *Christ!* Another swing. More blood.

He dropped to one knee, but still he came at me. I jumped on him, hitting him harder. A crimson river of blood painted my arms. I raised the weapon back up above my head to finish the job, but the blood-soaked shaft flew out of my hand and disappeared into the abyss. I looked around to see where it went.

*Fuck . . . I forgot the whore.* She was still standing in the doorway with eyes the size of saucers. I fished the envelope out of my jeans and tossed it at her feet.

"There's an extra fifty in there. Keep your mouth fuckin' shut or you'll get the same," I hissed. She snatched up the envelope and fin-gered through the bills. She smiled and wiped the transferred blood off her hands onto her shirt.

"It was a pleasure, baby," she said as she stepped over the limp, out-stretched arm of The Whale and scurried off to the dope man.

Behind me, a shallow cough followed by gurgling sounds emanated from the mountain of meat. He was coming around. Unable to locate the tire iron, I desperately searched for a substitute. Out of the corner of my eye, I spotted a bumper jack propping up a rusty silver Ford some twenty feet away. I sprinted over and kicked the car's rear bumper several times, causing it to rock until the jack kicked out and the car came crashing down. I picked up the long steel handle off the jack and spun back around to see The Whale staggering to his feet.

I couldn't let him get his feet settled under him. Death waited for any man this beast squared off against. I cocked the notched bludgeon back and lunged.

The jack's pump-head tore into the man's flesh and ripped it away with ease. I didn't let up until his bones were broken and flesh hung like meat curtains from his face, at which point I leaned in close to relay the message, "You're fuckin' done, don't let me see you again."

He responded with deep apneustic breaths.

The beating had taken both no time at all and all the time in the world—a dichotomy that only a handful of readers are cursed enough to understand. I had rolled onto my ass and tossed the jack aside when I heard the clanging of someone unlocking the outer gate. There was no time to clean up the mess. I was busted by whoever walked through that second gate.

"Jesus fuckin' Christ," a familiar voice cried out. "You caved his fucking head in!" It was my uncle Toby. I watched him bend over and grab the bottle The Whale had been nursing. He took a two-second hit and killed it, then slapped his palm to his forehead and ran it down his face, ending the exaggerated expression by tugging at his fat bottom lip. "The fuck were you thinkin' Sean-O?" he said.

"Gonna hafta get 'im to the hospital 'fore he croaks," interjected my uncle Joe, who appeared out from behind Toby. To this day, I don't know how or why they happened to stop by the shop that night at that hour; could have been a guy I didn't know about who was working the shop that phoned them or some twisted divine intervention. Either way, it was a stroke of pure Irish fuckin' luck.

"My pops is gonna kill me," I was able to get out after registering the severity of the situation.

"Go wait in the office. Don't call anyone and don't you dare fuckin' leave," Joe barked. "Let's go, Toby, help me load this fuck inta the car."

My legs carried me inside on lifeless autopilot. As the door was closing, I caught the beginning of Toby's rant. "I *am* liftin', fer chrissakes. This bastard weighs more than a goddamn engine block . . ."

I sat in the office among The Whale's shit. The scarred paneling, the newspapers, the old Wonderland schedules, the overflowing ashtray, the empty bottles, the dirt, the grime—it all stank. I hated The Whale more than ever in that moment. *Why did he make it so it had to go down this way?*

Toby came in, covered in sweat and secondhand blood. Joe had taken The Whale to the emergency room alone.

"The fuck was that out there?" Toby asked.

"I dunno . . . I was told if I felt wronged . . . do somethin' about it. So I did," I said.

"You didn't gotta do 'im like that. *Shit.* Ya beat 'im to an inch a death," Toby said. I hung my head; there was nothing else to say. We waited quietly until Joe got back.

The first rays of amber sunlight spilled into the office with Joe when he returned. He sat down across the desk. He looked tired. Toby did too. I'm sure I wasn't faring any better. Toby broke first.

"He gonna make it?" Toby asked.

"He'll pull through," Joe said. "Gonna be in the hospital a stretch."

"And what if he talks?" Toby prodded.

"He won't. I doubt he'll eva talk again," Joe said. "More 'n' a mumble."

"We shoulda threw 'im in the crusher, Joe. Got ridda him," Toby concluded.

"The kid did plenty," Joe said calmly. He took a breath and shifted the conversation over to me. "Here," he said, extending a busy key ring with half a dozen brass keys on it. "These are yours now. It's what you wanted, right? Jus' remember, you take these an' you get everythin' that comes wit 'em."

After what I'd just done, the gravity of Joe's statement came crashing down on me like a ton of bricks. *Was this really what I wanted?*

I closed my fingers around the metal ring and nodded.

The keys were heavy in my hand, but they felt good. Felt right. It wasn't exactly a heroic David-versus-Goliath story or anything, but *shit*, nothing in the real world ever is. I knew that was only the beginning, but give me one hundred lifetimes and I couldn't have imagined how deep and dark the path would go. Hindsight is a fucking cancer.

# FOUR

## LEARNING THE GAME

A warm summer breeze blew through the junkyard. The first car of the day rolled in, and someone closed the gate behind it. It was 1987, and I'd been running the crew for around eight months. The operation was smooth and efficient, and everyone was making more money than ever before. I had to install a large solid-steel Boston Lock & Safe Co. combination safe in the back office to accommodate the increased cash flow. Profits had almost doubled, even with paying my guys fair.

I leaned back in my new office chair that wasn't new anymore. It had almost gotten comfortable. *Shit* . . . Hank had warned me from the beginning about that feeling. Contentment can render the ambitious lazy. And being lazy in this world can get you killed. *Quick.* I knew that meant it was time for me to expand beyond the junkyard. I guess my pops agreed because later that week, he came to me with a new assignment: commercial fishing.

I had heard my uncles talk about the industry before. It was steeped in organized crime. Criminal co-ops dictated where captains were allowed to fish, purchase fuel and bait, off-load their catch, and at what price the "market value" was determined. On top of that, a fishing boat itself is an invaluable tool in organized crime. The benefit of owning and operating your own boat is based on the premise that each state only controls twelve nautical miles off its coastline; however, they can legally punish crimes up to twenty-four miles out. All it meant for us was that twenty-five miles out became our playground.

Real freedom lies in international waters because the North Atlantic keeps her secrets better than any dead man. Her inky-black bottom covets and conceals a whole helluva lot better than a hastily dug pit in the ground. Ultimately, bodies can be unearthed, trace evidence can be recovered, and empires can topple, which is why most of the crime on the high seas happens at the bottom. If it sinks, it stays. *Last time I checked, they still haven't found Atlantis, right?*

I was being sent with my uncle Bill Harvey to work on James "Big Mac" McCoy's boat, *The Real McCoy*, for two months. I was told to learn how to operate a commercial fishing vessel, navigate channel markers, and how to work a Loran-C system, radar, autohelm, and course plotter. Before I left, I had to promote whoever I trusted the most to oversee the stolen car ring while I was gone.

Just like that, two days later, I found myself standing on a dock dressed in an orange Grundéns bib and matching twelve-inch deck boots that Hank had given me.

It was too goddamn early on that dock in Green Harbor. Couldn't have been quarter past four. I listened to the small waves lapping against the pinewood pylons and watched as boats rocked peacefully in their slips. Each boat would have been practically indistinguishable from the next if every hull hadn't been painted a different color. It was low tide, and the air smelled like the hooker I lost my virginity to.

It was another fifteen minutes before Uncle Bill and Big Mac arrived in an old rusted-out pickup. Big Mac dropped the tailgate and loaded some equipment into my arms. He retrieved a cooler of food from the cab, and Bill carried a second cooler filled with Hamm's Premium lager and ice. We walked down the dock until we came to the second-to-last boat, the one with a pastel green hull. It was thirty-five feet long with a hydraulic winch mounted midship and a wide-open transom, and it held enough fuel to fish for three days at a time. The perfect fishing vessel. There was a cramped cuddy cabin below deck with a small kitchenette on one side, and on the other were utilitarian bunk beds—identical to the prison beds I'd spend a majority of my nights in later in life.

Big Mac stood at the helm and turned the key. The throaty growling of a big diesel engine echoed across the calm marina. Bill and I untied the cleat hitches from the dock and climbed aboard. As we exited the harbor, Bill gave me the rundown on different commercial fishing techniques.

Commercial bottom trawling was done by dragging a giant wide-mouth net along the seabed a quarter mile behind the fishing vessel. Clipped to each side of the net were two metal wing-shaped trawl doors, which, when towed at slow speeds, would be hydrodynamically forced outward to keep the mouth of the net wide open. Fastened just in front of the net was a row of heavy chains. Similar to tin cans tied to a wedding getaway car, these chains, known as "ticklers," would drag and bounce off the bottom and knock loose the flounder, cod, and other bottom-feeders to be caught in the net. Every three to four hours, you had to haul back the tow so the winch wasn't overloaded by the weight of too many fish.

We had been underway for three hours before setting the net. Uncle Bill showed me how to do it the proper way. It was carefully coiled around the drum of the winch so it didn't get tangled as it was fed through the A-frame gallows at the stern and into the water. Bill pulled the hydraulic lever on the starboard side of the winch and lectured me to always mind my hands around the net; never get the two tangled.

"Boat's no place ta be careless," Bill warned, keeping an eye on the net as it slipped into the ocean. Swelling waves tossed the boat around without much effort. He went on to describe the various accidents he'd witnessed while fishing. He explained how rats seldom had their sea legs, nor were they famously talented fishermen: a dangerously accident-prone combination amidst an unfriendly crew.

Furthering my education, Big Mac went on to explain how there's no better place in the world for a dead drop than at the bottom of the ocean in a lobster pot. He told me about how Frank LaPier used lobster pots to become one of the largest international narcotic smugglers at the time. The larger freighters came up from the south but could not navigate inland without authorities taking notice and wanting a proper declaration of goods aboard.

Between his boats and the freighters waiting to enter Boston, Frank had a network in place. They would pull only his pots, the buoys marked with his colors; fill the trap with narcotics, twenty kilos per pot; and reset the pots, all before coming into port. Every second day, lobstermen routinely pulled and reset their pots. LaPier's fleet would find hundreds of hydraulic-pressed kilos of coke, no larger than the size of this book, along with the red crustaceans.

A fishing boat is designed to smuggle drugs; the features are too convenient to be argued otherwise. A lobster boat, most anyway, has a livewell running along the keel; it is filled with water and oxygen to keep the daily catch alive until the fishermen can return to the shore.

Setting lobster pots is done with surgical precision, mastered by each captain. They are released from the stern, one at a time, in a string of ten to thirty pots. A marker buoy is attached to the two end pots. Each trap is separated by a one-hundred-foot section of groundline, meaning there is anywhere between one thousand and three thousand feet between buoys. An experienced fisherman often sets the traps in one direction, north to south or east to west, in multiple parallel lines to cover their territory. This makes it easy to tell when someone is fishing your spot; their pots will overlap, and pulling up one string ends by pulling up a twisted clusterfuck.

Commercial lobster pots are required by the Department of Fish and Game to have a plaque with the license ID numbers, making it easy to establish the fuck-head that was stealing from you. It happened to Uncle Bill's younger brother, Donny.

I forget if it was Big Mac, Bill, or my pops who told me the story, but it went like this:

Donald Harvey was nervously waiting on the dock. It was already late morning, and he normally would have been halfway to his first pot by now had it not been for instructions to wait. He stood by the stern of the boat that occupied the slip he was ordered to wait by. The engine of the boat revved as the transmission was engaged, and the diesel wet exhaust coughed up from under the water, all comforting stimuli to a real fisherman. The accident happened quickly, as most accidents do. Someone was walking by on the dock when they lost their footing and stumbled into Donald. He fell into the whirlpool of choppy water. The boat's prop, which would normally not be spinning, was spinning, and the brass prop cut deep into Donny's back, severing nerves and arteries and shattering bone. The damage was done. By the time he was pulled out, Donny's left arm was paralyzed, and he lost partial mobility in his back. I learned later on that I was filling the vacancy that Donny left behind.

For three days straight, I was utterly exhausted and very wet. When we finally docked, I had an inch or two of stale water lingering in my boots. The damp had crept into my bones. And I'd loved every second of it.

In total we caught roughly one thousand pounds of flats, six hundred of monkfish, six hundred of cod, two hundred and fifty of haddock, and a couple hundred pounds of lobster. A refrigerated truck was waiting for us to take our catch to the market. The fridge fan hummed as we unloaded fish tote by tote into the back.

After every outing, Big Mac would take the three of us to a restaurant called the Blue Fin for an early lunch. It became our ritual. Big Mac got the chowder, Bill got fish and chips, and I ordered the grilled salmon. Every time. Without fail. It was the best food around and one of those places where the back door was always open to guys like us.

When we weren't out on the water, Big Mac brought Bill and me up to a hunting cabin he owned in Maine. I always knew when we crossed over the state line because a potent whiff of pine sap filled the car. The property was naturally overgrown with twenty-five or so acres of dense woods. The house itself was hardly larger than his boat. The amenities were utilitarian and primitive: one sink that emptied into the crawl space below, two twin-size beds (Big Mac took out an old army cot for me to sleep on), one long rectangular kitchen table, and four chairs. There was a sooty potbelly woodstove in the corner of the room and half a cord of dried pine stacked next to it. We got water from the rain-catch barrel. There was an outhouse a short walk from the back door.

But that little house had everything we could have needed. There, Big Mac and Bill taught me about the other side of the fishing business. Big Mac would unfurl dozens of big nautical charts out onto his kitchen table and explain how each boat had its own territory determined by the historical parameters drawn up by mob surveyors and how ownership of each area was determined by loyalty. Whatever you were going to do on the water, you only did within your territory. He shuffled some charts aside, looking for a particular one. When he found what he was looking for, he oriented it in front of me. It was a detailed mapping of our first territory, Stellwagen Bank, where we had bottom-fished that first time. He explained how it had a soft sandy bottom perfect for bottom trawling. It became a protected marine sanctuary later on in '92, but prior to then, we certainly overfished it.

I remember Big Mac smoothing out the creases in a second chart and carefully looking it up and down before tapping the words "Jeffreys Ledge" printed in dark blue letters amidst a light blue background. It was our second, and arguably more useful, territory. Sixty-five miles off the northeastern shore of Boston, this underwater cliff defines the precipice of the world, denoted by the overcrowded contour lines. Any further east and the ocean floor plummets one hundred fifty meters, and with it, any chance of recovery. Big Mac explained that you can wrap a body with ten to twelve feet of chain-link fence and secure it with a couple padlocks, and the three-hundred-pound problem will sink to oblivion, protected by the impregnable edges of rocks that make up the seafloor of Jeffreys Ledge. Fishermen avoid a jagged bottom so they don't lose or damage any gear. If the body lay on soft sand somewhere else, the ticklers of law-abiding men may resurface what needs to remain lost. That's why not all ocean floors are created equal in the eyes of the mob.

I learned more from Big Mac and Uncle Bill than I ever could have in a traditional classroom. I could pen a full shelf of textbooks and not scratch the surface of what I was taught up there in the backwoods of Maine. It went beyond boats and the sea too. One weekend in particular, instead of handing me a chart and a compass, Uncle Bill placed a Weatherby Mark V sniper rifle and a box of high-powered .30-caliber rounds into my hands. Big Mac had set up half a dozen bottles on the far end of his property, about a quarter mile from the house. Bill showed me how to create and read a DOPE card and how to adjust the Tasco scope accordingly.

I notched the butt of the rifle into the crux of my shoulder and took aim at the little green bottle in my sights. I held my breath and pulled the trigger between heartbeats. I heard a click. Big Mac and Bill burst out laughing.

"Fuckin' thing's useless if you don't load it," Bill snickered, shaking the box of golden bullets in his hand. I pulled the bolt handle back to open the chamber. I reached over and fished one of the bottleneck bullets out of the box and inserted it tip first into the gun.

I punched the bolt forward, back into place, and retook my aim. *Bang!* The glass exploded and the rifle stock dug into my shoulder blade. The ringing in my ear lasted all afternoon.

# FIVE

## RUNNING THE RACKETS

I turned sixteen years old on September 10, 1987. It was a Thursday. Reagan was in his second term in office, and "Livin' on a Prayer" was played on an endless loop by every radio station throughout the country. I didn't give a shit about any of that, though—my birthday included . . . *my birthday especially*. The only person throughout my whole life who ever seemed to care about my birthday was Hank. And that year was no exception.

That morning, after my pops indulged in a breakfast-time jelly donut he wasn't supposed to have, we went for a car ride. Over the past eight years, Hank's eyesight had steadily deteriorated due to the mismanaged diabetes, and he now wore a pair of black-framed glasses when he drove. He hated wearing them. The thick lenses gave him exaggerated bug eyes, and you'd never catch him outside the car with them on.

Traffic was light. We drove south for forty-five minutes, making small talk about my maritime training with Big Mac and Uncle Bill. Hank took the exit for Scituate, Massachusetts. Ten minutes later, we rolled to a stop in the harbor marina parking lot. The lot was covered in a layer of shattered white shells. The fragments crunched under my feet as I followed my pops to the marina office. I sat outside on a sagging rope fence while Hank went in and talked to the dockmaster. He came out wearing a Cheshire Cat smile.

"Happy birthday, son," he said, tossing me a set of keys. A spongy orange key float was attached to them by a short brass ball chain. "Go on, go check it out . . . down end-a the dock, one on the left."

I had never seen anything so beautiful in my sixteen years. I walked around the boat to get every angle. The newly painted wooden hull gleamed in the reflection of the water, and the sleek silhouette of the gunwale ran into the horizon. It was a Cape Islander, a Nova Scotia lobster boat. Thirty-six-footer. The keel was shaped like a banana, with a high bow and stern hovering six inches above the water, which allowed you to load an extra couple thousand pounds on board. On the deck was a stack of brand-new lobster pots, rigged and ready to go. I wandered up the finger dock. The name *Sean's Dream* adorned the port bow and was accompanied by a hand-painted shamrock.

"Whaddya think?" Hank said, watching me scrutinize the gift like a thorough crime scene investigator.

I didn't know what to think. I was at a loss for words. I will never understand why my pops chose me; after all, I wasn't his blood. But I was his son. I threw my arms around my father, and one of us shed a tear. *I'll never fucking tell you which one of us it was, though.*

I had worked out a seven-part business plan ten different ways in my head before we even got back in the car. There's money in the sea, and now I had the tools to extract it. I captained the boat like a pimp turning out his bottom bitch. I put close to fifteen hundred hours on that motor in under three months. There were more jobs and opportunities than one boat alone could handle: I needed reinforcements. I took every penny of profit from those first months and added three more boats to my burgeoning fleet of quasi pirate ships. Four ships: each equipped with its own crew, its own territory, and its own reputation.

Sometime around New Year's, I pulled *Sean's Dream* out of the water to have work done on the engine. While a mechanic overhauled and rebuilt the motor, I decided to make some modifications to the boat itself. The boat had a wide and shallow cavity below deck. There was a hollow skeg running down the boat's centerline and transverse support beams running perpendicular, which made the space resemble the rib cage of a blue whale. The empty space was full of potential.

My idea was to install a dummy fuel tank and have a way to inconspicuously transport whatever it was I didn't want seen. I started by finding two almost identical tanks; the only difference being one measured an inch longer in regard to its height, width, and depth. I mounted the smaller of the two tanks into the hull, opposite the existing tank, with long bronze wood screws and cleanly cut the entire top panel off. I then cut away and removed the bottom panel from the bigger tank so it would slip overtop of the smaller one like a large metal shoebox. Once it was on, I hooked up fake fuel feed tubes and return lines to the decoy tank to camouflage it further. I now had an inconspicuous twenty-one-cubic-foot vault under the deck that couldn't be found by the prying eyes of any intrusive Coast Guardsmen. They could search with the thoroughness of an elbow-deep proctologist and still be none the wiser. The space was only just large enough to hide a couple hundred pounds of cargo or one large man.

My next idea was designed to increase stealth. I took a circular saw and cut ten inches out of the wheelhouse walls to lower the roof. It wasn't my best work, but it did the trick. By having a lower water profile, Sean's Dream became hidden from view at only three miles away and disappeared almost entirely in the trough of a rolling swell.

As soon as Sean's Dream was back in its slip, I put it to use. I became notorious for taking the boat out in weather conditions a craft its size has no business going out in. It leaked like a sonofabitch, but you're less likely to be bothered that way. The more inclement the weather, the better.

My second boat was a fifty-five-foot DMR, which had been aptly named Leviathan by its previous owner. Whitey had told me to find a seaworthy boat down in Ocean City, Maryland, and that he'd give me a job for the vessel once or twice a month. He had a connection overseas that would send us a package aboard a transatlantic freighter. The ship would have to drop anchor and wait for up to days at a time for the harbor pilot (whose job it was to guide the freighter safely inland) to be shuttled out.

The *Leviathan's* job was to meet the container ship while it waited in the unpatrolled international waters before it got to port. When the *Levithan's* red hull came into sight, the freighter's crew would load packages onto a soft-sided launch boat and carefully lower it into the water to meet us. They would tie off and unload the packages aboard the *Leviathan* under the cover of nightfall. When they weren't handling shipments for Jim, I had the crew running longlines for tilefish as far down as the Outer Banks in North Carolina.

I had another reliable three-man crew running a boat off the southern coast of Rhode Island. It was a beneficial stronghold due to its geographical location. To the east was Buzzards Bay, giving my crew access to the southern coast of Massachusetts, and to the west was the confluence of New York and Connecticut waterways. Averaging fifteen knots, it only took two hours to reach the tip of Long Island, New York. My crew rendezvoused with our narcotic suppliers and other contacts on the water, then delivered whatever packages they received to a runner on the mainland.

The runner, a young kid around my age, would drive up to the junkyard, and I'd disperse the bricks to mid-level handlers outside the organization to cut and repackage and distribute to lower-level handlers to do the same. A cascade of impurity that I wanted nothing to do with.

I kept my last boat in the armada stationed on the North Shore. It was a forty-eight-foot gillnetter with a green fiberglass hull that handled jobs from Boston all the way up to the Hague Line at Canada's maritime boundary.

This racket ran its course for a few years until my boats either sank or caught fire tied to the docks at various times. Thank God they were fully insured . . .

With my decision to live in the shadows of civilized society, I quickly adapted to the dark. I could see down here and always kept an eye out for new opportunities. Before long, my gaze was drawn to the art of garbage removal. It should come as no surprise to the reader that organized crime generates a mountain of trash that can't simply be placed in the bins at the end of the driveway, nor can it be loaded into the bed of a pickup, driven to the dump, and be disposed of in front of an audience of regular workers. Waste must be handled with the skill and tact of a military strategist on the brink of war. I devised a two-part battle plan: collection and disposal.

Collection was the easy part. My pops let me borrow the construction company's eight-yard dump truck that was used to haul gravel. I would get calls from restaurants, clubs, construction sites, flower shops, *you name it*—any business that required discreet removal started phoning me. I even did house calls if I knew the customer and the money was right. I came, loaded whatever it was into the truck bed, and left. No questions asked, no questions answered.

The one thing I didn't dispose of were dead bodies, although I did hear how it was done. It's not like any of that Hollywood *bullshit* either. You don't use chemicals; they're messy and slow, and afterward you still have to deal with the barrel. And if you *were* going to use chemicals, you sure as shit are not using hydrochloric acid like they do on TV. And if you did, you got a mushy mess. Nevertheless, if you wanted to go the chemical route, you'd have to use a high-concentrate lye: sodium hydroxide. It completely dissolves the flesh and compromises the integrity of the skeleton, diminishing bone density. You can easily pulverize what is left into a fine dust with a wooden mallet. It was easy to get your hands on enough of it too—plumbers often kept drums of it on hand, and if they didn't have a sufficient supply, they could get it and not draw any attention.

While equally messy, another option you have when disposing of a human body is to take the remains to an animal farm. Second only to the ocean's appetite for a body is a pig's. However cliché, pigs do, in fact, eat *anything*. They don't discriminate or hold prejudices; they just eat. And similar to serving a body up to the sea, the body has to be prepared for consumption by swine. The larger bones (i.e., femur, humerus, tibia, fibula, radius, ulna) have to be broken up into more manageable portions. And though a pig will eat anything, that doesn't mean it can digest everything. For that reason, hair must be shaved and any teeth must be pulled. Clothes, on the other hand, don't necessarily have to be removed, but it is common courtesy to strip the body beforehand out of consideration for the animal's digestive tract. You can rid yourself of the hair and clothes by tossing them into an incinerator. Teeth can be flushed down any public toilet or thrown out the car window on a road trip—say, one every five miles or so. The other hassle of using pigs is to find a farmer with aligned morals and enough pigs. It takes anywhere from twenty to twenty-five pigs to consume a body overnight. Any less and a partial body would still remain in their trough when a different farmer scatters oats for the pigs' morning meal.

Another fallacy on the Hollywood screen is how they portray the process of burying a body. The locations are always wrong; and no killer would ever have a victim dig their own grave—it'd take too long. General thinking among mobsters is that there are only two places bodies should ever be buried: under concrete or in a grave. Concrete is effective because it cannot be unearthed by weather conditions or a shovel. The easiest place to hide a body under concrete and not draw attention is at a construction jobsite. Every construction blueprint is built from the ground up, starting with the structure's foundation. Once the foundation is dug out, a large plastic sheet is rolled over the soil to act as a vapor barrier and protect the longevity of the concrete. A sturdy rebar grid is then laid out onto the plastic to provide structural support, and finally, concrete is poured over top. To ensure a body is buried and never recovered, a stiff is sometimes placed underneath the plastic and entombed in the concrete. Most major cities across the globe are built atop the dead.

If one does not have access to a construction site, a cemetery will do just fine. Ordinary people die every day, which is actually quite convenient for criminals. When a regular funeral is planned, a grave is dug days in advance. If someone finds themself in the predicament of having a corpse on their hands and desperately needs to unload it, they might grease the palms of the gravedigger to go a few extra whacks with the backhoe and deposit your liability into the grave a day or so before another casket is laid to rest on top of it. It's like having an unobtrusive squatter in the basement someone didn't know they had, except they're both dead. The family of the deceased whose last name is on the tombstone provides an additional impediment for law enforcement who might want to dig up the double grave, looking for evidence that may or may not be there.

The best—quickest and most efficient—way to completely wipe away any trace of a body's existence is through proper incineration in a crematorium or a foundry. Most cremation ovens burn their dead at 1600°F (871°C). That powderizes everything besides tooth enamel; but at the end of the day, thirty-two small teeth are unquestionably easier to make disappear than a fully intact body.

Multiple crematoriums around Massachusetts had at least one of these cremation chambers in their basement. They were built in the uncongested, rural parts of the state because of the unpleasant smell that came out of the smokestacks. Uncle Joe was a silent partner in some of them, but over the years I have forgotten which ones.

Easier than crematoriums are foundries. Foundries are where metals are cast into new shapes. Molten metals are poured into a mold and allowed to resolidify. After cooling, the mold is removed, and the metal retains its new form. To get most metals above their melting points, foundry furnaces must reach significantly higher temperatures than a crematorium oven. If one puts a body in with liquid iron, which has a melting point of 2,800°F (1,538°C), it instantly becomes an undetectable powder, which is then mixed into the solid block.

Sometime in the mid-'80s, Uncle Joe bought a smaller, more portable version of a foundry furnace for the chop shop. Ironically, the kind he purchased was called a crucible furnace. It was mostly used to melt down scrap metal. Condensing the scrap into dense geometric cubes allowed tractor trailers to haul an extra ten tons up to Canada per trip.

Once Joe had given me permission to use it, the furnace became an indispensable tool in my garbage business. Though I never threw bodies into it, I threw in whole arsenals of weaponry. They were mostly firearms, though the occasional knife or baseball bat went in too. Whatever the client wanted to get rid of. I also recall frequently melting down dental extraction tool kits.

Between the calls in need of my services, and with my crews operating self-sufficiently, I found myself inundated with useless leisure time. Most kids my age either took up baseball or football or were practicing for their driver's permit test. Organized sports never had the same allure to me as organized crime did, and not having a license wasn't going to stop me from driving, so I decided to take up the only true, authentic American pastime: making more money. But I took that idea quite literally.

It started as most of the stories have so far: in Toby's basement. Nothing in the basement was different, but my role had changed. I now had a seat at the table, my own highball of gin, and my own rummy hand to play. My balls had dropped too—if you were wondering.

One day there was a sixteen-wheeler waiting in the driveway to be let into the garage. I went up to unload it. After unlatching the four safety bars on the rear and swinging open the doors, thirty state-of-the-art office printers greeted me. Capable of printing twenty pages per minute in full color. Retail was $19,995 each. They were neatly arranged in two rows with a narrow aisle between them. They were tied down to pallets, one pallet per machine, and generously wrapped in plastic wrap. Each stood waist-high and must have weighed five hundred pounds. I dragged over the yellow pallet jack and waited as the driver lowered the trailer's hydraulic platform to the ground.

"Long drive?" I asked, trying to make small talk.

"Mhmm," the man grunted. He was old and had a hard face with solemn features. I wondered how many more trips like this he had left in him. I wheeled the jack onto the platform, and he raised us up. I carefully positioned the two tines of the jack under the first pallet and pumped the handle until it lifted the printer an inch. I maneuvered the printer onto the platform and was lowered back down to the ground. "You got it from here, kid. I'm goin' for a smoke," the old man said, fingering his breast pocket for cigarettes. He walked away before I could respond.

*Asshole.* I got all thirty machines out by myself.

"Big fuckers, aren't they?" Uncle Toby said, walking into the garage. He must have heard the garage door shut and the truck leave. He took out a folding knife from his pocket and cut away the plastic from one of the printers. "How the fuck's it work anyway?" he said, absentmindedly pressing buttons.

I picked up the power cord and plugged it in. The machine came to life. Turquoise letters welcomed us as they glided across a black screen similar to stock information on the Wall Street ticker.

"Got any paper?" I asked.

"Go ask Kitty where she keeps it," he said. "She's foreva typing poetry."

I went inside and found Toby's wife in the kitchen preparing a platter of sandwiches for lunch. She had a green checkered apron tied around her waist and a matching headband pushing her hair back. A mile-long menthol cigarette with two inches of ash dangled from her mouth.

"Hey, Kitty, you know where I can find some paper? Toby sent me in to ask ya," I said.

She wiped her hands on her apron while she thought. "If we got any, it's in his office, honey. You know where it is? Down the hall, second door on the left," she said, smiling.

I thanked her and followed the directions. The door was halfway open. I pushed gently and it swung in. The room was cluttered with piles of paper and magazines and unemptied ashtrays. Slid under the oak desk against the far wall was a lemon-yellow W.B. Mason box with three reams of paper left inside. I grabbed one and returned to Toby. He was still pressing buttons at random.

"Find some?" he asked.

"Yeah," I said and opened the top tray, sliding in the stack of blank office paper. "Let's try it out." I grabbed a twenty-dollar bill from my pocket, flipped open the scanner, and placed the bill onto the glass. I shuffled through the menu until the ticker read "COPY" and hit the green Start button. The printer hummed with excitement. Seconds later a warm piece of paper was ejected into the output tray. Toby snatched the paper up and spun it this way and that way. He held it up to the light.

"Well, *shit*. Ain't no difference," Toby said in a half chuckle. "Looks real . . . at least one side anyhow."

"Sonofabitch, I need one of these," I said.

"Then take it, s'all yours, Sean-O," he said.

I set up the counterfeiting operation on the second floor above a taxi company in Braintree, Mass. It was an old historic brick building with high ceilings and an open floor plan. A century of carelessly sliding heavy desks around had scarred the wooden floorboards. A wall of frosted glass windows provided the office with plenty of soft natural light. I scheduled small crews on alternating shifts to guarantee a minimum of two Winter Hill guys working at all times. Counterfeiting was easier in the eighties because there weren't any security threads, 3D ribbons, watermarks, or color-shifting ink on bills. Every bill had the same dimensions, weight, ink, and cotton-fiber paper.

We used a technique known as "bleaching." Essentially, we were turning bills of low denomination into bills of high denomination. I learned the technique from an old forger named Arturo "Arty" George. Arty had swarthy olive skin, thick Portuguese eyebrows, and a big hawkish nose; on either side of his head were the largest ears I have ever seen on any human being. Tufts of hair grew out of them like weeds. He printed and distributed the tickets for the illegal underground daily lottery for as long as anyone could remember. And he was always grumpy about something, but between his impossible accent and his frequently slipping back into his native language, you likely never knew what he was going on about. However, everyone in the criminal underworld turned to him for their forgery needs. He was a master, and he took his craft very seriously. So, when the opportunity came, I sought him out to work through my plan and ask for guidance. He began by giving me a list of everything I would need to furnish the shop.

The next day, I took the gravel truck over to a secondhand appliance store and picked up an open-top belt-driven washing machine, the accompanying dryer, and two clothes irons. Then I made my way over to the pool supply store to get chemicals in bulk. Arty had given me a list to get. The last thing I needed was printer ink. I bought the local office supply store out of their ink cartridges and placed an order at the register to get cases of it shipped straight to me.

With the equipment and chemicals on hand, Arty came by the shop to walk me through the process. The first step was to fill the washing machine with a concoction of chemicals and one-dollar bills. Exact proportions of the caustic chemicals were imperative. Too little and there would be no effect; too much and the bills could disintegrate. After the wash, we transferred the wet bills into the dryer. We repeated the wash-n-dry cycle three times or until we were left with completely blank off-white bills. We then laid the bills on the table and ironed out the wrinkles. With the bills flat, they were ready to go into the printer. We test-printed a few prototypes until Arty was satisfied with the color and alignment; after all, he was putting his reputation behind the product.

And the product was completely indistinguishable from the real thing. At first glance, the bills might as well have come straight from the Bureau of Engraving and Printing. If, however, you got your hands on a bill at that point, you might be able to spot the counterfeit. The feel was off. The bill became soft and limp due to the strong alkaline chemicals.

But Arty already knew that. He had come up with a cheap and easy solution years ago: Aqua Net Extra Super Hold hair spray. He brought up a case of the tall purple cans from his car and handed me one. Similar to how a housewife irons her husband's suits, we sprayed and starched every bill and ran the electric iron over them one last time.

Arty gathered a stack of the fresh bills and began rapidly shuffling them into his other hand one at a time. After a few seconds, he stopped, singled one of the bills out, and began rubbing it with his thumb. The feel was perfect, and the ink didn't smudge. He raised the stack next to one of those gigantic elephant ears of his and flipped through the bills again. The sound was perfect too. He smiled.

"Same way ever' time," he said. "No 'little more this, little more that.' No! . . . Same way ever' time, yes? You understan'?"

I had just turned one hundred dollars into ten grand in only four hours. I wasn't going to change a *fucking* thing.

The major issue with counterfeit money is that it's worthless unless you can spend it or exchange it. Knowing this beforehand, I strategically chose to move into the vacant loft above the taxi office. We had an understanding where I would supply them with the money the drivers used to make change for their customers, and in exchange, I received a portion of the total profits. The added advantage of sending the fake money through the taxi office was that it was spread around the country. More often than not, the taxis were exclusively hired as airport shuttles, and because it was a cash-only business, customers were required to receive at least a few counterfeit bills if they didn't have exact change. These travelers would then unknowingly transport and distribute our phony money wherever they landed, making it impossible to trace back to me. I had similar arrangements with other cash-only businesses. Odds are good that if you brought your car to a Massachusetts car wash in the late eighties, you drove away with a wallet full of my fake bills.

# SIX

## CONSEQUENCES

Anonymity is a blessing that never returns once it's gone. From the moment you get a reputation, you have to defend it, to back it up, to prove it every day. It was too late for me. In my world, losing a reputation was a death sentence. *I could never let that happen.*

I wasn't a kid anymore, though I hadn't been for quite some time. At seventeen, my reputation entered a room before I did. In a way, that had been what I was working toward. Respect. And not just from my family but from everyone. I had been so focused on building a reputation that I'd turned a blind eye to the dangers of actually having one.

I was in a popular Yugoslavian bar in East Boston called the Rakija Lounge. It was a private club for Slavs, which meant my red hair made me stick out like an albino gorilla. But I didn't give a fuck: the bar was on Winter Hill turf, and I was there on business. I was picking up an envelope for Jim. In addition to the bar operating on our turf, we had been supplying it with liquor at a heavy discount for a few years and got a cut of their net profits. I would come by quarterly to collect. I still handled all of the larger collections myself so that the payments wouldn't be short. *You never brought an envelope to Whitey if it was light*—it was an ironclad rule that might as well have been carved into a stone tablet.

Nikolas, the bartender and owner, was always good about paying on time and in full. This time looked to be no different. The bar was busy. I didn't recognize many faces—one, maybe two at most. I got a frigid greeting from a group of Yacs sitting at a booth by the door. It wasn't so much a greeting as an ostracizing glare. The few faces I knew gave me a grunt or a nod in acknowledgment and respect. An unfamiliar face sitting at a high-top tipped the corner of his cap as I passed. A couple of the other barflies that must have known of my reputation paid their respects on my way to the last stool beside the service station, where Nikolas always stood to get a view of the television.

There were two old white guys on the screen sitting in a press box and talking loudly into microphones. A Sox-Yankees game was about to start, which explained the crowd. Only two things unite all Bostonians: crime and the Red Sox. The Yacs were no exception.

"Ayy, Sean-O," Nikolas said with feigned enthusiasm as he looked away from the pregame commentary. "Here for the game? Clemens is on the mound, you know. Should be a good one."

"Not today, Nik. Got a few other stops to make after this," I replied. He knew why I was there without us having to get into it in front of his other customers.

"All right, you give me minute," he said. "Got it in the back office. You want drink?" he asked. I nodded.

I was still in the honeymoon phase of the addict: that short window when I actually enjoyed the liquor. Most addicts misremember this time period as being in a happy, healthy, and manageable relationship with their fix. I was no different. I started most mornings with a shoulder of Smirnoff to feel good, not to thwart off sickness. There wasn't a psychological or physical dependance yet; I just liked the stuff.

Nikolas turned around and reached behind the front rows of liquor bottles to grab an unopened bottle of Jack Daniel's. He placed it down in front of me. "On the house," he said half-jokingly.

The old barfly on the stool beside me had watched the entire interaction with the ravenous eyes of a drunk. He wasn't dressed in any sports apparel. He was a professional. Knew all the tricks. The moment the whiskey bottle hit the bar, his performance began.

"You need help with that?" he salivated with a thick Balkan accent. I tried to ignore him. I was there on business, not to be bothered. He persisted. "C'mon, my friend, we drink together. No need to drink alone, we are all friends here, and friends drink together."

*Fuck, what was taking Nik so long?* The drunk flipped his shot glass upright on the bar. I couldn't ignore him much longer. He moved impatiently around on the stool and opened his mouth to make another plea.

I cracked. I poured him a double. He twisted his face into a grotesque smile. Suddenly, the bar exploded with Bostonian patriotism: Clemens had struck out the side. The drunk saw the opportunity and clumsily grasped it.

"You see that? *Jebeni* Yankees can't touch 'The Rocket' if their lives depended on it. You pour another one for the two of us, yes? To celebrate," he persisted. "This is year they break the curse, you know.'"*

"Every year's the year they're gonna break the curse," I said.

"Ack, you give me drink either way, you not going to finish bottle by yourself," he demanded.

"I'm not handin' out free fuckin' drinks to every drunk who's too cheap to buy their own."

"*Irska pička.* You watch that tongue, you little shit. You better show some goddamn respect and pour me fucking drink when I tell you to. Now—pour," he said, punctuating the demand by picking up his shot glass and slamming it back down again.

"Fuck off," I said, attempting to brush off the drunk. I heard a set of heavy bootsteps tramping up behind me.

"He giving you any problems, Milos?" a deep, cavernous voice said, addressing the drunk. I turned around to see its point of origin. A towering gargoyle stood behind the two of us at the bar. He was dressed head to toe in all black and had the stoic face of a man with just one

---

* The Curse of the Bambino refers to a superstitious baseball curse arising from the drought of World Series Championship wins after the Red Sox sold Babe "The Bambino" Ruth to the Yankees, their rivals, in 1920. This curse would go unbroken for a total of eighty-four years until the 2004 season.

THE DEVIL TO PAY

expression: hatred. He was one of the two Yacs that had been sitting in the booth by the entrance when I arrived.

"My friend here was just pouring us shots, right?" The drunk smirked at me with smug satisfaction.

"I think I'll have one too," the tall Yac said. "Oleg, c'mon over. Our generous friend here is offering to share his bottle." The second, shorter but equally burly Yac from the entrance booth joined us. The drunk added two more shot glasses to the table in jittery excitement. The tall Yac reached his arm in front of me and took hold of my Jack Daniel's bottle. He uncapped the bottle and filled three of the glasses up to the top. He took a long pull from the bottle, tilted his head, gargled the whiskey in the back of his throat, and spit it into the glass in front of me. A small crowd had forgotten about the baseball game and turned their attention to us.

*Fuck. Something had to happen now. I had a reputation to protect, right?*

I reached back across in front of the tall Yac, picked up his glass, and took the shot. I repeated the process for the glass in front of the shorter Yac. (The drunk had emptied his glass the second it was poured.) I then slid the regurgitated shot between the Yacs and said, "This one's on me. You filthy fucks can share it." I ripped my bottle out of his hands and turned back to the television. A dumbfounded gasp came from the on-lookers; ears bent, eyebrows raised, assholes puckered.

"Fuck you," the tall man said in his deep voice. I felt a smattering of spit speckle the back of my neck. I spun back around.

"The fuck d'you say to me?"

"Fuck. You. Bitch," he repeated in staccato.

A concoction of survival instinct and Tennessee whiskey ran hot through my veins. I still had the almost empty bottle in my hand, so I whipped it around like a baseball bat, swinging for the fences. And unlike the Yankees that day, I made solid contact. The bottle exploded. Shards of glass burrowed into the Yac's face. A shower of whiskey and glass poured into his eyes. He staggered and slumped to the floor.

The shorter Yac jumped at me, flailing his arms. I ducked under a clumsy right hook and landed a succession of heavyweight haymakers. He helplessly lurched forward again, grasping for his life. He managed to grab hold and pin my arms by my side in a defensive clinch. He let out a couple laborious breaths, praying for a reprieve.

But it wasn't enough to just teach him a lesson. I had to set an example, a precedent. *Why teach one when you can educate the masses?*

I snapped my neck forward, driving my forehead into his face. He winced in pain, recoiling his head a few inches. That's all I needed. I sank my teeth into the bridge of his nose and snapped my head backward, ripping flesh and cartilage from his face. A crude, jagged outline traced where the bulb of his nose used to be. The Yac let out a shrill and fell to his knees. He cupped his hands to catch the river of blood that flowed from the new hole. I spit the chunk of meat on the ground, back to its rightful owner.

But I wasn't done yet. I had one more thing to take care of. Walking around the bar, I got a second bottle of Jack and headed back to the Yacs. I looked down at the taller Yac, still slumped face down on the floor. He was conscious but just barely. I bent down next to his ear.

"Fuck me?" I shouted. "No! Fuck you!" With my free hand, I pulled down the seat of his pants and shoved the neck of the bottle deep into the man's ass. He screamed in pain. I straightened up, rolled my shoulders back, cracked my neck, caught my breath.

The only sound in the bar was the Major League announcers continuing as if nothing had happened.

"What the fuck?" Nikolas shouted, emerging from the back office. "What the fuck, Sean-O!" he repeated, pushing through the crowd of bodies to get a better view. Terror filled his eyes when he got to the front. "Fuck, man . . . You gotta get outta here, Sean. *Now!* . . . Take this and go," he commanded, thrusting an envelope with twenty to twenty-five grand into my stomach.

The sea of bystanders parted, clearing a path to the door. Nikolas guided me to the exit with a firm hand pressed into my back. As the door closed behind me, I heard Nik address the bar. "Nobody fuckin' saw a thing, you hear me? *Nothing!* Next round's on the house." The door shut with a click.

Outside I was ambushed by harsh sunlight. I had a pounding headache. The black Mercedes I was driving that month was parked a few cars down. I went over and sat in the driver's seat. I flipped the sun visor down. I found a pair of sunglasses under the armrest and put them on too. Nothing could stop this throbbing. I popped open the glove compartment, looking for something, anything, to help. There was a half-empty fifth of Smirnoff which I polished off to calm me down. With my head on straight, I threw the car in gear and drove away; I still had a job to finish. Southie was only a fifteen-minute drive. I found a spot and parked outside Triple O's Lounge, where I knew Whitey would be.

In the late sixties, a small-time crew used the building to run a nascent loan-sharking operation, and they'd hired Whitey as extra muscle. In May of 1972, the bar's owner, Donald Killeen, was shot fifteen times in the head. It was at his son's fourth birthday party. The murder went unsolved, and the bar fell into Winter Hill hands.

From the outside, the bar was unobtrusive and unassuming: standard neon signs hung in each of the street-facing windows advertising cheap beer; a small set of three concrete steps led up to a plain front door. Nothing special. Nothing that would raise suspicion or draw attention. There was even a police station not three blocks down. But that was the point: to hide in plain sight. With Whitey paying a supplemental salary to the captain, he could safely call the shots from right under the department's nose.

Those days, I hardly saw Whitey at Toby's anymore. Instead, he was using Triple O's as an unofficial South Boston courtroom. *The dishonorable James "Whitey" Bulger presiding, all rise.*

Inside, Whitey sat at a table with Flemmi, the bailiff and executioner. Whitey was wearing a tight-fitting argyle polo and had his hair neatly combed back.

"What the fuck did you do?" he said, seeing the dried blood on my clothes as I walked up. He wasn't showing me worry or concern; he was hungry for any details about a victim.

"Was painting the side of a fuckin' barn," I said. "Here's the money." I tossed the envelope onto the table. It landed with a thud.

"Any problem?" Flemmi said, chewing a cigar butt.

"I handled it," I said.

"If you made a fuckin' mess, you betta clean that shit up yaself," Flemmi spat. "We don't run no fuckin' daycare 'ere."

"I said I handled it, didn't I?"

"Yeah, shut the fuck up, Stevie." Whitey took over. "Kid said he handled it, so I think he handled it." He smiled and flashed me his big stained front tooth. Flemmi grunted a disapproval, but fuck him, I didn't care what he thought anyway. "How's Hank holdin' up these days?" Whitey asked.

"Doin' good," I replied, not in the mood for polite small talk. I didn't like being at Triple O's. I belonged on the other side of the bridge on the South Shore.

"That diabetes is a real serious matta, ya know. Gotta keep on topa it. Nothin' to laugh at," Whitey continued. "You keep a good eye on him for me, will ya?"

"Sure, Jim. Look, I gotta go. Still got some shit ta do taday."

"O' course Sean-O, o' course. Don' wanna hold ya up. Keep doin' whatcha doin'. Ya goin' places, kid."

Jim's eyes never left the stains on my shirt as I left. They followed me back out to the car and all the way down the street.

I drove over to my sister Tina's house to lay low. It had been a while since I had seen her. She distanced herself from my world—or maybe I distanced my world from her. Thankfully, she was home, but when she opened the door, she looked less than pleased to see me. *Must have been the bloody clothes.*

"What the fuck did you do?" she bawked, barring the doorway with her arm—the second time that day I was asked the question.

"You gonna let me in or what?"

"Fuck . . ." She paused. "Go get cleaned up. Bathroom's there." She pointed to a shabby door and lifted her barricade. I slid past her and into the washroom. I spun the faucet marked Hot and waited. Tepid water gushed out. I cupped my hands under the stream and began scrubbing the blood off my exposed arms and face and hands. I looked in the mirror. It wasn't kind, so I looked away. The wall creaked with the weight of Tina leaning against it outside. I heard her fatigued exhale and suppressed sobbing on the other side of the door.

"Love what you've done with the place," I said through the wall.

"It's all right . . . Seany, you okay?" she softened. "Are you in trouble?"

"Everything's fine. Just a misunderstanding, nothing serious."

"You betta not bring the cops 'round here, Seany. I don't want nothin' ta do with that."

"Nothin' happened, Sis, don't worry," I lied as I finished washing up. I didn't bother with my clothes; they were permanently stained. *Like the rest of my life.* I turned the cold faucet on full blast and splashed frigid life into my face.

Tina was shouldering the wall with crossed arms, waiting for me outside the door. She looked the same as she always had, but she'd become a beautiful woman. She was smart and stubborn and the spitting image of Doris Day. And she never took any shit from me.

"Don't fuckin' lie to me, Seany, I know you did somethin'," she punctuated. "I jus' hope you weren't too stupid this time. C'mon, I'll make you some dinner, I'm cookin' chicken and pasta."

"I'm not hungr—"

"You're eating." She cut me off. "Now sit at the table in the kitchen, I'll make you a plate." I followed her down the hall.

"Any beer?" I asked, entering the kitchen.

"Get it ya-fuckin'-self," she said.

I took a beer from the fridge and collapsed into one of the four chairs surrounding the table. I sipped my beer and listened as Tina danced on air around the kitchen; she opened cabinets, shuffled pans, and hummed softly to herself. Tina walked over and set a plate down in front of me. She returned with a base layer of noodles, then chicken, then dumped a ladleful of pasta sauce on top. Tina was a wonderful cook, and the meal was delicious.

We ate without saying a single word.

Finally, as she sipped a vodka cranberry, Tina said, "Tell me the truth, Seany, are you all right?"

"I missed you, Tina. I'm all right . . . really." I sipped my beer to empty. "Need another cocktail?" I asked, noticing her rattling the ice cubes around her empty glass. "I need one."

"No."

The police arrived an hour later. Someone knocked on the door with the brutish cadence of a cop. Tina opened the door just enough to see an Officer Wagner standing on the top step. His posture was stiff and arrogant. A revolving blue-and-white light behind him painted his acne-pitted face.

"Responding to a disturbance call, ma'am," he said to Tina and politely coughed into his fist.

"What?" Tina feigned surprise at the officer's presence.

"We got a call about a disturbance at this address," he repeated.

"Nothin' goin' on here all night, been quiet . . . Musta got a prank call or somethin'," she said.

"Are you here alone tonight, ma'am?"

"Brother's in the kitchen, but ain't no disturbance here or nothin'," she said adamantly.

"Get him out here," the officer commanded.

"Why? You 'n' me are talkin' just fine by ourself."

"It's all right, Tina, I'm here," I said, walking up the hall. "The fuck you want?"

"What's your name?" the officer asked.

"I'm Colonel fuckin' Sanders, what's it to you?"

"Were you at the Rakija Lounge earlier today?" the officer questioned.

"Been here all fuckin' day, mindin' my own fuckin' business," I said.

"Hey, I thought you was here about a fuckin' disturbance call or some shit," Tina cut in.

"Where'd that blood on ya shirt come from?" the officer said, ignoring my sister.

"Cut myself shavin'," I said, trying a different excuse.

"Bull-fuckin'-shit," the officer barked. "You were there this mornin'. There was an altercation that left the owner's son without a nose."

"The fuck that gotta do wit me?"

"Turn around, takin' you inta the station. We'll finish this conversation down there."

"Fuck that, I ain't goin' nowhere with you," I said, much to the pleasure of the officer. He was salivating, waiting for the opportunity to strike. He grabbed a handful of my shirt and tossed me against the wall as if I weighed nothing. His strength caught me off guard. He pressed his full body up against me, pinning me against the wall, and took the handcuffs off his utility belt.

He wasn't overly cruel or unjust. After all, I did shove that bottleneck up the Yac's ass. But an impetuous rage took root inside of me. I'd managed to stave off a pair of bracelets for seventeen years, and this pig-fuck Officer Wagner was popping my cherry—*so to speak*. Tina refused to look at me. I don't think it was because she was angry or ashamed but because she was sad. She had been holding on to a thin, diaphanous hope that I could still turn back, retrace my steps, and change my ways, that I hadn't gone too far. In her eyes, this was the precipice before the fall.

But the truth was that I'd been in free fall for years, though I wouldn't hit the bottom for another thirty-one. Maybe she knew that part of it too, and that's what she was grieving for. Maybe not.

Looking back, I don't know why I went to Tina's that night. Freud might offer up some fucked-up reasoning, but it was simple: Tina was one of the only people I felt safe with.

The question of my guilt was a moot point. There was no further discussion at the station. I was booked and processed in a series of soon-to-be-familiar steps. An officer took me by the wrist and aggressively guided my fingers to a pad of ink. The officer maneuvered my inked fingertips as if I were a toddler incapable of controlling my motor functions and stamped and rolled them onto a grid of ten boxes. Ten incriminating miniature self-portraits arranged in two neat rows. From there I was walked over to get my mug shot taken. A black sign with white numbers was hung around my neck like a necklace. I was directed to stand in front of a backdrop that had graduated height markings.

Bright lights on tripods were aimed at my face. I was hot, sweating. I heard a snap of the camera's shutter closing.

"Turn to your right . . ." *Click.*

"Turn to your left . . ." *Click.*

A young cop with a virginal face took me to the communal holding cell. We paused for a moment while he identified the correct key from his crowded ring. There was no need to have so many keys, I decided. He got the door open and callously pushed me in.

There were three of us in there: me and two others. The other two were drunks who knew each other, no doubt from countless nights spent together in the drunk tank. They were talking loudly about some toothless whore named Tammy, but I wasn't really listening.

My mind ran wild elsewhere. *Would they pin this to me as an adult?* I knew they would try. When you're a minor, the judicial system has the memory of a goldfish. But when the ink touches your adult record, you're fucked. A scarlet letter *A* is sewn into your forehead. From then on, it will ostracize you, keep you at arm's length from reentering the general population, much like a zoo animal. You'll have to lie on every job application or stay unemployed (not that this applied to me, I just think it's bullshit). The hypocritical and continued use of the word *rehabilitation* in our justice system has driven good men to the brink of madness. Every worst-case scenario torments a captive their first night behind bars.

I don't remember falling asleep, but no one ever does. I only recall waking up, and it was less than pleasant.

"Hicks . . . Hicks, wake the fuck up!" a new voice shouted. "*HICKS!*" A solid object struck the cell bars three times. *Clang! Clang! Clang!* "Your lawyer's here . . . For chrissakes, Hicks, wake the fuck up already!"

I sat up. The bench I had slept on was hard but not entirely unpleasant. The drunks were gone. They'd be back tonight or tomorrow or the night after, I thought. The officer's wake-up call finally registered through my morning fogginess.

*Lawyer?* Tina must have phoned Pops and told him what happened.

I was taken out of the holding cell and led down a hall to an attorney-client interview room. The room was grey and depressing, likely by design. A stainless steel table and two chairs were arranged in the center of the room. I sat down in one of the chairs.

An elfish and bespectacled man in his late sixties, sporting a neat snow-white Friar Tuck tonsure, sat opposite me. He was overweight but not fat. He wore a nice tailored suit, and his shoes had recently been shined.

"Milton Fischman," he said, introducing himself. He extended a warm hand across the table and gave me a genuine smile. I liked him immediately. "Let's get down to business, shall we?" He removed a file folder from a briefcase he had under the table. There were about fifteen pages inside. He chuckled when he got to a copy of my mug shot.

"Wouldn't have taken you to be six feet tall," he said, spinning the file around for me to see. When I saw it, I laughed too. In the mug shot, an Alfalfa-like needle of my red hair stood up, adding two inches to my height.

For the remainder of the morning, Milton told me what to do and say when we went into the courtroom. I was going to be charged as an adult, he said, but it wasn't a problem. (Back then, in the state of Massachusetts, juveniles aged seventeen and above were charged as adults.) After the judge read the charges and questioned me on the nature of my plea, I was to respond with "Not guilty, Your Honor." Besides that, I was essentially instructed to shut the fuck up. He would handle the rest.

Later, as we walked together into the courtroom, Milton comforted me with a story of his long-standing relationship with the judge, stretching back to their childhood together. Everything in the courtroom was wooden: the doors, the walls, the judge's bench, the gavel, all the pews. Even the people had a wooden quality to them.

The judge addressed the courtroom with little enthusiasm but gave a slight nod to Milton before taking his seat. My case was on the top of the docket. A completely foreign legal lexicon was used, but I remember the gist of what was said:

"Case number [redacted]. We are here today for the arraignment in the case of Oleg Salka and Uros Zeljak versus Sean Scott Hicks. Mr. Hicks, you are being charged with one count of assault in the first degree by digital penetration, a felony punishable by up to fifteen years in prison and a fine of up to $10,000; one account of mayhem in the first degree by facial disfigurement, a felony punishable by up to eight years in prison and a fine up to $10,000; one count of assault with a deadly weapon in the first degree. How do you plea?" *That was my cue.*

"Not guilty, Your Honor."

Bail was set at $20,000.

Hank posted my bail and was waiting for me outside the courthouse. He was wearing his nicest camel-hair suit, and he looked tired. Like he hadn't slept. He moved toward me slowly at first, but after two steps he broke into a run. He wrapped his arms around me and held me tight. He was crying.

"I'm sorry, Sean. I'm so sorry." There was a quiver in his voice. He apologized one hundred times, though I wasn't sure what for. He let me go, fished a damp handkerchief out of his jacket pocket, and blew his nose into it. "C'mon, let's go home," he said.

"Yeah, let's."

My pretrial hearing was in three weeks. During that time, Hank wouldn't let me out of his sight. He had me come to his construction jobs with him, and if I had to go check on one of my crews, he drove me. Milton came by the house on two separate occasions and had conversations in private with my pops.

At dinner after the second meeting with Milton, my pops was in better spirits. He told me not to worry about the trial, that he and Milton were working an angle, and that everything was going accordingly.

"We'll get you ova to Maurice, 'The Pants Man,' and getcha a suit too, for the trial. And a haircut too," he said. "Cheers, son." He raised a toast to the information he was keeping secret. I raised my glass. We were both drinking gin that night. I didn't mind him keeping things from me; it was just good to see him happy—if only for the night.

The trial came two days later. I was in a stiff, scratchy suit that Hank insisted I wear. I felt ridiculous. *Who the fuck cares what I'm wearing?* I thought. *As long as I don't show up buck-ass naked, it shouldn't matter.* But again, it made Hank happy, or at least at ease, so I kept it on. I put my foot down when it came to a tie, though. And I left my shirt untucked. So, we compromised.

I was right about the meaningless outfit: the judge didn't even look up before throwing out the case for a "lack of sufficient evidence." From start to finish, my hearing took no more than sixty seconds. The two Yacs didn't show up to testify. Neither did any eyewitnesses. Without them, there was no case.

When the gavel fell, I turned to Milton and said, "Thanks again, Milt."

"Congrats. But be sure to thank Hank too. Crazy bastard sure loves you."

Milk, butter, eggs, cigarettes, gas, freedom from prosecution—anything could be bought in those days. I found out that Hank had paid out ten grand to the right people for my case to go away.

I walked out a freer man than ever before. That was my first "real" consequence as an adult, and it was hardly a slap on the wrist. If I took anything away from the whole ordeal, it was that there are no hard-and-fast rules in our justice system; everything is speculative . . . Not to mention, those who enforced the law were on our side—or they could be bought for pennies on the dollar. It wasn't cops versus robbers out here; it was cops and robbers against whoever was left. The corrupt versus the righteous is hardly a fair fight. *The wicked prosper in this life, the virtuous in the next.*

# SEVEN

## GREEN EGGS AND HAM

A few short months after my altercation with the Yacs, I found myself back in the courtroom in front of the same judge facing separate but similar charges: another drunken fight.

The judge wasn't pleased to see me. This time my immunity had its limitations. The judge had to keep his job. He would be no use to us if he was unemployed, so a conviction was necessary—an unavoidable consequence in my line of work. They were minor charges anyway: one count of assault and battery, and one of destruction of property.

Even though it wasn't the impunity I would have preferred, when it came to my sentencing, I was given the "friends-and-family" discount. I got the least amount of time the judge could give me.

It was my "first" offense, after all.

When you go to prison, you always get a psych evaluation. Some shrink asks you questions about nothing important. Boring stuff. And because of the nature of my offense—fighting—I was also given a physical exam. I had a few bruises, nothing major. Last but not least, I was sent to the optometrist for an eye exam, all standard procedure.

I had had an eye exam before and passed it with flying colors: twenty-twenty vision. But in truth my eyesight wasn't great. I had cheated, prepared ahead of time so I wouldn't need glasses. Seeing Hank wearing them with those lenses getting thicker and thicker, I knew I didn't want them. Hopefully, I could remember the answers this time.

The optometrist was five foot six at most. He had his hair buzzed to the scalp and was clean shaven. There was a conceited air about him. Even with his short stature, he seemed to look down at each new patient in disgust. When I walked into his office, he positioned me in front of the eye chart.

"Start with line four," he instructed.

I skipped the first six letters I had memorized, then rattled off the next four aloud. "L, um . . ." I stumbled for a moment and continued, "B, E, D."

Close enough, I thought, pleased with how much I had remembered so far.

"Line five," he ordered.

I froze up. My mind went blank. I knew that line five had five letters but couldn't remember which ones. I paused, trying to figure out what I was going to say. I looked at the chart. The letter was a stick with a half circle coming out of the right side. It looked to me like a child's rendition of a flagpole, but what the fuck was it called?

"Just read whatever letters you can," he said, checking his watch. A few more seconds went by in complete silence before he smirked. "You can't read, can you?"

"I can see it just fuckin' fine," I said adamantly. I was telling the truth. I could *see* everything; I just couldn't read it.

"Then read line five to me." He smiled.

"Fuck you."

"Jesus Christ. How old are you? And you don't know the alphabet yet? My niece knows all of it 'n' she just turned six." He chuckled and shook his head, writing something on his clipboard. He began complaining under his breath just loud enough for me to hear snippets. ". . . Dumbass doesn't know letters . . . too stupid to be anything but a criminal . . . throw the lot of you in the hole for sheer stupidity."

He was taken by surprise when I hit him. He must have thought he was protected by the threat of severe punishment if any harm came to him. Idiot. Did he not realize I was a fucking criminal? Consequences and punishments don't deter us. When we are disrespected, we retaliate. *A six-year-old would know that.*

I was thrown into solitary confinement. And while I was there, his words got to me. I didn't sleep the first night, nor the second. I ruminated on what he had said. I stayed awake countless hours, arguing against the blank wall and losing every time. I came up with case after case to defend myself. I knew all my numbers. I knew ounces in a pound, and pounds in a key. I could add, subtract, and multiply within reason, so fuck him. I knew most of my letters . . . just not $P$ . . . It's a fucking stupid, good-for-nothing, piece-of-shit letter anyhow.

It wasn't until the acute insanity wore off that I realized what had been bothering me so much. It wasn't that I didn't know all twenty-six letters of the English alphabet, and it wasn't that he had called me stupid either.

What bothered me the most was that I couldn't disprove him. He was right: on paper I had the formal education of a fourth grader, but in reality, I couldn't even read or write.

That night—three days after assaulting an optometrist in frustration because I didn't know the letter $P$—I vowed never to allow anyone the opportunity to call me "stupid" again.

When you think about it for more than a second, education in general is fucking daunting. It's impossible to know everything, and it's impossible to know exactly what you'll need to know before you need to know it, so why bother?

Educating oneself parallels the Greek myth of Sisyphus, pushing a boulder up a hill only to have it roll back down when it nears the top. The process is never-ending and seems pointless. The deeper I thought about it while sitting in that cell, the more I realized that I was just concocting every excuse to give up before trying. I didn't need to know anything, but I needed to try. I owed it to myself, the kid whose mother had traded his chance of a normal education for a high and a fuck. I realized the only way I would ever come close to a normal life would be when she had no part of it.

Locating elementary-level educational material in a prison library is like being in a perfectly round room and trying to piss in a corner. The Department of Corrections places inmate education toward the bottom of their budget, and they have a hair-trigger knack for diverting the funds elsewhere. It's more common to see the warden getting a nice Christmas bonus than it is to find new academic material on the shelves, suitable for all education levels. Because of that, most prison libraries are filled by virtue of outside donations. They were generous but infrequent, and soon after their arrival, the shelves resembled a looted market. That's not to put all the blame on the administration staff; the guilt lies on us convicts as well. For one, most prisoners don't give a fuck about books, and naturally, no one is going to go out of their way to appease the small population who do. Second, the inmates I knew who checked out books ruined them. I've seen guys wipe their shitty asses with pages torn from literary masterpieces. The few guys who liked reading and respected books coveted the best titles and hoarded them. If they got their hands on a good one, they wouldn't give it up easily. But those caliber books weren't even on my radar yet. I needed books to learn the fundamentals, the basics—books that started at ground zero. These books, the ones I required, weren't in the prison library, but they *were* in the prison. Children's books are in the only place children are allowed to be in prison: the family visiting room. Go figure.

When their parents engaged in adult conversations, sons and daughters were left to be distracted by hundreds of illustrated children's books and activity workbooks and crayons. The shortage of designated coloring books caused a youthful rebellion of incoherent drawings defacing the other books. And those children drew dogs and cats as if they'd never seen dogs and cats in their lives.

One day Quinny was visiting me, and at the end of his visit, I gathered a stack of the materials and tried smuggling them back to my cell under my loose-fitting prison uniform.

Leaving the parloir, I was searched, and the guard found everything. I tried explaining how I was going to use the books' illustrations to trace little drawings onto a letter for my daughter. Whether he believed my cover story or not was irrelevant; he couldn't let anyone take anything for any reason. If another convict had been given a photograph of his newborn child, it would have been confiscated too. There were no exceptions; nothing from the visiting room could come back into the prison. Nothing besides the convicts, of course.

Well, that plan didn't work . . . *fuck*. It would have been too easy, right? Much too convenient. Prison doesn't work like that. If I wanted to learn how to read, I was going to have to show some humility, humble myself. There was no other way. So, I put in a request to go to the library—not for the books, but for the librarian.

Despite being one of the only women the male prisoners encountered while locked up, she was the least sexualized among them. Even if you had the most resourceful imagination, it was impossible to fantasize about her. She looked old enough to have voted for Lincoln. And as expected, she was a no-nonsense gatekeeper. However, she was fair with her judgment: she'd give anyone a first chance, but no one got a second. Seeing as how I'd yet to piss her off, she'd likely help me.

A week later, my request was approved, and I was granted one hour in the library on the following Thursday. I had gotten used to the slow nature of prison administration reacting to a petition.

On Thursday I went to the library and explained how I was trying to teach myself to read. I asked the librarian if she could acquire the materials from the visitation room and have them delivered to my cell. She said that she respected my initiative and agreed to help.

Everything between the two of us was said in confidence; I didn't want word of my illiteracy to spread.

Saturday morning, she sent me what I had asked for, a few workbooks and some simple stories. In addition, she sent an alphabet reference chart with upper- and lowercase letters. Regardless of how small an act it may have seemed to her, it made a great impact on me.

I started immediately. At first, all I could do was trace the ABC diagram. It had little red arrows I could follow, which indicated how to achieve proper penmanship. I committed both forms of all twenty-six letters to memory in a day, separating vowels and consonants on day two. Within a week, I got comfortable writing the symbols until they no longer felt foreign. After that, I developed a religious devotion to the workbooks. I wrote my answers in pen around the chaotic crayon graffiti. When I ran out of exercises, I reworked the pages and waited for another visitor so I could get a new stock of workbooks.

The first book I ever read was *Green Eggs and Ham*. Most people could have finished a series in the time it took me to read those thirty-something pages, but I finished them, and I did it myself. One book became two, two became three, and so on . . .

It was never easy—far from it. It was too foreign, maybe as difficult as that optometrist's six-year-old niece trying to run a series of criminal enterprises. Although, of course, you can't learn everything in a book.

With a rudimental understanding of reading and writing, and a functional grasp of mathematics, I thought it only right to get a GED. I didn't have a reason to get it, but I didn't have a reason *not* to get it . . . so why the fuck not, right? I certainly had time to kill. To get it, I was going to need to pass a standard comprehensive test that covered five subjects: reading comprehension, writing ability, math, science, and social studies. Unless the science section focused on cooking crack cocaine and the social studies section asked questions pertaining only to Boston's seedy criminal history, I was fucked. Essentially, I was starting from scratch.

That was fine. I wasn't going to get my GED right away—not during this stretch, anyway. But I had to start the process sometime, and I figured this was just the beginning of my rap sheet. I'd find myself behind bars again, at which point I could pick up my education where I'd left off.

I managed to condense the curriculum of grades one through twelve into two years of studying. However, those twenty-four months were not consecutive. It took me three or four additional arrests to prepare for the GED exam, but I passed with flying colors—all without cheating.

# EIGHT

## BECOMING A MONSTER

There is not a single person on this godforsaken planet who isn't capable of getting blood on their hands. And yes, that includes you. But before any of you *fucking* lunatics show up to my home with torch-fire and pitchforks as if I'm some blasphemous heretic (effectively proving my point), let me explain . . .

Say, for instance, that you're sleeping soundly in bed next to your beautiful spouse. You wake to your well-groomed golden retriever, Max or Tucker or whatever-the-fuck, barking at something. Really yapping its head off. You decide to check it out. Swinging your legs out of bed, careful not to wake the love of your life, you slip your feet into the slippers you laid out for the morning and readjust your sleeping cap. The barking has stopped. You shuffle down the hallway, pausing to check on your two adorable children. First door on your left. Lucy, four years old, and Jack, five (although his sixth birthday is at the end of the month, and you really need to start planning the party), are deep in their colorful dreamworlds; they are okay, so you continue to the kitchen. Still nothing out of the ordinary; you keep going. A watery moonlight has spilled into the living room through thin lace curtains. At the far end of the room, beside the display cabinet, which holds your grandmother's china, you see the silhouette of a slender man. He is holding, in both hands, your brand-new color television. Before you open your mouth to confront the thief, he drops the TV set, reaches into his waistband, and points something small at your chest. *Bang!* Like a flash of lightning, the room is illuminated by the muzzle of a handgun. You feel the force of a small-caliber bullet hit your shoulder, although to you it feels like that punch from the grade-school bully all those years ago. The true pain hasn't registered yet. Suddenly something comes over you, you don't know what it is, but it drives your legs and propels your body forward. The slender man raises the gun again, but you're in time to grab his wrist and wrestle it skyward. A second bullet fires into the ceiling. The two of you fall to the floor. One thing leads to another in the ensuing struggle, and a third shot goes off.

Behind you, an incandescent lamp is switched on. Your spouse lets out a horrifying shriek, seeing you covered in the blood, brains, and facial bone fragments of the dead thief. You and your wife's once-matching pajamas no longer match, but at least both of you and the kids are alive. You're hailed as a hero who saved their family. Congratulations. But now you've got blood on your hands. And whether the blood got there for your survival or otherwise, there was a perceived necessity to act. Hesitation or nonaction could have caused you or those close to you to suffer grievous consequences. Looking at it through the utopian lens of logic, it becomes hardly an act of condemnation.

Bending that rock-solid morality of yours a little further, the idea of some degree of violence for the sake of personal, financial, or career-oriented prosperity becomes almost palatable. We see and condone varying degrees of violence every day, in fact. I watched a whole arena of fans get off on Ray Bourque breaking an opponent's nose during a Bruins-versus-Canadiens hockey brawl. Would you punch your boss square in the jaw for a million dollars? How about one hundred thousand? Ten grand? I bet some of you would do it for free. How about receiving a cut of the $30 million purse to go toe-to-toe with Tyson? Sure, you don't stand a chance, but that's the type of money that buys freedom. I'd jump into the ring for that level of prosperity. Regardless of what we are desperate to believe, we haven't evolved so very far from the sands of the Colosseum.

Now, I'm not saying any of you would beat a man to the brink of death to take over a chop shop, nor would you bite a nose off to keep a reputation intact, but there is a crumb trail of logic that hopefully can be followed to my fucked-up rationale *thus far.*

But there *is* a limit; there *is* a line in the sand, over which no human can cross. Crossing it is to lose one's humanity. To become a barbarous beast, a monster among men. It's an enigmatic threshold, this line. It can only be seen in the hindsight of those who've stepped over it. And it's not pretty on the other side. It's a place where "right" and "wrong" are nonexistent, a labyrinth of pain and misery. It's inhabited by cursed, faceless creatures who crawl around piles of filth on their bare stomachs. The most brutish of brutes stand on corners under flickering streetlamps sucking at cheap foreign cigarettes. It is a place that would make King Hammurabi look like Mr. Rogers.

I am, of course, exaggerating to highlight the depravity. In truth, it is a lonely place. So lonely, in fact, that you cannot find any comfort within the sanctity of your own mind. Thought, feeling, and sanity are poisoned upon that first step. There is no antidote and no turning back. The only way is forward. There's no guarantee you'll make it out the other side and no guarantee there will be anything there even if you do.

Fresh out of prison at eighteen years old, I accepted the job that would take me over that line. It's different for everyone, but I crossed the moment violence transformed from necessity into a form of currency.

Since my altercation with the Yacs and the second brawl after it, Whitey had begun keeping a fond, watchful eye on me and my work. He was an admirer of sorts. He liked that I had not only a proclivity for violence but a talent for it. You see, most guys won't get their hands dirty at the instruction of another person. They only turn to abhorrent violence as a last resort, backed into a perceived corner, lashing out like an abused dog. My pops was that way, and so were Toby, Joe, and the other guys.

Whitey saw that I was different, that I could be molded into an asset for his agenda: a soldier, the perfect weapon. With Johnny Martorano on the lam since '79 for his involvement in fixing horse races, Whitey had to call on Flemmi or Kevin Weeks, guys he could trust, to take care of the dirty work. And his list of reliable guys was growing short. What he couldn't pass off to others, Whitey had to handle himself. I think that's part of the reason why he chose me: I could be trusted.

I remember parts of that day in '89 as if it were yesterday. I even remember what shoes I had on: a crisp pair of Air Jordan IVs, the Black Cement colorway—the same ones Michael Jordan had worn earlier that year when he made "The Shot" at the buzzer against the Cavaliers to win the game. I was, and still am, an avid collector of sneakers, a "sneakerhead" they call it. The moment I saw Run-DMC wearing those milk-white Adidas with three stripes, I was hooked, as were a lot of kids back then. It didn't take long for other hip-hop artists to follow suit—Tupac, N.W.A., Grandmaster Flash, the Beastie Boys, you name it, and they were wearing a pair of shoes I wanted. And I was able to get most of them too. I had access to a direct supply line coming into Toby's house. Every few months a shipment of the newly released shoes would show up in his garage, and I always made sure I was there to unload. Before I knew it, my closet was filled with every coveted shoe imaginable. I had every limited edition and every sold-out pair in its original box.

That morning at Hank's, I decided to put on the Air Jordan IVs, completely unaware of the violent torrent of events I was about to be swept up in. I was eating breakfast—a cup of black coffee and a cigarette—and watching the TV when the phone rang. I let it ring, waiting for Hank to pick it up.

The ringing stopped, then started again. We didn't have an answering machine. Again, the ringing stopped, was silent for ten seconds, and started back up. I dropped my cigarette into the last gulp of coffee and stood up. I went over to the receiver and ripped it off the wall.

"What? What is it?" I said curtly into the mouthpiece.

"Sean, I'm calling from the Quincy Police Department. We, uh . . . We got your pops ova here at the Fore River Bridge. He was drivin' home from the Adams Heights Men's Club, but uh . . . we think he musta forgot ta take his insulin this mornin'. He was swervin' all ova the road and he's not walkin' or talkin' straight. You might wanna come ova 'n' pick him up."

"Yeah, gimme a half hour. I'll be there." I hung up the receiver.

I don't remember what the weather was like that day. I just know that it wasn't raining. I wouldn't have worn those shoes if it were. And of the shoes, I am certain. The roads were busy with oblivious men and women in their blue-collar vehicles commuting to work. It took me an extra fifteen minutes to drive there.

I pulled up behind the police cruiser, which was parked in tandem with Hank's familiar white Mercedes-Benz. Hank had somehow managed to get over the Fore River Bridge, pull through the breakdown lane, and drive into a thicket of weeds before shutting his car off.

The officer got out of his car to greet me. I recognized his face but only faintly. I apologized for the traffic, and he smiled politely. He helped get Hank out of his cruiser's front passenger seat and into my car. Pops reeked of liquor; you could see the alcohol vapor radiating off him in the morning heat. He was shit-faced from drinking all night. The cop knew it too. But instead of slapping Hank with a DUI charge, the cop called me, even knowing I didn't have a license to drive Hank home. (I never bothered to get it until I was twenty-one.) The officer took Hank's keys out of his pocket and handed them to me. We'd have to go back for the Benz once Hank sobered up.

"Get home safe, Hank," the officer said, leaning his head through the window. He thumped the side of the car, letting me know I was good to go, and he took two steps back. I pressed the accelerator to the floor and pulled back onto the throughway in the opposite direction.

The phone was ringing off the hook when we walked in the house. Unaffected by the irritating sound, Hank took two steps and collapsed into the leather recliner, snoring in a drunken slumber. I picked the phone up, figuring it was the cop checking to make sure we got back all right. I was wrong.

"This Sean?" the voice on the other end said.

"Yeah."

"Whitey wants ya ta come by the liquor store."

"When?" I asked.

"Now," the voice said. "There'll be a car waitin' outside for ya." There was a click, and the line went dead, followed by an endless hollow beep. I went to the large front window and pulled back the dated curtain. A champagne-colored Chrysler pulled up to the sidewalk on cue. Flemmi was driving.

They were in the back room, Whitey and a few others. Six or seven guys in total. They were gathered around a table, and on the table was a large pile of money. A large old billiard chandelier hung over the table, providing dull yellow light. Whitey was surrounded by his loyal sycophants, incapable of anything beyond nodding at their master's bark.

Seeing that I had arrived, Whitey waved me over. He seemed to be the only one who was glad to see me. Steve Flemmi showed indifference (which, actually, was an improvement to his usual), and everyone else had a sullen expression painted on their face.

"I want you to do somethin' for me, Sean-O. Ya see all this?" Whitey said, pointing to the scratch. "I want you ta count it for me."

"Count's good, Jim," one of the guys said. "Did it myself . . . twice."

"I don't give a fuck if Albert *fuckin'* Einstein counted it a hundred goddamn times. I want Sean-O ta count it in front-a me. I wanna hear it from him. If I wanted to hear it outta your cocksucka I would fuckin' ask ya, wouldn't I?" Whitey said with a venomous temper. "Go on, Sean-O," he directed.

Whitey leaned onto his elbows and interwove his fingers together, watching me closely as I counted. The pile was large but had already been separated into smaller, easier-to-count piles. It didn't take long to add up.

"Five hundred grand," I said.

"What'd you say?" Whitey said, not hearing me.

"I counted five hundred large, Jim," I said louder and clearer.

"Same as I got too," said the other counter.

The room became quiet and crypt-like as we waited for Whitey to speak. The silence was suffocating, asphyxiating, deadly. There was a chill in the air. We all nervously watched as Whitey mulled the number over in his head, turning it over this way and that, trying to make sense of what he'd just heard. He was slowly choking the blood out of his fingers. Behind the strangulated fingers, I heard the rhythmic tick of Jim's tongue flicking against his teeth. *Tick, tick, tick, tick.*

Whitey exited his trance. "You read the paper this mornin'?" he asked me.

Before I answered, he threw a copy of the morning newspaper on the table in front of me and fingered one of the articles. "Read 'ere what it says."

I picked up the paper. The article he pointed to was on page five and had no pictures and not many words. Under any other circumstances, I would have missed it. I understood the gravity of the situation from the first sentence. New details had emerged in the case of an underground gambling parlor that was hit by two masked assailants over two weeks ago. The two men, whose names were either unknown to the reporter or purposefully left out of the article, entered a known gambling den and held up the constituents to the tune of $1.65 million before escaping into the night.

*$1.65 million.* I did a rough calculation in my head. Jim's cut on a score this size should have been 40 percent, and piecing together that the money on the table was what was given to Whitey for his cut, the payout was light. It was light by $125,000, to be exact. And you don't do that. Not with Jim. Not unless, of course, you make it a habit of playing Russian roulette with five bullets in the cylinder instead of one.

What it really meant was that the thieves reported less than they took and thought they'd get away with it. Bad luck for them: they got ratted out by a hardworking journalist. The last line of the article instructed the reader to call an anonymous tip line with any pertinent information regarding the crime. I almost laughed reading it. All the information called in to those tip lines was funneled straight to our ears anyway. Plus, Whitey already knew who'd pulled the job. They'd handed him their own death warrants when they dropped off the wrong amount of money.

I folded the newspaper and placed it back down onto the table.

"Those stupid fucks stole from you, Jim," I said.

"No, Sean-O, no . . ." Whitey said with a calm timbre. "Those fuckin' no-good, dirty Italians lied to me, but they stole from *you*." He paused to shake his head and click his tongue three times, as a mother (not mine) scolds a naughty child. "You see, they stole from us . . . from the family. And it's not a good look to let such a crime go unpunished. Someone else might get the wrong idea, tryin' ta think for himself, ya know? Like they don't gotta follow the rules, like maybe they're above them. Disloyalty spreads like fuckin' wildfire, Sean-O. And no disloyal cunt has got a place in my fuckin' streets. No. Not in Southie."

A few of the faceless men nodded in approval.

"Whatdya wan' us ta do, Jim? Take 'em on a trip ta Australia?" one of them asked.

"Whatdya say, Stevie?" said Jim, looking to Flemmi but not looking for an opinion contradicting his own. "We give the kid a shot?" he said, referring to me.

"He done good for us in the past," Flemmi said.

"You think you can handle the job?" Whitey asked me.

"Course I fuckin' can, I'll getchu your money back tonight," I said with the naive confidence of every eighteen-year-old who feels impervious to the harsh reality of consequences.

"It's a lotta money, now," Whitey said with fake concern. "And ya gunna hafta teach those thieving pricks a lesson or two. We gotta drive the fuckin' vermin outta our streets like some kinda Pied Piper or somethin'." That got a laugh or two from the audience.

"Jus' tell me where ta find the fuckin' pricks, and you'll have the money and their fuckin' heads on this table by tomorrow," I bragged. "All of the money."

"All right, I'm puttin' my faith in you, Sean-O." Whitey smiled. "Don't make me regret it. We'll see whatcha got. Stevie'll walk out wit ya 'n' tell you where ta find those cocksuckas. Take his car, it's got everythin' ya gonna need in the trunk . . . Stevie, give 'em ya keys."

Flemmi and I stood up from the table and went downstairs. When we got outside, he filled me in on where I could find the thieves. They had been lying low in a duplex on the East Side for the past couple days. We got the drop on their location from a drug dealer that had been selling to them. The dealer was making drop-offs to their building around ten o'clock every night. I needed to get the thieves out separately, one at a time, to avoid the complications of getting two men into one trunk.

The dealer agreed to meet up with whoever Whitey sent (me) and help isolate one of the targets. He would set up the deal on the corner to draw one of them out of the apartment. I was on my own for the second one. Flemmi gave me the address and a small piece of paper with the dealer's license plate number and begrudgingly handed over his keys.

"Got yaself a promotion, kid, don't fuck this up," he joked as I shut the driver's door. "And don't fuck up my car neitha . . . Oh, and Whitey told me ta give ya this." He reached behind his back and pulled out a small snub-nose handgun that had been tucked into his waistband. A six-shooter with wooden grips. The gun was heavy and fateful.

I pulled onto the busy city streets and headed northeast.

It was sometime after seven o'clock, and the sun was dying a beautiful death when I left the liquor store. I took my time getting over to the East Side, driving slow and absentmindedly, without much thought or purpose. I had time to kill. I didn't want to get there too early and have to sit with my thumb up my ass, waiting around for the inevitable. When left to my own devices, my mind often wanders, and I've found that to be a bad thing.

I saw a sign for McDonald's and pulled in. I had never eaten at one before and figured I'd give it a try; that night was as good as any other. The drive-through attendant sounded annoyed when I didn't instantly fire off my order and instead asked for more time to look over the menu. I read through every item and decided on a regular cheeseburger and a large Coke. I sat in the parking lot and ate. It wasn't very good, though I'd come to learn that it was gourmet compared to the slop served in Massachusetts prisons. I threw out the bag and drove off.

I reached the address Flemmi had given me just after nine o'clock. I parked the car three buildings down and angled it to get a good vantage point of the corner and the apartment complex. I had one hour, and I decided to empty the contents of the trunk into the back seat. That way there'd be enough space to transport the two men without attracting unwanted attention.

Maybe I shouldn't have been surprised, seeing as how I was driving a car that belonged to a psychopath. However, nothing could have prepared me for what I found in the rear of the car.

Lifting the deck lid, I found a vast collection of zip ties, duct tape, trash bags, hedge trimmers, garden shears, hammers, framing nails, drills, drill bits, a propane blowtorch, an extra bottle of propane, a handheld ice pick, some rope, a half-full can of gasoline, hypodermic needles, smelling salts, vials of epinephrine, brown bottles of rubbing alcohol, a dozen IV bags, IV tubes, and the metal stand that the bags hang on. And there was a green garden hose too. The car contained all the makings of a psychopath's wet dream. All that was missing were the bodies. I had no idea where the lunatics got their hands on half of it, and I didn't have time to speculate. I took the gun out of my pocket and put it under the front seat, out of sight. I began discreetly carrying armfuls of gear from the back into the rear seat. I made quick work of it and was able to transfer the shit into the back seat before the dealer showed. I went back to the front seat, retrieved the pistol, and waited.

A black Cadillac drove up to the corner and killed its engine. The plates matched the scrap of paper Flemmi had supplied; it was their drug dealer. I paused before getting out of the car, making sure the thieves were not waiting somewhere out of sight. But the street was dead. The only sign of life was a pair of rodents humping to stay warm. I slipped the gun into my waistband and took a roll of duct tape from the back seat, then left the car. I skirted along the edge of shadows created by silver moonlight and tall buildings.

I opened the Cadillac's door behind the driver and slid in, stowing the roll of tape on the floor and the pistol in my lap. We made brief eye contact in the rearview mirror, acknowledging one another. We spoke very little, sticking to the essentials. He was going to tell whichever thief approached the car to get in the back seat. I'd take it from there.

After that, we fell into silence. The hands on the dashboard clock read a quarter till ten. Any minute now. Cokeheads and junkies tend to show up early. The eagerness to score compels them to do so.

The situation reminded me of a story told to me in my childhood by Gene Roberts, the Hells Angel who hit and fucked and married my mother. He used to say that a rabbit is most vulnerable when leaving its hole to forage for a meal and that there's no telling what danger might come to that rabbit if it scavenges for more than it needs. "There's wolves in the night," he'd always say, "wolves waiting in the dark." Gene had used the story to ensure I never complained about being hungry and the lack of food, but now the story took on a whole new meaning.

For those faint of heart, or those who do not wish to learn the basal nature of this book's author, I implore you to skip the next few pages of this chapter. However, if you continue, note that I will not offer any excuses or exonerating explanations for my actions. I certainly don't expect sympathy, nor would I accept it.

For the purposes of proper storytelling and to ease the burden of character differentiation, I will, from this point onward, refer to one of the men as "No-Nose" and the other as "The Shiv."

No-Nose exited the apartment building alone, made his way across the street, and stood under the light of the twenty-four-hour corner store. He wore a black hoodie with the hood pulled up. I knew it was him by the way he walked. I sensed trepidation in his posture, a slight hunch, a shuffled gait. There was caution in his movement, as if he didn't want to be seen, much less found. It was him all right.

I tightened my grip on the gun. The dealer rolled down his window and instructed No-Nose to get in the back. The door swung open, and he climbed in. He shut it before realizing he wasn't alone.

"Who the fuck are—?" Before he got his question off and his guard up, I lashed out with a succession of viperous pistol-whips. My aim was guesswork in the dark, but it didn't matter. The gun made contact against his head, and that was enough. The traumatic blunt force caused compliant grogginess, and No-Nose put up minimal resistance to the duct tape restraints I was applying to his wrists, mouth, and eyes.

I would wrap his feet once he was in my trunk. I didn't want to have to carry the fuck. Deadweight hangs heavier.

The dealer drove us over and double-parked beside my ride.

"You done a good thing," I said. After hopping out, I dragged my semiconscious prey onto his feet and placed him into the trunk. I hit him again, a knockout blow, then bound his feet with a generous amount of tape and closed the hatch. *One down, one to go.*

The building was a shithole. It was a low-income, subsidized two-family complex that had been long forgotten by a neglectful landlord. Its front stairway was littered with cigarette butts and crushed beer cans. The plywood boards covering the first-floor windows were tattooed with meaningless graffiti. The Shiv was held up on the second floor.

My plan to smoke him out was quite literal. I took a bottle of the isopropyl alcohol and the blowtorch from the Chrysler and made my way around back of the house. There was a dark black patch of decaying wall that had started to buckle. I peeled the curling wood shingles off to expose equally rotted boards beneath. With one hand, I was able to fracture a wallboard and get access to the inner chamber. The building was insulated with dried-out brittle newspapers and decades of cobwebs; old homes in New England are essentially volatile tinderboxes.

I unscrewed the stopper on the orange-brown disinfectant bottle and emptied it into the wall, splashing some onto the exterior, creating a makeshift fuse. I clicked the trigger on the blowtorch a few times before getting a steady flame. I held the fire to the fuse. You would have assumed the entire building was doused in rubbing alcohol by the speed it went up in flames. Once the flames reached the second floor, The Shiv would have no choice but to come out. And he would come out the back to avoid the main street.

The Shiv burst out of the safe house in a coughing fit, accompanied by a cloud of black smoke. Had he known what he would face in the next twelve hours, he might have chosen to stay inside and go down with the house.

The Shiv was easier to detain than No-Nose. The smoke had done most of the work for me. He collapsed onto his knees and began convulsing, his lungs fighting to replace the smoke with clean air. I approached him from the side, kicking him in the stomach as hard as I could. He didn't let out a cry; he just crumpled into unconsciousness. I had knocked out the oxygen he had left in his system, and his brain shut off.

The Shiv was no taller than five foot six and weighed around a buck sixty. He was more portable than No-Nose, at least, so I threw him over my shoulder and returned through an alley back to the car. I stuffed the second body into the trunk, rearranging the two men like condemned Tetris pieces, and shut the lid without being noticed; any potential witnesses would have been busy watching the flames consume the house. I have noticed that whenever fire is involved, people tend to act like dumbfounded cavemen and divert their undivided attention to it. Fire has kept me out of prison more times than some of my lawyers.

I needed somewhere to take No-Nose and The Shiv to have our "talk" about where the stolen money was. Somewhere hermetically sealed and soundproofed, where we wouldn't be noticed, interrupted, or heard. *Somewhere like that in Boston? Fat fuckin' chance!*

"Fuck it," I said under my breath in the car and turned south. I knew of a dirty bar in Brockton that had an equally dirty basement, but we'd be left alone down there. And we could go through the service doors on the side street, enter directly into the cellar, and remain largely unnoticed. I had never been before, but it had been used on other Winter Hill jobs, or so I'd heard.

I got there around midnight, not more than a few minutes on either side of the hour. It was a quiet night. The moon was clear and crescent shaped, and the sky was freckled with stars. On the side of the building, a concrete staircase was cut, descending into the earth, leading to heavy steel doors. I went down and gave the doors a try.

They were open. I was lucky; I wouldn't have to show my face inside the bar. The basement floor was hard compacted dirt, and the air thick and musty. The space was cluttered with decommissioned bar objects.

"Who's there?" an unfrightened voice called from the stairs against the basement's far wall. It was the owner, carrying a crate of liquor bottles to restock the bar above. I stepped under the light from a naked bulb in the center of the room so he could see for himself. His face had a vague familiarity. It was an ugly mug, but I was certain I had seen it before. I hoped he remembered mine enough to at least know my affiliation. I decided to give him as little information as was necessary.

"Doin' something for Jim. Need the basement tonight. That a problem?" I said, avoiding the question of my identity with a vague threat and dropping Jim's name.

"Nobody told me nothin' about it."

"What? We supposed to give you a fuckin' two weeks' notice or somethin'?" I asked.

He grunted and shrugged; he understood that resistance was stupid and futile—not worth the headache.

"S'all yours," he said. "Just make sure ta clean up after yourself. I don't wanna see nothin' here in the mornin'. The last time I let one of you guys use *my* bar, the prick left a goddamn mess. Took me days to get my shit back in order."

"Gonna need two chairs too," I added before he went back upstairs.

"Spares are in the corner behind ya," he said, using his chin to motion toward the corner over my left shoulder. He left with his crate and his deniability, and I never saw him again.

A thick layer of dust covered the stack of chairs. I took two off the top and positioned them to face one another underneath the bulb. I went back outside to the car. I decided to bring in all the tools first and set up. I wanted to be prepared for whatever the fuck was about to happen.

I wasn't sure if I would use all the tools, but I had an idea of how to use each item if neither of the thieves talked. Zip ties and duct tape would bind the two men to the chairs. The medical equipment would keep the men conscious and hydrated. I had never used an IV needle before, but fuck it, I'd probably hit a vein after a few dozen attempts,

right? I figured that I could just stab them anywhere with the epinephrine if they started passing out; precision isn't always necessary. I could
drive some framing nails into their hands, one nail per wrist and a few
into the palms. The ice pick could be inserted into a precise cut along
the clavicle; scraping the pick against such fragile bone should get even
a mute to sing. The garden trimmers could be used to remove whatever protrudes from the body: fingers, toes, nose, ears, penis, testicles.
Shears and trimmers are quite useful, the jack-of-all-trades in the realm
of torture, but I hoped not to have to use them on No-Nose and The
Shiv. They could be messy, and cauterizing wounds with a blowtorch
produces a foul odor. Burning flesh smells fucking horrible.

All that was left to figure out was what the green rubber hose was
for. I had no fucking idea. Maybe Flemmi was watering his lawn or some
shit and just threw it in the trunk. That was it! *Shit.* A person can only
take so much before they lose control of their bowels. The hose was to
spray off any piss and shit so that it doesn't get on you.

I was ready, I think. *Fuck it. It had to be done, right?*

I delivered the sinners to purgatory: No-Nose first, then The Shiv.
I watched their desperate eyes dart from the medical instruments to the
contractor tools to the gardening equipment until finally settling their
gaze on one another.

Tears began flooding down The Shiv's cheeks. No-Nose didn't sob; he
kept his composure for the time being. I respected that. His will would be
harder to break, but it would break all the same. Some men cling to life,
others to loved ones, others hold out just as a "fuck you" to their captor,
and although each man is distinct at the beginning of the process, all three
are indistinguishable from one another by the end: shitty and crying and
begging for it all to stop. And they always talk. Don't believe otherwise.

In moments like these, a million and one uncertainties run through
the captives' heads while one certainty occupies the mind of the captor.
I know this because I have been on both sides of that green garden hose.

As per torture's protocol, you always give them one last chance to give
up the information before you begin. Fuckin' Shiv cracked in less than

two hours. I guess seeing Flemmi's gear set up made him shit his pants. He told me everything in exchange for my word that I wouldn't kill him.

I gave it to him. That wasn't my job. Sure, they'd be punished, but not by me. It was my job to get the money, and now they'd given me its location.

However, it didn't matter whether or not I tortured the two men; I had made the decision to do it and came to terms with it, so the damage was done. My humanity was lost. I was a beast. My morals were neither bent nor broken; they'd vanished altogether. I had visualized using every one of those objects on those men. I had imagined them screaming their muffled screams and pleading and even telling me what I wanted to hear as I continued the torture. To this day, there are still times when I visualize those horrid acts in such vivid detail that it makes me question if I actually did torture them that night. *Did I? How deep can one's mind bury something?*

The Shiv confessed to stashing the money in the air ducts of a warehouse in Brockton, about twenty minutes away. I put the duct tape muzzle back on The Shiv, fortified the bonds on both men with extra zip ties and all the remaining duct tape, and left them in the basement.

I'd have time to go check out the address and make sure the information was good before figuring out what to do with the thieves. They couldn't stay in the basement forever, not above the dirt floor at least. There was a map book conveniently tucked away in the Chrysler's glove box. I flipped through the pages until I found the map that could lead me to the warehouse and drove off into the night.

The money was right where The Shiv said it would be. It was separated into two forest-green L.L.Bean duffels behind a vent cover in the warehouse's office. I slung the first bag's shoulder straps over my head and picked up the second bag on the other side of my body to counterbalance the weight. Depending on the denomination of the bills, $1.1 million can weigh anywhere from 24 pounds to 2,200 pounds. In my case—holding a mixture of ones, fives, tens, twenties, fifties, and hundreds from the gambling den—I would have guessed the bags weighed around sixty pounds apiece.

A blanket of exhaustion wrapped itself around me the moment I picked up the bags. My muscles felt sore, my joints ached; the burden of the night was much heavier than the contents of a couple duffel bags. I couldn't think about it, though; I didn't have that terrible luxury yet. I still had to get the money to Jim.

Only then could the aftermath of my decisions settle in and cause the damage that would screw me up for the next thirty fucking years. That would come. It did come, but not quite yet.

Whitey was proud of me the following morning at the Liquor Mart when I told him everything. And just like that, I was in. In with his side crew. I became someone he could, and did, call upon for the dangerous jobs, the brutally violent jobs, and the jobs in which failure would mean lifetime prison sentences for practically everyone I knew. It was no longer stealing cars or printing money; these jobs wound up plastered across newspapers and television broadcasts.

If Whitey decided a job was important enough, and he didn't want to dirty his own hands, or if he wanted to hide the profits from his colleagues (Flemmi, Weeks, et cetera), he'd call on me. Nothing was off-limits. The point of no return was a lifetime behind me, and I had no intention of looking back. Now, however, the burden of living with myself, this new fucked-up version, had begun. Skipping manhood, I went from boy to monster. Thanks, Jim.

That stark reality struck me like a ball-peen hammer the minute I stepped out of the Liquor Mart and onto the sidewalk. I puked, right onto my new shoes—which is the reason I remember the exact pair I wore that day.

*What the fuck have I done? That wasn't me . . . I couldn't have . . . Who am I?*

I couldn't fully grasp the truth. Questions ate away at me. Inside my head, one thousand voices screamed and argued with each other. A battle between ethics and realism ended with the desire to drown myself in booze.

Seeking shelter in the bottle was the only way I saw forward. Maybe there were answers in there, maybe there weren't. I didn't care. Liquor would quiet the thoughts and questions I couldn't face. The more I drank, the quieter they became. At that moment, the angel on my shoulder went on a thirty-year bender, leaving the devil to call the shots.

# NINE

## THE ISABELLA STEWART GARDNER MUSEUM HEIST

Let me preface this next part by making one thing crystal fuckin' clear: I wasn't there, and it wasn't fucking me, all right? How this all went down, as presented in this chapter, is just my theory. *Good*, now we can begin.

## I.

To this day, law enforcement has followed every lead and theory under the assumption that the Isabella Stewart Gardner Museum heist had to be done by either the Italians or the Irish, but every time, the trail they were following hit a dead end, ran dry, or was bullshit to begin with. Basically, the FBI as a collective couldn't find its prick with both hands. The way I see it—my theory—and the only way all the evidence makes any sense is that it had to be the Italians *and* the Irish. And even though that rat-bastard Whitey told the FBI that I was involved, the trail of dead bodies, greed, cocaine, corruption, and the missing paintings traces back to Bobby Donati: he started this whole fucking mess, which is exactly why he's dead.

I knew Donati back in the day before he became a buffet for maggots. He drove around a high-up caporegime, a "captain" in the Patriarca crime family, and he was a mid-level bookie on the side. I saw Donati working down at TRC Auto Electric in Dorchester every time I went in there to pick up Jim's cut for any business being done together on Winter Hill turf. The place was an epicenter for the local Merlino Gang, which was loyal to the Italian Mafia, but was also used as a front for a sizable coke trafficking operation. Guys were always going in and out to drop off the shit or pick it up or place bets with Donati. He took bets from half of the North End; and practically everyone, from degenerate gamblers to addicts to wannabe rock stars, owed him money. I heard from someone that the idea for the museum job was hatched to settle a fucking debt. Donati was told that one of the night security guards at the Gardner Museum was a musician with a substantial drug habit and that he'd be an easy mark.

Donati was familiar with the museum. A while back, Donati cased the Gardner with his friend Myles J. Connor Jr. The two had worked together on other jobs, and in 1972 they'd been arrested for stealing five paintings. Myles was able to exchange artwork he'd previously stolen—a Rembrandt—for a significantly shorter sentence. Years later (if you believe a fucking word out of Myles's mouth), the two visited the Gardner Museum on multiple occasions and noted which items they'd be able to quickly unload.

Donati took a liking to a Napoleonic finial in the shape of an eagle, possibly expecting the flagstaff ornament to be made of solid gold. Also, he thought a Shang dynasty gu, a drinking vessel that was one of the oldest objects in the museum, had to be worth a fortune—*right? Wrong.* Fucking idiot.

After the museum closed, Myles claimed that he and Donati climbed trees around the building to get a better vantage point and time the guards as they made their rounds, which sounds as stupid as it is. Myles? Maybe he did that; at least he was in shape. But Donati? The only shape he was in was round.

After some planning, they agreed that the best way to get in would be to dress up as police officers, as they'd done together on previous jobs. But for whatever reason, the two never pulled off the Gardner job back then.

Now, however, things would be a little different: this time Donati had an inside man. And whether the security guard knew it or not, he was in . . . all the way up to his fucking neck.

Now for a little background. Jump back four months before the heist went down: November of '89. Myles got arrested and charged with attempting to sell stolen property. He was sentenced to ten years. That same month, Donati's boss, Vincent "The Animal" Ferrara, was arrested in a monumental RICO case that put away six other high-ranking members of the Patriarca crime family.

Donati feared for his boss's safety on the inside, reason being that before being arrested, a power-hungry Ferrara had put an unsuccessful hit out on his competition. According to a source, Donati visited the prison several times, informing Ferrara that he had plans in motion to secure him an early release. Presumably, this was a plan to ransom stolen artwork for a reduced sentence, as Myles had done previously. Monkey see, monkey do.

But with Myles in for a dime, Bobby Donati would have to look elsewhere for help.

That's where Robert Guarente enters the picture: the clear choice to assist Donati with the scheme. Not only were the two childhood friends, but Guarente was a frequent sight at TRC Auto Electric.

There, in the back room after hours, they worked out the plan for the museum heist. The first step was determining how big the crew was going to be and who they trusted enough to let in on the plan. Both men were a half century old and around an extra hundred pounds away from peak physical form; to pull off a job of this magnitude, they'd need someone who could, at the very least, climb a set of stairs without getting winded. Guarente knew the perfect man for the job: David Turner.

Guarente was Turner's friend, mentor, and quasi father figure. The two had known each other since Turner's high school days more than a decade earlier. Turner was a hothead and a seasoned thief, but he mostly just trafficked Colombian coke from Florida back up to the auto shop.

In addition to Turner, they'd need to find two low-level patsies to actually go into the museum—and who'd take the fall if something went wrong. Turner knew just who to get. Georgie Reissfelder was a fucking junkie and a friend of Turner's, so he'd be perfect for the job. The other low-level chump would have to be Lenny DiMuzio. According to a close associate of Turner's, Turner had worked with Lenny on a robbery in January of 1990, in which the two dressed as deliverymen to gain entrance into a house in Canton, Mass.

Coincidence? *Yeah fuckin' right.* Dressing up worked once for these dopes—why fix what ain't broke?

What's more, just prior to the Gardner job, Donati was seen walking into a club in Revere, Massachusetts, carrying a paper bag that contained two authentic Boston Police uniforms. He was meeting Guarente there.

Word about the museum robbery would have to reach the head of the Italian Mafia beforehand in order to get permission to pull it off. The job was being planned in the wake of an internal power struggle among many Italian underbosses after their former boss died. The de facto godfather, Frank "Cadillac" Salemme, had forged strong ties with Whitey to solidify his claim to the throne. And that's how the Irish got involved with the heist.

Guarente was a made man, and he reported directly to Salemme. Once Salemme knew about the upcoming art museum heist, he would have informed Jim. There's no fucking way the Italians would dare to pull off a job of that magnitude in Winter Hill territory without including the Irish. With their ranks weakened by their boss's death, the Italians couldn't risk going to war with Jim. No matter what, Whitey always got his tribute . . . his *pound of flesh.*

The last piece of the puzzle was their inside man, the security guard: Rick Abath.

After learning about Abath's music aspirations and his insatiable quest to get high and live the rock 'n' roll lifestyle, it would be easy for Donati to exploit, influence, and corrupt him. When a person, especially one who's constantly wasted, is caught in a stranglehold of delusional dreams of grandeur, they become as malleable as a lump of clay in the hands of a potter.

*Just open the fuckin' door, Abath, and you can keep getting as high as you want.*

The only ingredient missing was an introduction to Abath. A friendly face was needed to enlist Abath's help without scaring him off.

Guarente's longtime friend James "Irish Jim" Marks was the key. Marks was a street dealer with an affinity for getting high on his own supply and placing long-shot bets on losing horses.

Whether it was through dealing drugs to Abath or sometimes partying with him, Marks could provide the connection that Donati and Guarente needed. Once introductions were made, it would be as simple as supplying Abath with as much weed, blow, and booze as the kid wanted in conjunction with empty promises to broker the deal that his band needed to make it in the music industry (at the time, known to have strong ties to the Patriarca crime family). The general consensus on Rick Abath was this: "Once this fish was hooked, there'd be no fight; it would practically mount itself on the wall."

With the crew complete, the final step was to decide which of the more than 2,500 works at the Gardner Museum would be taken. While working the midnight shift on New Year's Eve, just months before the robbery, Abath let a group of people into the museum. He later claimed these "friends" had been there to party, *not* to scout the artwork.

Gaining knowledge of the available paintings, Donati, Guarente, and Whitey would each have their own self-serving stipulations for what would go on the "shopping" list. Donati needed a masterpiece that was valuable enough to secure his boss's early release from prison. He knew that his friend Myles had successfully used a Rembrandt as a bargaining chip in the past and likely set his eyes to the same painter's work, *The Storm on the Sea of Galilee.* This was Rembrandt's only known seascape and at the time was valued at around $100 million.

Initially, Guarente's concern had been what the *fuck* he was going to do with a bunch of stolen art. But on second thought, at the time about 74 percent of all the coke that entered the US was coming from Colombia. And with Guarente's drug trafficking connections, he would have a pipeline to the ideal art patrons: members of the Medellín Cartel.

Around this time, the heyday of their manufacturing and distribution, the cartel was raking in over $60 million of dirty money per day. Americans then (and now) consumed so much cocaine that nine out of ten US bills in circulation would test positive for cocaine residue. The laundering of these illicit gains through the fine art world would be exceedingly easy, considering how unregulated and anonymous the transactions were. Basically, all you had to do was find one of the many less-than-scrupulous auction houses that ignored an item's provenance, and you were allowed to astronomically overbid and secure masterpieces. The auction house naturally would take their cut, and you'd have the clean money in your account before law enforcement had a chance to catch on.

This was a common practice by the cocaine kingpin of the world himself, Pablo Escobar. That he flew his wife, who had an affinity for fine art, all over the world to collect masterpieces was common knowledge. To her credit, she had a curator's eye and a sharp instinct. The crown jewel of their legally acquired collection was *The Dance*, an oil painting from 1957 by Salvador Dalí depicting two people dancing. It was his wife's favorite.

Moreover, Escobar's business partners, the Ochoa family, were also well-known fine art connoisseurs. It would be no problem trading artwork to either Escobar or the Ochoas in exchange for enough coke to take over the New England market. Having knowledge of the Ochoas' obsession with horses (they owned over a thousand thoroughbreds) as well as the affinity of Escobar's wife for artwork depicting fluid dancing movement, Guarente likely added to the top of the list five sketches by Edgar Degas that involved this appealing content. Also, the small size of the sketches would make them simpler to deliver to Colombia. For example, they could easily fit into a contractor's blueprint tubes.

One obstacle Guarente faced was setting up a deal with the Medellín Cartel. However, as a made man in the Boston faction of the Philadelphia Mafia, Guarente could manage a connection to the Colombians.

The Philadelphia Mafia had close ties to the Sicilian Mafia, and they, in turn, had a close relationship with the Medellín Cartel. The Colombians sent cocaine to the Sicilians in exchange for money and strategic military advice. Once the Sicilians gained possession of the cocaine, they'd forward it to Philadelphia; then Guarente would bring it up to Boston.

Guarente could use this pipeline in reverse to sell the stolen masterpieces to Escobar.

But there was a backup plan in case Guarente's channel to the Medellín Cartel was too labyrinthine. David Turner had a more direct network through his drug smuggling operation in Florida. Turner made frequent trips to his second home down there, picking up shipments of coke to take back to Boston. Assuming Guarente couldn't set up the deal with the Colombians, Turner could use his outlet to make the deal. Either way, Guarente could use one of these connections to off-load any stolen artwork in exchange for copious amounts of cocaine.

Jim's cut would be used in an attempt to save face with the Provisional Irish Republican Army (IRA) in Northern Ireland after a pretty big fuckup a few years back.

In 1984, he'd promised to deliver them seven and a half tons of weapons and ammunition in support of their cause and to establish a profitable relationship. The shipment would contain 163 AK-47 assault rifles, 25 mini-machine guns, 12 shotguns, 12 bulletproof vests, 71,000 rounds of ammunition, and a literal ton of military-grade explosives. To amass the munitions, Whitey had each individual part separately mail-ordered from magazine publications like *Shotgun News*. He tasked underlings with assembling the cache in and around the Boston area.

Problem was the Irish Navy got tipped off about the shipment and intercepted the fishing trawler, the *Valhalla*, that was smuggling the weapons. After Whitey and Flemmi learned the name of the informant from a corrupt FBI agent, John "Zip" Connolly, they personally tortured, killed, and interred the rat in the basement of a South Boston home.

Because of the munitions seizure, the IRA lacked sufficient weaponry in their fight and suffered numerous casualties, severely bruising Jim's credibility.

However, being the narcissist he was, Whitey wouldn't think twice about offering up two of the world's most valuable masterpieces, a Rembrandt and a Vermeer, in order to restore his good standing in the eyes of the IRA. He wouldn't have trusted the Italians with *his* masterpieces and would have insisted on sending a separate vehicle to the Gardner with one of his own guys to get his hands on the art after it was removed from the museum. With what was at stake, he would not have allowed the heist to occur under the sole control of another faction of organized crime, and he would have insisted upon having one of his own men present to immediately take his cut of the haul.

That just left the compensation promised to "the tampons"—individuals deemed disposable. In exchange for playing their part, Georgie Reissfelder and Lenny DiMuzzio were likely misled about what the phrase *taken care of* meant, and Abath would have been given enough coke to keep skiing down the Colombian slopes until his heart gave out.

All right, look. I'll make the theory real fucking simple: Donati, Guarente, and—to a lesser extent—Turner planned the heist. Lenny and Georgie would dress as cops and be let into the museum by Abath. Jimmy would send his guy in a separate van to take his cut. A few of the stolen sketches would go to Colombia for the coke, one painting would be used to negotiate for Ferrara's early release from prison, and two more would go to the IRA to make up for the *Valhalla* disaster.

That's it. It was only supposed to be three goddamn paintings and a couple little sketches, but I guess when you give a fat kid the keys to a candy store, shit's bound to happen.

The day came, and a tidal wave of beer and shots drowned the streets of Boston as St. Patrick's Day celebrations continued into the late hours of March 17, 1990, my uncle Howie's sixty-first birthday.

Instead of joining the party with the rest of the city, Rick Abath and a second security guard punched in for their shift at the Gardner Museum. That night, Abath took the first walking patrol. His footsteps echoed down the dark hallways and quiet galleries as he cleared his floor without interruption. Just after midnight, now March 18, halfway through clearing the second floor, the fire alarm pierced through the void.

Abath radioed down to his coworker at the desk. The entire alarm box had been triggered. With no indication of any fire or broken windows in the museum, he quickly returned to the security desk to check the box. After resetting it, the same malfunction instantly occurred, so Abath decided to power it off and made a note of the issue for the morning crew to deal with. As per museum protocol, he would have to restart his rounds from the top.

This second patrol followed Abath's usual routine except for a single small detour. On the ground floor, after spending a few minutes in the Blue Room gallery for a second time, Abath buzzed himself into the small lobby of the trap room near the security desk, which securely separated the employee side entrance from the rest of the museum.

He quickly opened and closed the outside door leading onto Palace Road and returned to the security desk to swap duties with the other guard. He maintained later on that he had performed the "door check" on multiple occasions. Ironically, no evidence of this alleged door check exists, and his claim was later refuted by other employees.

As Abath was opening the door, two men, perfectly fitting the descriptions of Georgie and Lenny, dressed as Boston cops, were seen sitting in a dark hatchback one hundred yards from the entrance. Many believe that Abath opened the door just then to signal that he was "in place," but it was definitely more than that. This was the first of many greedy fucking side deals that ultimately led to the murders of practically everyone involved.

Unbeknownst to the others, Abath, Georgie, and Lenny likely had plans to take a few extra paintings for themselves. Abath could use his required walking patrols as an opportunity to take the artwork and as an alibi to proclaim his innocence. Upon opening the door, Abath could hand off the first painting, a small portrait of a man by French modernist Édouard Manet, then return to the security desk and exchange roles with the other officer.

Abath then manned the desk for a half hour without incident. At 1:20 a.m. the dark hatchback was caught on one of the museum's three cameras pulling into the employee parking lot. Four minutes later, the two men in police uniforms pressed the buzzer on the side door, stating they were responding to a disturbance in the museum.

Against the standard protocol of calling the police station to confirm they had sent over the officers, Abath buzzed the men through *both* doors and into the museum. Standing face-to-face with the cops, Abath was ordered to call the other guard back to the office, prior to finishing his patrol.

After radioing his partner, the shorter of the two "cops" (who looked identical to Lenny) supposedly accused Abath of fitting the description of a wanted criminal and commanded him to come out from behind the counter and present identification. Abath obliged and stepped away from the panic button affixed to his station.

Once Abath's coworker reappeared, the "officers" handcuffed the two watchmen and informed them that the museum was being robbed. Abath put up no resistance as he and his partner were wrapped and blindfolded with a roll of silver duct tape the thieves had brought along.

Low voices reciting unintelligible code cut through the static emanating from the fake officers' radios, indicating the presence of a second, and possible third, team outside. The robbers seemed to know the layout of the museum, and they ushered the two guards directly into the basement without hesitation. After descending the stairs, the security guards were separated; the thieves handcuffed Abath's partner to a sink and then led Abath down a long hallway and shackled him to a workbench, out of earshot from the other captive. No movement was captured by the building's motion sensors for the next thirteen minutes.

The theory that the thieves remained quiet in the basement for those thirteen minutes to be certain that the police had not been alerted is a load of shit. It makes no fucking sense. There's no way a couple of thieves—even ones as fucking dumb as Georgie and Lenny—would sit around with their thumbs stuck up each other's asses in the midst of robbing the place. The only rational explanation in my mind is that Georgie and Lenny used that time updating the others over the radio and talking to Abath about their side deal. Throughout the night, one of the thieves repeatedly returned to the basement and checked on the guards, asking if they were all right—an action that Georgie's sister swears he would certainly do.

After leaving the guards in the basement, the thieves unskillfully and haphazardly went about stealing the artwork and artifacts on the list Donati and Guarente and Whitey had made. Motion sensors caught their movement in only two of the galleries where artwork went missing, both on the second floor: the Dutch Room and the Short Gallery.

At 2:40 a.m. the side door was opened to deliver the paintings to Jim's guys, and five minutes later it was opened one last time to hand over Donati's and Guarente's cut. The robbery was over, but the real fucking story was just beginning.

## II.

For four hours, the crime scene sat untouched, waiting for the morning security officers to relieve the night crew. The morning guards arrived around 7:00 a.m. and rang the bell a few times without response. Not having a set of keys, they used a pay phone to call the museum's deputy director of security, who showed up ten minutes later and let them into the Gardner.

The second he entered, he noticed one thing more troubling than the next: an unwound wire coat hanger on the ground next to the candy machine (Georgie and Lenny must have gotten hungry waiting for the pickup crews); the absence of guards manning the security desk; and lying empty in the supervisor's office behind the security desk, the small hand-carved frame that had held *Chez Tortoni*—the masterpiece Abath had likely handed off.

The deputy director phoned his boss, then the police. Four Boston Police officers arrived on the scene and began searching for the missing security officers. While two patrolmen wandered into the basement and found Abath and his partner, the other two officers walked up to the second floor and discovered the extent of the theft. *Holy shit!*

Jurisdiction over the scene rapidly exchanged hands from the police officers to the local detectives. By lunchtime, the FBI had seized it.

Which begs the question: *Why the fuck did the FBI even get involved?* Robbery isn't a federal crime unless the stolen objects crossed state lines or if what was taken had a connection to the federal government. At this point, neither was the case. The museum's paintings were part of a private collection, not federal property, and there was no evidence to conclude the paintings had crossed state lines. There was no recovered DNA, hair, or conclusive fingerprints. In fact, besides the security computer printout, a roll of duct tape, and two sets of handcuffs, there wasn't anything to go on. The FBI's bullshit excuse was that they had authority because they *believed* the artwork had left the state.

In a criminal's lexicon, this translates to the FBI taking the case in order to cover their ass for crimes of their own.

By this time, Whitey was a fuckin' full-blown rat for the feds: a "top echelon informant," in their words. In exchange for feeding the FBI a bullshit monthly report, Whitey was untouchable. And on top of the protections sanctioned by FBI supervisors, Jim's handler, Zip Connolly, was tipping off the Winter Hill Gang and falsifying reports to cover up a slew of Jim's crimes.

If the relationship between the FBI and the crime lord was uncovered during the Gardner investigation, Whitey could drag many high-ranking federal agents and politicians behind bars alongside him. Hell, he'd be able to show that the FBI were goddamn criminals too, de facto mobsters in their own right, the only difference being that the government signed their fucking paychecks. By taking control of the Isabella Gardner Museum investigation, the FBI could steer it straight into a fucking brick wall. To effectively ensure the case disappeared, they placed it in the inexperienced hands of a young agent, Daniel Falzon.

Falzon was an FBI virgin fresh out of the academy and had just been assigned to his first permanent post in Boston. He had proven himself somewhat useful on other less significant cases, but as he was only twenty-nine years old and an outsider to New England, the thought of handing him the reins under the assumption he'd be able to crack the case was a fucking joke.

Quickly and unsurprisingly, the only physical evidence recovered at the scene that could provide DNA—two sets of handcuffs and the silver roll of duct tape—vanished into thin air. Any hope of success withered within the first three months as the number of agents actively working on the case was reduced from over forty to just Falzon himself.

As the FBI continued derailing the investigation, the artwork slowly began to move, and in its wake, bodies started to drop.

Sometime in April 1990, a month after the heist, the first piece surfaced: the bronze finial. Bobby Donati brought it to a jeweler named Paul Calantropo to get it appraised. Calantropo, a personal friend of Donati's, claims to have told Donati it was worthless because "the whole world knew it was stolen." Frustrated, but not giving up, Donati kept the eagle and left. Realizing the art was too hot to handle, he stashed it away, deciding to wait for the steam to blow over. In due time, he planned to bring it out again and negotiate for his boss's early release.

It wasn't long before things took a sharp, violent turn.

In February of '91, "Irish Jim" Marks was returning home to Lynn, Massachusetts, after spending the day with Guarente. He took two point-blank shotgun blasts to the back of the head. He was the first to drop dead.

And when one domino falls, the rest are fucked.

Lenny DiMuzzio disappeared in March, last seen visiting his sister in the hospital. His body resurfaced in June, stuffed into the trunk of his car, his skull riddled with bullet holes. Georgie Reissfelder was found dead the following month in his Quincy apartment. Cocaine poisoning.

Prior to his death, *Chez Tortoni* had hung on Georgie's wall, a claim first made by Georgie's brother. "I know I saw it in his possession," he told law enforcement after his brother's death. Georgie's sister-in-law backed the claim. "I distinctly recall that painting—the man in the tall hat," she said, remembering that the painting had been awkwardly hung in a secondhand frame. But seeing how the painting wasn't recovered at Georgie's apartment after his death, it must have been removed beforehand by someone who knew exactly what it was.

Unsurprisingly, the first three deaths connected to this case were those of the disposable pawns. That just left Rick Abath alive. What the fuck made him so special?

First off, he was smart enough not to snitch, although he knew little to nothing. All he could have offered the detectives was info regarding his own involvement; he would have been kept in the dark about everything else. However, he stuck to his story of complete innocence and refused to provide the investigation with any useful information. He went on later to tell a news outlet, "I remember at the time thinking, there's no way they're going to catch these people from [the information I provided] . . ."

But equally important to Abath's continued residency aboveground was the fact he wasn't a criminal—not a real one, anyway. He wasn't playing the game, and in adherence to the code of not fucking over people who weren't criminals, he wasn't touched. Still, the fact he was involved in a robbery of this caliber and came out in one piece . . . Abath is a lucky sonofabitch.

The same cannot be said for Bobby Donati. In September of '91, on the twenty-first, in broad fuckin' daylight, he was abducted by a group of men off his front porch. To make matters even more suspicious, this happened while Donati was under twenty-four-hour FBI surveillance. He disappeared out from under their noses . . . supposedly. Three days later, his body was discovered in the trunk of his white Cadillac, a half mile from his home. He had been badly beaten, stabbed twenty-one times, and his throat had been cut. Pretty brutal, even by my standards.

Two months after Donati's death, the Chinese gu was spotted in the hands of David Turner. The state police had him under surveillance and spotted him carrying it into a lawyer's office in Boston. The police never stopped and questioned him about the incident. What makes the timing of this interesting is that the vase, according to Myles Connor Jr., had caught Donati's eye years before and would have originally been in his possession following the heist. So how did Turner get it?

In the months leading up to his abduction and murder, Donati had become somewhat of a recluse, staying indoors and withdrawing from social situations. He had mentioned to a friend that two suspicious men dressed in all black were following him. Fearing for his safety, Donati gave his share of the artwork to Guarente for safekeeping in the event of his demise. After the handoff and subsequent homicide, Turner likely told Guarente that he could flip the vase to one of his usual customers of stolen goods—the Boston lawyer.

Then, for a number of years, the reports ran cold. The paintings were held "on ice." Guarente's daughter claimed that while they were living together, her father had hung *The Storm on the Sea of Galilee* on the mantel above the fireplace, although there has been no corroboration of this claim. But for authorities, there were no new leads. No reliable sources came forth. No sightings. Nothing. It wasn't until 2002 when the artwork saw the light once again.

The artwork was moving in tandem with Guarente's slowly approaching death: he was diagnosed with terminal cancer. And with unavoidable death on the cards, he sought to cash in his chips to provide for his wife after he was gone. So he reached out to his connections in Philadelphia for help.

According to the FBI, it was around this time that the artwork came up for sale on the black market in the Rittenhouse Square art district of Philadelphia. The problem was that the art was too hot; nobody would touch it. It didn't sell. Unable to rid himself of the paintings at auction, Guarente returned to Maine with his troubles still intact. Running out of options and time, he gave the small Rembrandt self-portrait to his wife, Elaine; everything else went to his longtime associate and friend Robert Gentile. Elaine reported that after a lunch with her husband and Gentile at a seafood restaurant in 2002, Gentile was given two of the paintings in the parking lot, and in exchange, Gentile promised to look after Elaine when the time came—a promise he kept after Guarente died in 2004.

Years passed by with the art in Gentile's custody. Gentile's cousin, an FBI informant, recounted the bronze eagle finial on open display in Gentile's auto shop. The cousin also recorded conversations in which Gentile offered to sell the paintings at the low price of $500,000 apiece, a bargain when taking into consideration their true value. But no sale was ever made.

At last, in May 2012, the location of most of the artwork was discovered. Its final resting place. Gentile had been indicted on drug-related charges, and the FBI got a no-knock warrant to raid his house in Manchester, Connecticut.

The FBI sent over twenty agents to the residence, an outrageous number for the relatively mild charges Gentile was facing. Combing the yard for freshly dug soil or other neoteric hiding spots, the agents found shit. Inside the house, however, they found a *Boston Herald* newspaper with an article detailing the Gardner heist. Along with the newspaper, they found a sheet of paper listing each stolen object. Next to each item was the price that the item could fetch on the black market.

When asked to explain the list, Gentile stated a broker had written up the numbers and gave a bullshit story of how he was attempting to buy them from his deceased friend Guarente. It made no fucking sense. What makes more sense is that Gentile knew he couldn't sell the artwork himself, and without the same connections as Guarente, he needed a third-party broker to arrange the sale.

Not long after discovering the list, a second search warrant arrived at the house hours later. This time, it expanded on the original search warrant to include the shed in the backyard. Quickly, agents scoured the shed. Nothing. The artwork wasn't there. Had Gentile managed to sell it? No, probably not. The answers to what happened to the art lie with Gentile's son, who arrived on scene soon after the second warrant.

The first thing he told authorities was that his father didn't have the connections nor the wherewithal to sell stolen masterpieces, supporting the idea that Gentile Sr. would have tried to enlist outside help. But Gentile's son wasn't done talking.

The next thing he divulged was that his father had installed a false floor in the shed. *A false floor?* A frenzy of agents rushed to the shed to double-check the floorboards. Had they missed something? Yes and no . . . the wooden boards did cover a long dug-out pit, and sitting in the pit was an equally long plastic container. Removing the lid revealed nothing; it was empty. A fool's last hope.

Robert Gentile had no explanation. If the art had been in the plastic box at some point, he wasn't saying anything. His son, on the other hand, provided the last piece of the puzzle. Bad news: Some years back, torrential rain had flooded Connecticut, submerging the shed and all its contents. Whatever had been in the container was ruined. It was the most upset Gentile Jr. had ever seen his father; whatever was in there had meant a great deal to the old man.

Such is the likely fate of *The Storm on the Sea of Galilee*, along with the rest of the shit the Italians stole. With the works ruined, they would have to be destroyed. Safer that way. The only value they had at that point was to get you multiple life sentences. It's a shame how something so precious can become worthless in the wrong hands.

*Now, to account for the remainder of the stolen art, we must return to the morning after the heist and follow a separate yet concurrent storyline plotting the two paintings on the Irish front.*

The Irish courier would have delivered the paintings to Whitey right away, operating under the fear of a fate worse than death should they not arrive when expected. Even so, as soon as Whitey got ahold of them, he would be in no rush to move them. For the time being, he wouldn't even be able to. Not safely.

There would be a handful of FBI agents knocking on his door come noontime; Whitey knew that if he wasn't there to open it and answer a litany of questions, he'd be the robbery's prime suspect. Not even Zip Connolly or his brother or anyone he had in his pocket could protect Whitey if that happened. His life would be hell.

He'd have to wait until the opportune moment to make his move—when the heat was off his back.

Around this time, my name started getting tossed around where it didn't belong. From my understanding, the FBI added my name to the list of potential suspects when Whitey fed it to them, pointing fingers every which way but toward himself. It was a bullshit move to pass the blame onto me. And as history shows, when Whitey opened his mouth, the FBI took his word as gospel; it didn't take long before I was under the magnifying glass.

I found out this information years later at a transfer hearing when I was applying to be moved from a maximum-security facility to a lesser-security lockup. A document presented to the court arguing against my transfer reads verbatim as follows: "In addition—since the arrest of James J. 'Whitey' Bulger, Hicks and his uncles' names have been linked by the FBI to the Isabella Stewart Gardner Museum art heist . . . [which is] 'justification' for [Hicks] remaining at maximum-security . . ."

Working under the assumption that I had some part in the heist, law enforcement started fitting extraneous evidence to support the accusation. Specifically, there were multiple reports that I had been seen near the museum on the days and nights leading up to the robbery . . . which was true. At the time of the robbery, I had been working on a construction job a street away from the Gardner. I was replacing windows in a brick building for a wealthy doctor, and the client was out of town for a few days and wanted the project done by the time he returned. It was common for me and my crew to work into the night at the property and have my van parked outside on the street. It was mere coincidence the construction job matched up with the Gardner heist, nothing more. The fact that the artwork was rolled up when it was removed strengthened the FBI's suspicions against me because if I had been a part of anything (which I wasn't), I could have easily hidden the artwork in blueprint tubes, a common item in every builder's van. The whole theory was complete bullshit.

This flawed investigative technique may have led the FBI to ignore other vital information, occasionally missing it altogether. Case in point: the brick mason who was working with me on the window job. His name was David, and he was doing ledge work for me, repairing some of the broken bricks on my client's windowsill. In addition to working with me two streets away from the Gardner, David was doing other brickwork inside the fucking Gardner Museum itself. Yet somehow, he was never even interviewed, questioned, or interrogated. David had his own truck, equipped with building tubes, was in the vicinity at the time of the heist, and had access to the grounds leading up to the robbery, yet wasn't even a suspect as far as I know.

With my innocence clarified, we can continue.

Not long after the heist, six months at most, Whitey went to Ireland. He traveled using fake documentation—a forged passport under a solid alias, stolen credit cards, and possibly donned a disguise—to keep the FBI in the dark, a necessary precaution to take if he was carrying the stolen Gardner art. It was how Whitey always traveled back then. It was how most of us traveled, to be honest, me included. And at this point, Whitey wasn't yet on the FBI's Most Wanted list, so it would be easier to get in and out of the country without raising any flags. Accompanying Whitey on the journey was Joseph Murray, the owner of the *Valhalla*.

In an attempt at reconciliation and to repair his "good" name, Whitey would have met with his contacts in the IRA and handed over two works of art worth over $250 million: *The Concert* and *A Lady and Gentleman in Black*.

But the moment the paintings left Jim's hands, they seemed to vanish off the face of the earth. Solid leads dried up. Many people who held on to hope for their recovery had to let it go. The chance of a break in the case was nothing more than a fool's pipe dream.

That is, until 2019, when a renowned art detective by the name of Charles Hill entered negotiations with a notable Irish criminal to recover the lost works. Hill was an ex–Scotland Yard detective and celebrated art recoverer most known for returning such stolen works as Edvard Munch's *The Scream* and *Lady Writing a Letter with Her Maid* by Johannes Vermeer.

A criminal, Martin "The Viper" Foley, claimed to know the whereabouts of the art and agreed to help Hill make a deal with the members of an Irish gang who had the lost masterpieces in their possession. The claim by Foley was not to be overlooked; there was a good chance it was legitimate. Foley was a well-known associate of "Ireland's biggest fence," Tommy Coyle, the only person capable of moving the two paintings on foreign soil. Foley and Coyle were spotted together on multiple occasions over the years following Jim's 1990 trip.

But what happened next, after Foley came forward with a promise of progress, was a disaster. Somebody fucked it up. This time, however, it wasn't law enforcement who ruined the chance of solving the case; it was the media: a tabloid journalist recklessly chasing a headline.

The journalist, a BBC correspondent, had been filming a documentary about the heist when he caught wind there might be a break in the case after almost thirty years. And like a toddler entrusted with a big secret, he plastered Foley's name across the news, identifying The Viper as the tipster who would lead authorities to the art.

Soon after, Foley disappeared. Never to be heard from again.

Now, for the life of me, I cannot remember who told me this, but I heard the paintings were eventually bricked up behind a church wall somewhere in Dublin. West Dublin, maybe. The rationale being that no one would dare desecrate a wall in the house of God on the off chance an old Dutch masterpiece was stashed behind it.

Wherever the art is today, you won't find it, assuming it hasn't been destroyed. There are too many unsolved crimes still connected to the heist. It's safer for whoever has the paintings if they remain lost forever. I don't know for certain where any of it is. All I know for sure is that anyone who has come close to the stolen artwork seems to vanish, is killed outright, or is dead already . . . everyone, that is, except that one Irish courier . . . I almost forgot about him. At this point, though, it's safe to say whoever he is, he's a ghost.

# TEN

## GHOST

The Gardner heist fucked us. Without convictions, solid leads, or progress, the blatant corruption within the FBI was too obvious to be swept under the rug. And to make things worse, in the throes of the heist's aftermath, Zip Connolly—the FBI's rat tamer who had been a lifeline providing vital tip-offs and protection for Whitey and Flemmi—retired from the bureau to take a cushy union job as the director of security/public affairs at the Boston Edison. The FBI cut its ties with the Winter Hill Gang, Whitey and Flemmi were no longer denoted as protected informants, and the "hunt" for Whitey Bulger began.

Every agency wanted a piece of the action, to get in while the getting was good. They were on our asses like a chronic case of hemorrhoids. If anyone so much as breathed in the direction of a known associate of the Winter Hill Gang, they'd be brought in, questioned, and have a gloved hand jammed up their rectum, probing for shit that could be used in court. Agencies started filling their files with whatever evidence they could find. When the time was right, you could be certain that whoever had the fattest file would conduct a flashy raid while the other agencies watched from the sidelines. The winner of the fattest file contest would send in troops in full combat gear holding assault rifles and shotguns, with high-caliber sniper rifles positioned on neighboring rooftops aimed at exit points (everyone with a weapon secretly hoping for a shoot-out), and, of course, the bulletproof vests with large block letters identifying which agency finally "took down the criminal over-lord, Whitey Bulger." The whole choreographed spectacle was being performed for the six o'clock news broadcast.

But it took four years and the unlikely cooperation between the DEA, Massachusetts State Police Department, and Boston Police Department to compile sufficient evidence for a case against Jim. The FBI was purposefully excluded from any cross-agency communications and all evidence sharing. Meanwhile, in a relatively successful attempt to keep operations running smoothly, monthly payoffs had increased, reaching the hands of more badges than ever before. Sure, bribes only prolonged the inevitable, but it gave us some extra leash to run around on for the time being. And it proved to be more than enough leeway to continue as if the eyes of the world weren't on us. Our collections were still being collected; our cocaine trade flourished; Jim, Kevin Weeks, and two other Micks found a way to get their hands on a lottery ticket to win $14 million; and I, now with a drinking habit to rival André the Giant's, managed to rack up the first seven pages of my rap sheet.

But I am getting ahead of myself because a lot happened in those four years, and it should be told in chronological order.

Six months after the Gardner heist—as the signs of a cold winter began to appear—I decided to take a sabbatical from day-to-day operations in the South Shore and travel abroad. Seeing tensions rise between my family and law enforcement, I felt it would be as good a time as any to go. Spending the majority of my life within the boroughs of Boston and neighboring areas (with sporadic time spent in Florida), I knew little of foreign countries. In fact, there was only one that I knew anything about: Northern Ireland.

I remember bits and pieces of stories told around the card table years ago, and as a child I filtered out any reference to business deals and relationships, instead remembering the details about Northern Ireland's beauty and it being an "ancestral home." For all his flaws as a psychopath and general piece-of-shit human, Whitey was able to tell wonderful stories of the people and the countryside that stuck with me for over a decade and made me decide to visit.

I purchased a first-class plane ticket because I'd heard a rumor that alcohol was free up there. Not only that, but I wouldn't have the person to my left breathing hot air on my neck, nor would I have the person's stomach to my right spilling over the armrest and onto my thigh. The seats in first class were designed to accommodate the average-sized human instead of the inhumane sardine packing that occurred in coach. The flight attendant, a talkative redheaded broad, offered me a cigarette and went off about some new smoking ban on planes. She said it didn't apply to international flights yet, and that made her happy; then she said to ask for her specifically if there was anything I needed.

I immediately asked her for a drink.

She informed me that she was prohibited from serving alcohol until we were airborne to some arbitrary height. I reminded her that she'd said, "anything I needed," but she held her ground and replied that she would be more than happy to serve me once the plane had taken off.

I began wondering how authority over airways worked. Was it considered international airspace above that noted alcohol-serving height? And if so, could an organized crime syndicate use the boundary in the same way as the international waters? I couldn't think of an effective exploit. The issue of gravity seemed to be an issue—any business conducted in the air would inevitably have to reenter the dominion of some country. If, however, there was a way to overcome the need to return to Earth, the opportunities were endless. If you could launch a body into space, it would be impossible to retrieve, compared to the same body dropped to the bottom of the ocean; although the coordination of a contraption that shoots something beyond Earth's gravitational pull instantly killed the plan's viability . . .

Finally, the need for distracting thoughts vanished as our plane sped down the runway and the nose lifted off the tarmac; a series of mechanical noises indicated that the wheels had been retracted into the underbelly and that we were officially airborne. I called over to the flight attendant and requested a few airplane bottles of whiskey even though the plane hadn't yet leveled out. I figured that by the time she got them, we might be in that international airspace.

She shook her head playfully but gave in all the same. She unbuckled her three-point crewmate harness and, using the overhead cabinets and passenger headrests to stabilize herself, procured me a shot.

I quickly ripped off the plastic cap and sucked down the bottle. I asked for ten more. She smiled, laughed, said that she really shouldn't, then went and got them for me. The man next to me—an old, properly dressed businessman with a nicely trimmed Teddy Roosevelt mustache—looked horrified as I downed the bottles with ease and ordered five more.

I explained to him that "I don't do well on flights" and that the alcohol helped calm my nerves. The flight, from what I can remember, was smooth, easy, and enjoyable as I flirted with the flight attendant for more and more whiskey. I was loaded when the wheels of the plane touched down on foreign soil; however, it wasn't in Northern Ireland. Fuck.

"The Troubles"—the violent conflict between Northern Irish nationalists and the British loyalists occupying Irish land—made it virtually impossible to travel from Boston nonstop to Belfast, so I had flown into Dublin and planned on taking a train across the border.

And I would never have gotten there had it not been for Danny McCaffrey. I met Danny at the airport bar in Boston. We had been the only two people ordering liquor straight that morning, the only two dedicated drinkers. I had known by his accent that he was from the north, and we happened to be on the same Aer Lingus flight. We got to talking and found common ground when I recalled some of the nationalists Whitey had spoken about over the years. Danny had heard of a couple names or at least knew their families. He was close to a decade older than me, putting him around twenty-eight years old; he had dark hair and a tough face that turned splotchy and red when he drank, which, like me, was most of the time.

Not having the endless supply of free liquor on the plane as I did left Danny in better shape when we touched down in Dublin.

"Oi! Oi! Seanie-boy!" Danny called to me. His accent thickened the

closer we came to his home. "Jeeesus, yousens deaf or what? Been callin'
yeh fer awlmost five minutes seems like. Not a windie-licker are ye?"

To be completely honest and sincere, I had no fucking idea what he
was saying. I just nodded my head and shrugged my shoulders.

"Ahm juss takin' a piss, mate! Seems like yeh had the fun witout me
up there wit themuns posh feckers, eh? . . . Ahm jealous 's all, yer two
sheets ta the wind 'n' ahm not even half-cut meself. Waddya say the twos
of us go git a pint 'n' somethin' ta eat? Ahm so hungry ah could eat the
arse of a baby through the cot bars."

"Ahh, sorry Danny, I can't. Gotta find my way to Belfast tonight . . .
Supposed to be staying with someone my uncle set me up with," I said.

"Ahm goin' there meself. Want me ta run ye over? Train's not fer
another couple o' hours anyways. C'mon, ah'll show yeh what a proper
drink tastes like, none o' that watered-down piss ah been served fer the
past month."

"Know anywhere good around here?" I said, deciding that it would
be easier to get to Belfast if I had a guide.

"The food's better up north, but ahm sure we can fine somethin'
'round here," he said, smiling. "More importantly, looks like ah got some
catchin' up ta do." And with that, Danny flagged a taxi, and we deposited our suitcases into the trunk. He then spoke quickly to the cabby
in what sounded like a jumbled foreign language, and we shot off into
the busyness of morning's traffic.

We did get to Belfast eventually, God knows how. We missed the
train that first day, of course. One pub became two, and two became four,
and four became an all-night drinking affair. The next morning—more
likely, sometime around noon—we woke up in a shoddy, pay-by-the-
hour hotel located in northeastern Dublin, in an area ironically called
Summerhill.

We slipped by the receptionist to avoid any complications with the
unpaid bill and made our way to the nearest train station, where we
nursed our hangovers with cigarettes and a carbonated pale-orange drink
mixed with vodka. I am not sure how he did it (or how I understood
what was being said), but it only took the short train ride for Danny to

convince me to abandon my travel plans, rent a motorcycle, and take a two-week trip around Ireland with him—he would act as tour guide.

After arriving in Belfast, we dumped our luggage into Danny's apartment and set out to find me a bike. Danny already had his own. We found a repair/rental shop less than a mile down the road and rented an old Honda cruiser that proved to be reliable beyond expectation. We set out the following morning. In less than an hour, our bikes were humming cheerfully as we drove along the buttery roads tightly wound around Ireland's royal-green hillscapes. The roads were smooth and well cared for (albeit not always wide enough for two motorists to pass one another) compared to the shitty pothole-ridden motorways I was used to in New England. Over the 1,500-plus miles I spent on the rugged, well-built street bike, I spent them without incident—that is, except for the one hiccup early in the trip.

It was the morning of our third, possibly fourth day. A friend of Danny's, Tommy, had let us stay in a spare room built off the back of his house. His home was modest but could be considered charming and was within walking distance of the previous night's pub. There were only three of us in the house—Tommy's wife had taken their children on holiday—and the lack of his wife's supervision proved disastrous.

I was awoken by the laughter of two childhood friends reminiscing loudly over a hearty breakfast of eggs, beans, bangers, and mash. When I walked into the breakfast nook, Tommy was reenacting a drug-fueled day he and Danny had sometime in the eighties at a music festival. The animated story culminated in Tommy running out of the room and returning with a big bag of magic mushrooms he said he was saving for a special event and that our presence fit the bill . . . if we were interested in a trip for old times' sake.

Danny loved the idea. Groggy from having just woken up, I heard myself saying, "Fuck it, why not?"—despite never having taken psychedelics before. It is safe to say that I had no idea what the fuck I was getting myself into. Up until that point, my main reference to getting high came from smoking a little pot here and there with Scott Quinn while the two of us unloaded cargo trucks.

Tommy excitedly ran to the stove and put a kettle on. He hated the taste of eating the mushrooms raw and insisted that brewing the drugs into a tea was the best way to take them.

The tea was fucking terrible. I mean, *really* fucking terrible. I can't imagine how bad the raw mushrooms tasted if this was the preferable way of ingestion. I had no idea how potent the tea was, but I assume it was strong.

Thirty minutes after my first cup (I drank two), I started to notice the effects: things behaved differently, reality was compromised. I watched my hand extend toward the warm cup on the table in front of me. My hand moved one frame at a time, as if filmed in stop-motion. I picked up the cup and took a sip. The tea, once thin and putrid, was now thick and golden like honey sliding down my throat. I stood up. My chair began giggling, tickled with friction as it slid across the oak floor.

Danny joined in the laughter, then Tommy, then me. The three of us doubled over, howling at the lunacy of the mundane . . . of everything . . . of nothing at all. The cacophony of drug-fueled laughter slowly dulled until everything to me sounded underwater and lifeless. But it didn't last long before a voice broke through.

"We can't stay cooped up all day with a head full of mushroom tea. Why don't we go down to the pub, see what's happenin'? Pop in for a drink." I have no recollection of who said this; it could have been me, for all I know. Regardless, the words struck a chord, and we grabbed light jackets and went outside.

As I mentioned, Tommy's house was within walking distance of the pub. However, we were high—so high, in fact, that we decided to take the motorcycles instead of Tommy's perfectly suitable (albeit still dangerous) four-door sedan. We only had the two bikes, so Tommy hopped on behind Danny, riding tandem. Danny revved the throttle and took off, Tommy hanging on for dear life.

I took longer to get going. I was still seeing in stop-motion and was in no way, shape, or form to operate a motor vehicle. The other bike was out of sight by the time I started down the road. No matter—it was no more than a half mile to the pub, I knew I could find my way. The ride was surprisingly pleasant and easy. I noticed the green hills rising and falling on both sides of me, inhaling and exhaling ever so slightly. It started snowing . . . but from the ground up. Snow piles grew out of the breathing earth. Before I knew what was happening, a second winter descended, a whirlwind of snow flurries surrounded me, I lost control of the bike and slammed into a snowbank.

It should come as no surprise to learn that what actually happened was far worse. In truth, I had wandered off the road and into an open field, heading straight for a large herd of Blackface sheep. Most of the sheep scattered, terrified of the bike and the maniac driving it, but not all of them. The collision was quick and violent. I was thrown from the Honda and landed ten feet away on my back, the luckier of the two victims.

The sheep never separated from the bike. Its unsheared wool tangled in Japanese motor parts as it flipped over three times before coming to a halt, the heavy bike letting off black smoke as it lay on top of the animal.

I stood up, muddy and bruised, and walked over to the pile of steel and sheep. It was no use trying to save the animal; it was dead. The motorcycle's front wheel had flattened the sheep's torso in the initial impact, crushing its rib cage, hopefully killing it instantly. I picked the bike up by the handlebars and rested it on the kickstand so I could get down on my knees to pick the bloody bits of wool and flesh out of the motor. After I got it clean (the bike, not the sheep), I gave the kick-start lever a few tries before giving up. I dragged the dislodged carcass by one of the legs over to a large rock in a half-assed attempt to hide the thing, then went back and walked the bike back to the road. Danny and Tommy were walking out of the pub when I arrived.

"Tha fuck happened ta you, mate?" Danny said. I filled them in, inciting a fit of laughter that lasted a minute or so. Once it died down, I asked why they were leaving the pub.

"Ahh, fergot me fuckin' wallet and used up all me credit last night. Piece of shite won't give me nuthin', though he knows I'm good fer it," Tommy responded. "Besides, looks like we got ot'er things ta take care of, haven't we?" he said, nodding toward my Honda.

The bike cost one hundred dollars American (around sixty sterling) to fix. Seeing as how US banking policy inhibits the ease of depositing ill-gotten money into an account for convenient withdrawal around the world, I had decided to travel to Europe with a large bag of US currency, planning to exchange it upon arrival. I had never gotten around to it, but the mechanic who fixed the bike was kind enough to accept the foreign bills in exchange for his services as a favor to Tommy.

With a stroke of luck, as it turns out, Honda bikes weren't particularly uncommon in the country, and parts were readily available. The garage was able to put my crotch rocket back together before nightfall, good as new. And just like that, the trip resumed.

The remainder of the Irish itinerary consisted of drinking our way through a string of nationalist pubs in the northern country, the way irresponsible sightseeing goes, and continued to contain the appropriate amount of drunken debauchery. Danny was, as he put it, "a devout and orthodox" drinker, and I, on the other hand, was just competitive—although maybe it was the other way around.

Those two weeks were some of the best memories of my life, despite the irreparable damage to my liver. We were given carte blanche and treated it with total reckless abandon, and it was a perfect disaster. My only regret from that period, apart from killing the sheep, was losing touch with Danny. I could fill a second and possible third installment to this autobiography with stories from that time, but there are more pressing matters to include in this volume . . .

There was a higher purpose at play beyond just flying overseas to escape the mounting police pressure: I had business to attend to in Switzerland. In addition to the stranglehold Winter Hill had on Boston's cocaine market, Whitey wanted an early foothold in the budding ecstasy market.

In the late seventies, the majority of all US ecstasy production was in the labs of Boston chemists, a so-called "Boston Group." However, demand for the drug had remained relatively low for over half a decade until 1985, when the DEA announced an emergency Schedule One classification for MDMA on their controlled substance list. In conjunction with this reclassification, Nancy Reagan enacted her oblivious, doomed-to-fail "Just Say No" campaign.

And similar to a toddler being told no, an uncontrollable desire to rebel spread across the country like smallpox, which in turn sprouted a new consumer base. It took another six years for Whitey to become cocksure and brash enough to get involved—that's where I came in.

To cultivate sufficient commerce for a profitable harvest, we needed adequate supply and distribution channels. Aware of my connections with other transporters along the Canadian seaboard because of my ship fleet, Whitey put me in charge of import coordination. For production and supply, I was sent to meet a Swiss man named Renard and his chemist.

I flew into Zürich on a clear day. A watery outline of the Alps was visible far off in the distance. At baggage claim I was greeted by Renard. He was neither pleased nor displeased to meet me; the expression on his face was frozen in indifference.

But his stoicism vanished the second he got behind the wheel of his cramped Volkswagen Golf. He drove the cherry-red vehicle like an enraged New York City taxi driver, threading the little car through narrow gaps between neighboring vehicles whilst screaming death threats at the other drivers. There was an odd charm about his anger. Over the half-hour car ride, hanging on to the grab handle for dear life, I learned of Renard's role; he not only owned the laboratory and its contents but was the one who got his hands on impressive amounts of the raw, heavily regulated starting materials needed to cook the drug. His operation was primed and ready to expand into the US market, he explained after cussing out a Swiss-made SUV.

The laboratory was tucked into a factory that was large and grey with an aluminum roof and no windows. The building looked to be abandoned and not operational; the only lights on were in the laboratory room.

When Renard opened the lab door, I got a strong whiff of root beer followed by a ferocious smell of burnt chemicals. Inside, a small man in a stained lab coat was cheerfully talking aloud to himself. He was surrounded by giant metal vats of mixing chemicals, commercial chemical ovens and dehydrators, and ventilating vapor hoods. On a long black benchtop stood a row of propane burners shooting steady flames at smaller tubes; other vials were being continuously shaken and spun by whirring machines; precise scales were ready to measure to the microgram; running along the back wall were ten or so big plastic barrels.

I hadn't a clue what I was looking at but was impressed nonetheless. Upon noticing our intrusion, the lab worker bounced over to make an introduction. He pulled off his double-filter, full-face mask and extended a friendly hand. The man, Sadik, was a brilliant Bangladeshi chemist with a mouthful of titles and qualifications. He spoke the Queen's English with impeccable precision and enthusiasm. With introductions out of the way, we stepped out of the lab and sat at a table, where I assumed Sadik ate his meals, to talk business. "How much can you supply? Cost? How quick can you make it? What's the turnaround time? How do you package it? Can you package it to maximize efficiency of transportation? How good is the shit?"

The last question seemed to offend Sadik, who then assured me that every cook yielded a final product with 99.9 percent purity. There wasn't a better chemist in the world, Renard said matter-of-factly. We shook hands, and that was that. Sadik would produce one hundred thousand doses of pure MDMA every two months out of Renard's chemicals; from the lab, after packaging, the shipment would be flown to Nova Scotia, Canada, driven to Halifax, stashed aboard a boat, and taken to meet with my captain in the Bay of Fundy for pickup.

With business out of the way, I took what money remained and spent the next three months in Germany, France, and Scotland before returning home. Pops picked me up at the airport and said he missed me. It felt nice to be home; the imposing billboards, Sam Adams beer on tap, and Dunkin' Donuts signs on every corner were comforting in a strange way. Nothing had changed in my absence. Massachusetts—Boston in particular—will never change, I don't think. You could drop a nuclear warhead on the city, and it would stay intact.

My old second-floor bedroom at Pops's was exactly how I left it too.

The stacks of shoeboxes in the closet. The unmade bed. I unpacked what little I had and immediately fell asleep. Fuck jet lag, it took me a few days to get reacquainted to the longitude.

Not long after returning stateside, the police caught wind that I was back in town, and the harassment began. For once in this story, I wasn't breaking laws and was minding my own bullshit when a cop pulled up behind me and flipped on his lights.

I pulled over, and two additional cruisers joined the fucking party. The first cop out of his car was Officer Wagner, the pig-fuck who had arrested me at my sister Tina's house. The other cops from the other cars were equally familiar faces.

Five officers and one law-abiding citizen—not quite your routine traffic stop. Wagner walked with the swagger of a man whose penis hangs down to his knees; the fucking prick was just showing off to his compatriots. I wanted nothing more than to wipe that smug look off his fat face. I might have been able to take all five of the assholes too.

But the pissant wasn't worth it, I decided. I wasn't going to gamble in the courtroom now that our freedom walked on a shoelace tightrope after the Gardner.

Wagner rapped twice on my window with the bony knuckle of his middle finger. I rolled it down.

"Wha'da we got here?" he said, not to me but to the other officers who were walking up behind him. "Thought you was dead. We figured you got your drunk ass killed, didn't we, boys?" he asked, again addressing the other officers.

"I heard the Italians got to ya," another officer said, leaning on the open passenger-side window. "Picked up an Italian few weeks back who swore he saw someone put two slugs in tha backka ya head."

"Guess that makes me a fuckin' ghost then, don't it?" I said.

"You hear that, boys? Got ourselves a ghost, ain't that some shit?" Wagner mocked.

"The fuck you want, Wagner?" I said. "I wasn't doin' anythin'."

"Well, *Ghost*. The boys and I got a little welcome present ta congratulate ya for comin' back from the dead," Wagner said, scratching something out on his ticket pad. He tore a yellow slip off the top and slid it coolly onto my dashboard. "We'll be keepin' our eye on you, you Irish fuck."

"I'll tell my family you say hello," I said, fighting to remain calm. Wagner spit on the rear panel of the car as I pulled away.

I told Hank about it when I got home: "Motherfucker gave me a three-hundred-dollar speeding ticket. I wasn't even five miles over."

"Don't worry 'bout it, Sean-O. It coulda been worse, ya know? They was comin' 'round the club while you was gone, askin' for you—stoppin' by jobsites too. Tryin' to pin something to ya. They ain't got shit, though. I jus' told 'em to fuck off. They gave up after a month or so," Hank said, reading the ticket line by line.

"Fuckin' dimwits thought I was dead," I told him. "Heard a rumor I was taken out by the Italians. Two bullets, back of the head. I guess they didn't look too hard for the body."

"Ah, you oughta let 'em think that way, they'll neva catch a ghost, right? And it doesn't hurt ta have 'em thinkin' that not even a bullet in your head would kill ya."

"I guess there's worse things ta be in this world than a ghost," I joked.

"Hell, whateva you sold your soul to the devil for, it seems like ya got a good price."

The nickname stuck. From that day on, everyone referred to me as *Ghost*.

# ELEVEN

## ON THE LAM

It was July of '96. I was shooting pool and drinking with Pistol Pete and Mechanic Mike in a bar called the Cove in Revere, Mass. Both men had long, wily beards and faded prison tattoos. Pete's woman got us drinks from the bar at his command. She wore a jean miniskirt with an inch of her ass cheek falling out the bottom and a shrunken top that exposed her midriff. She was not pretty to look at, but she was a real woman and could drink any one of us under the table.

Mike and Pete were members of the Devil's Desciples MC, a motorcycle club that law enforcement considers to be a criminal or-ganization.*

For years, the Devil's Desciples had been a steady customer for our narcotics. They purchased massive quantities, enough to widely distrib-ute on the street, but I actually think they took all the drugs themselves. I had seen Mechanic Mike go on a three-day coke binge and finish three eight-balls by himself—on more than one occasion. And, as I have found in my experiences with them, bikers tend to pair their impressive

---

* The Devil's Desciples MC was established in 1964, in Massachusetts. They are a one-percenter motorcycle club, denoting them as an outlaw biker organization. In such clubs, it is common to require prospective members to commit certain crimes in order to show their allegiances prior to receiving full membership status. That's how the club's patch is earned.

drug intake with an equally impressive alcohol consumption, similar to a sommelier pairing cheeses with wine. The bikers are loud and rambunctious and don't give two fucks about what society's opinion is of them—suffice to say, we got along well. The most impressive characteristic of any biker is their ability to shoot a good game of pool regardless of how fucked-up they get. It's a sign of true professionalism in both playing billiards and the consumption of drugs.

On a typical outing with Mike and Pete, we would start drinking around four o'clock and not let up until our "grand finale" at last call. What made that night different at the Cove was the intrusion of five police officers and me being taken away in handcuffs.

Apparently they'd been on the lookout for me for more than a week in connection to a little altercation I may or may not have been involved in.

I was charged with assault with a dangerous weapon. And much to the chagrin of the perverted sadomasochists reading this book, I'm not going into the details of the incident; they aren't very important.

I will note, however, that there is a difference in the legal classification of a dangerous weapon versus that of a deadly weapon. The use of a deadly weapon in an assault exacerbates an assault charge straight to a felony offense. With a dangerous weapon—what the court deems an object capable of causing harm but one that is not necessarily lethal—assault charges start at a misdemeanor and can be adjusted on a sliding scale dependent on the extent of injuries caused. In my case, I got slapped with a felony. Fuck.

To make matters worse, it was a bad time for me to be incarcerated. Very inconvenient. I had things to do. I was in the middle of a job. There was an individual I needed to find, and I couldn't do that from a jail cell.

They brought me to the Rockland Police Department on Friday night to wait for my arraignment that coming Monday. The department was newer and nicer than most other Depression-era shitholes I had done time in up and down New England. Not a lot of time had passed since the ribbon-cutting ceremony—a problem because up-to-date facilities meant up-to-date security measures. That's bad if you, as an individual being held there, have no plans to remain in captivity.

I spent the first day studying the routine of every guard and probing the cell for weak points—there weren't any. I knew it wasn't going to be easy, but there had to be a way.

As far as Hollywood movies were concerned, I had two options to escape: like Andy Dufresne (*The Shawshank Redemption*, 1994) or Frank Morris (*Escape from Alcatraz*, 1979). Both pointless. I wasn't going to dig a tunnel behind a poster of a broad because they wouldn't trust me with a rock hammer . . . and they refused to give me a poster of Rita Hayworth. Those motherfuckers. The other option was an elaborate plan involving papier-mâché dummies and raincoat rafts. But seeing as how I wasn't locked up in Alcatraz and there was no surrounding water I could use to paddle off into the horizon, my aspiring papier-mâché career would have to wait. *There went my chance of a sexy Hollywood getaway.*

The literary world was no help either. Could I pull off the daring escape depicted in Dumas's *Count of Monte Cristo*? *Fuck no.* There wasn't some mad priest who conveniently died and whose body bag I could sneak into. Rockland PD didn't have that. But in my world, you don't always have a choice: necessity trumps theatrics. It had to be done even if it was ugly, even if it wasn't romantic.

I woke to a dissonant, atonal voice and an obnoxious clanging of metal on metal. It was my second morning, and I was being told that I had a visitor. I brought my legs around and placed my feet on the ground, sitting up straight. My lawyer had come.

I was siphoned out of the cell and diverted to a cramped private room.

Milton Fischman smiled professionally when I walked into the room. "You can remove his cuffs," Milton said, addressing the officer. The cop hesitated but obeyed, then left the room in a hurry. "How ya holdin' up?" Milton said, holding a Styrofoam cup of coffee. The cup looked comically small in his oversized hand. He sipped slowly, savoring his morning pick-me-up. I knew he wasn't going to like what I had to say.

Here goes nothing: "Look, Milt, I'm gonna need your help with somethin', just hear me out . . ."

I kept my head down and mouth shut, waiting for my arraignment like the good criminal I was. It was two days away, during which time I was a model captive. I wore the costume, followed the script, and played the part flawlessly. Any infraction could have me transferred elsewhere or screw up the date of my arraignment, and everything would go to shit—my job, I mean.

Every additional hour I wasn't on the street in active pursuit heightened the chance of never finding the person I was looking for. Time is crucial when trying to locate someone. The animal kingdom abides by the same principles of a chase; the more time prey is given to roam free, the harder it is for the predator. To further explain, let's say, for instance, that a cheetah has to find a meal for its family. The cheetah doesn't know precisely where its next meal will come from, but it has good intel about a specific gazelle that drank at a specific watering hole and grazed on a specific patch of savanna grass. Ordinarily, the cheetah wouldn't have any issue scouting the two locations, lying in wait for the gazelle, pouncing on the unsuspecting animal, and feeding his family. However, in order to get to the hunting ground, this cheetah must run around a gully—this takes extra time. Now, does this extra time give the gazelle a false sense of security, believing it has found a safe watering hole to drink from? Possibly. But let's say over the time it takes for the cheetah to cross the ravine, word of the cheetah's hunt gets around, and the no-good, loose-lipped warthog tells the gazelle, "Hey, there's a fucking cheetah out there that's going to find you unless you take all the money you stole from him and his family and fuck off to a different watering hole on the other side of the vast plain where you won't be found." See the dilemma? If the cheetah didn't have to waste his time crossing the gully, the thieving gazelle wouldn't have caught wind of the pursuit and skipped town, and the cheetah could have gotten his fucking money back . . . or whatever the moral of that story was supposed to be. A perfect metaphor, if you ask me, which is why I was on my best behavior—so I didn't add an extra gully to cross.

Milton came back the following day, carrying an urgent message. This time, we convened and spoke in my cell. He stayed fifteen minutes, spoke quickly, and left.

I noticed it five minutes after he left, small, silver, and hidden: a key balancing on the cell bars, in the right angle made from the intersection of horizontal and vertical rods. I jumped up, snatched it off the steel, and recoiled to the back of my cell. Fearing discovery by a passing guard, I scanned the naked, exposed cell for somewhere to stash the key. Knowing I was able to reach the overhead light by standing on the bed, I hopped up and slid the contraband safely atop the hanging fixture. It was a lazy spot, but the key would stay hidden up there for at least two days, and that's all I needed. The only thing left to do now was wait.

I was nervous, sort of. It was the calm that worried me. There was no rhyme or reason behind my uneasiness, just a nagging skepticism. Recently, it seemed like luck wasn't on my side. "If not for bad luck, I'd have no luck at all," as they say. The aphorism is attributed to some old racist from the 1920s, and although I can't appreciate his egregious caricatures, his quote summed up the last few years of my life out on the street. So why should today be any different? It shouldn't, in theory. But then again, nobody understands luck. Some people attribute luck to their god or some higher power, others swear we make it ourselves, and still others denounce the idea altogether. Whether it stems from some godly interference or is just entropy, I can't say, but I can tell you with certainty that we don't make it ourselves. That theory is built on the fallacy that we, as human beings, get what we deserve. Pure lunacy.

If fairness existed, crime wouldn't, and this book would be a lot fucking shorter. For every criminal who faces proportionate punishment for their crimes, there are a million crooks who go unpunished. Not bad odds, really. Consider it like a roulette wheel with 999,999 winning numbers and only one double-zero pocket. But as I was saying, it felt like my ball had started landing in that losing pocket more often than not, which accounted for my anxiety the morning of my arraignment. Something had to go wrong.

According to the itinerary—the Department of Justice's, not mine—I was set to appear in the courtroom on Monday at 9:00 a.m. That meant leaving the lockup at 7:00 a.m., with no time for breakfast. I didn't mind, I wasn't hungry. I could have used a stiff drink, though. A couple days had passed since my last drink, a fact I was constantly reminded of. The weekend had been hellish. My body went through the full gamut of withdrawal symptoms: sweating, stomach cramps, delirium tremens, and lots of vomiting. And after the physical ailments ran their course, the psychological shit took over. I needed out; I couldn't wait any longer.

6:50 a.m. I was removed from my cell and led outside. Sleepy sunlight peeked out from behind tall buildings, coloring the world. Following protocol, my hands and feet were shackled prior to entering the transport van. The novelty of handcuffs had worn off years ago. I had gotten used to the feeling of them being cinched one click too tight around my wrists.

In the back of the transport van, I felt us starting to move. Besides the one officer behind the wheel, I was alone in the van that morning. Less of an audience greatly increased my chances of success. I bent down and retrieved the cuff key I had hidden in the neck of my tube sock. My ankle chains rattled as the van went over a bump. It was a fifteen-minute drive to the courthouse, which gave me plenty of time to get the restraints off.

The van rolled to a stop. The door to the cab shut with a resonant thud, and I knew it was time. Ten seconds now. I positioned myself in front of the door, taking an athletic stance (five seconds). My nerve endings began screaming, my heart clawing at the inside of my chest (four). A key inserted (three), a handle popped (two), a sliver of light (one), fuck . . . *now!*

I kicked the door with everything I had, every fiber fighting for that freedom on the other side. The officer was thrown from his feet, taking the full force of the door's momentum. Had the door's hinges not been reinforced and made of heavy-duty steel, it would have ripped off the truck and crushed the officer. I sprang from captivity and hit the ground running, not daring to look back and find out if the officer was in pursuit or not—or if he had recovered from the fall.

I had to keep going. Propelled by massive amounts of adrenaline, I sprinted down the empty sidewalk and turned the corner. I kept running, hopping two fences and avoiding a snarling Rottweiler. An eighth of a mile later, there it was: the windowless panel van that would smuggle me to safety, its engine running and the side door waiting open. I dove in, and the door slid shut behind me. I had made it.

"What took ya so long?" Pistol Pete snarked from the front seat, maneuvering the getaway van into the lane leading out of town.

"You crazy motherfucker, Ghost! Ha! Ha!" Mechanic Mike said excitedly. He always loved a good crime, especially when he got to pull one over on the system.

"Never thought I'd be so glad to see you ugly bastards," I said.

"Didn't think we'd forgotten 'bout you, did ya?"

"I knew you'd be here. Hey, I need a fuckin' drink. You guys got anything up there . . . and I gotta get outta these fuckin' scrubs."

"We wouldn't show up empty-handed," Mike said, passing me an unopened bottle of vodka.

"Where to?" Pete asked.

"Head ta Quincy. I got somethin' to take care of."

The successful bounty hunter knows how to play cat and mouse. If the target's in hiding, they must be drawn out—it's no use playing against home-field advantage. To do this, a bounty hunter presents a scenario so tempting that their quarry is flushed from shelter. The scenario varies from case to case, but the results are the same. I once heard a story of a wanted criminal showing up to a lottery office, thinking he'd won a sweepstakes he'd never entered; he was apprehended without much effort.

The average criminal may require slightly more creativity than that, but you'd be surprised. In my case, after I'd been searching for three days with no results, the perfect scenario presented itself. You can call it luck if you'd like. A man was killed by a late-night hit-and-run: no suspects, no witnesses. The victim, dead on impact, was a cousin of the target. The two had been close, I was told—which meant my target would show up at the funeral to pay his respects.

I have heard of that method too—kill someone close to your target and stake out the funeral. It's a cruel and brutish tactic. There's evidence of Whitey and Flemmi doing it. I wouldn't put it past them. Nothing was off-limits as far as they were concerned. And funerals are like fly-paper: there's no better honey trap than the death of a family member, none that I've heard of anyway. I think a criminal's code of loyalty compels them to attend. The career criminal leads a lonely existence, rife with temporary relationships and betrayal. That lifestyle emphasizes the role of family and the sense of stability and loyalty that comes with it.

When I received news of the upcoming funeral, I knew it was only a matter of time before I found the guy I was looking for. However, I couldn't just wait for the funeral and assume he would walk up to the casket and kiss his dead cousin on the forehead right in front of everyone. He'd have more sense than that. I learned that he knew of my escape and that I was in pursuit of him.

The first place I checked was the funeral home. Who had contacted the funeral home? Who was fronting the bill? How was the funeral home instructed to contact the family in case of emergency? Unfortunately, those avenues led to dead ends. The parents of the deceased had taken care of all the arrangements.

I left instructions with the owner of the funeral home to call me with any news pertaining to that specific corpse. I left him a description of the man I was looking for and $5,000, letting him know there was another nickel in it for him if he gave me anything useful.

The second place I checked was the local flower shops. Oftentimes a person in hiding will order ostentatious flower arrangements to compensate for not going to the burial, and you can just follow the paper trail back to their hideout. I paid the florists five hundred bucks to check their books for any suspicious orders. No luck.

In the absence of leads, I started to worry. Then one day before the funeral, I received a call from the mortician informing me that an anonymous caller had requested a private viewing of the body. The motherfucker had finally come up for air, and I would be there, waiting, harpoon in hand, ready to spear the white whale. I fucking had him.

Except my part of the job was done. I had been told to stand down. From the start, I was only contracted to locate the individual. When it came to confronting the mark and collecting the money he owed, it would be handled by someone else. I had too much heat on me. It was too great a risk when we only had one chance. So I was out.

I should have been happy I wouldn't be the one getting the blood on my hands, but I wasn't. I was pissed. I felt cheated out of the opportunity to finish the job. All the foreplay, and I wasn't allowed to bust my nut.

I thought my escape had gone off without a hitch. I had no idea what had gone awry until it was later presented as evidence in the courtroom. As it turns out, the guard who was driving the transport van was two months from retirement. He had a commendable career spanning over a decade without a single complication or injury . . . until me.

When I kicked the door and the guard fell down, his head hit the pavement. The impact caused a severe concussion. It was ten minutes before he was found on the ground. He survived, but at his age (midsixties), the brain is less regenerative, and portions of his memory were compromised. I don't remember how I took the news back then, but now, as I reflect, I am devastated by what I did. I violated one of the only things I believed in, that a person was off-limits if they weren't in the game. That officer was innocent and could have been a good man. He didn't deserve to suffer the consequences of my actions.

# TWELVE

## MODEL INMATE

I was on the run for close to two years. It becomes easier after a while once the police stop actively looking for you. They figure you'll turn up sooner or later . . . and you always do. No criminal goes straight when they're on the run, not for good. They might walk the straight and narrow to cover their tracks, but when the cops lose their scent, the criminal reverts back to what they do best. So, like I said, it was only a matter of time.

Eventually, they found me. A separate investigation led them to the construction site I was working at: on the front steps of city hall. Maybe I had gotten a little too comfortable.

Earlier that year, a friend of the family had received a big construction contract to fix the granite steps of a South Shore city hall. The foundation under the steps had given way, causing them to become uneven and unsafe. The contract detailed the removal of the granite slabs, regrading the incline, and resetting the steps. My pops and I saw the contract as a promising opportunity to turn a good profit. It wasn't our contract, but that hadn't stopped us before. The company president was a friend, so it wasn't a surprise when he subcontracted the job to H&S Custom Home Improvements. I am sure the envelope filled with money that wound up in his mailbox didn't hurt either.

THE DEVIL TO PAY

State jobs were great because we could charge a premium for materials and labor. They say it takes ten government-contracted laborers to dig a hole—two using shovels and eight watching. On top of inflated foreseen costs, there is a wide breadth for any unseen "incidental" costs. The profit margin on a government contract is a powerful aphrodisiac for contractors; it's the reason that one bridge project in your hometown ran millions of dollars over budget.

The only issue we ran into when doing the job was that our lift operator was sloppy and lacked experience. In the first week on the site, he lifted the first slab into the air and dropped it on another slab. Both steps broke. And it took our stone supplier over a month to locate new slabs that were the same size. The remainder of the project went off without a hitch. However, after we finished, there was a slight controversy with the bill. We charged the state an extra $300,000 to replace the granite slabs we broke. They weren't too thrilled about that and sicced the district attorney on us. I was cleaning up the site when they arrived.

I was charged with conspiracy and extortion, which they bundled with my escape and assault charges. And in there somewhere, they tacked on an extra sixteen months for breaking a bottle over the head of a sixty-six-year-old strip club owner on a separate occasion (which was fair play because I did do that—the owner was being a fucking prick). When all was said and done, I got seven and a half years behind the wall. *Fuck it!* Just a side effect of my lifestyle. In many ways it's like a marriage . . . *for better or worse.*

MCI–Concord is the oldest running prison in Massachusetts. It is also one of the shittiest. To put it into perspective, I've done time in over a dozen different prisons throughout my criminal career, MCI–Concord is one of the worst (second only to my brief twenty-four-hour stint in Tijuana, Mexico—a story for another time). It's the type of penitentiary that inspires its criminals to contemplate suicide or shank one another on a regular basis—a real fucking hellhole. The facilities were rundown, dirty, and antiquated.

The diminished state of things was most apparent in the summertime.

The lack of air-conditioning in the old cellblocks essentially made the buildings a convection oven; it was oppressive heat, the kind that makes breathing laborious. Everyone was miserable. To combat those sweltering temperatures, we broke the windows, clamoring for a breeze. Seeing as how the windows didn't open, we had no choice but to smash the panes. They were the old nine-over-nine rectangular-pane windows. We broke them so often maintenance stopped replacing them. That was fine with us during the warmer months, but when winter came around, we froze our asses off. Guys would plug the empty panes with random bits of cardboard or ripped-off book covers just to stop the ice-wind.

I served out my sentence in the horseshoe-shaped building designated "East and West." My sentence was on the lighter side, but by no means did it mean I was someone to be fucked with. Word of my reputation preceded my arrival and excluded me from the traditional trial by fire many first-timers are faced with. I already had a seat at a coveted table, populated by other good guys, waiting for me. The respect I was shown on the inside, I had earned on the outside. Better still, I was met by a few familiar faces from the neighborhood.

The culture inside a prison is unlike anything on the outside, alien to anyone who has not spent time behind bars. The closest reference point I can provide would be to liken it to the barbarism of warring tribal nations. Instead of the unity among inmates as a common people, differences (most commonly ethnic in origin) fracture and segregate the inmate population, placing one tribe against another: a vicious dog-eat-dog ecosystem. Gangs run prisons, not guards and administrators. Even in moments without active conflict between two groups, tensions run high, and violence is anticipated. Blacks naturally mix with other Blacks, whites with whites, Mexicans with Mexicans, Asians with Asians, et cetera with et cetera.

Lone wolves are an enigma but do, in fact, exist. Those unfortunates without the benefit of alliances, bona fides, or pedigree must pledge allegiance to one group or another almost immediately or face complete ostracization without any protection.

A faction's power was measured according to four different categories: (1) the number of members, (2) the brutality level of faction members, (3) the faction's ability to corrupt and control prison staff, and (4) the faction's ability to acquire and distribute contraband.

I ran with the whites. The Blacks only outnumbered us, but we held our own when it came time for conflict. Most of us were in for violent offenses. But we derived the majority of our power from controlling the flow of contraband—specifically, drugs. Unfortunately, it's the primary commerce behind the wall. So, I set up our supply channel through my attorney, Milton Fischman. He visited two of the guards at their home addresses and put them on the payroll. Once a week, I would receive packages containing Suboxone, heroin, coke, marijuana, and tobacco.

In addition to the weekly shipments of drugs, I received cell phones on demand and an almost daily delivery of vodka. The booze was all mine. There was no fucking way I was going to stay sober for seven and a half years. *Fuck that.* Why would I want to? Inside I had the same access to alcohol as I did on the outside. I was given a Poland Spring gallon jug every couple days. It was cheap rotgut shit, but I didn't give a fuck. I was loaded by lunch, and the days went by quicker.

I was never worried about the guards' frequent shakedowns of my cell; they never found anything. I was often tipped off about any "random" searches the night before, which gave me time to prepare. I tried not to keep the contraband in my immediate possession. Cell phones were the exception. I stashed them in the wall cavity behind the electrical outlet faceplate. I'll admit it wasn't the cleverest spot, but it worked. The bags of tobacco usually didn't last long enough to be found; I moved hand-rolled cigarettes left and right at a massive profit and to gain future favors.

I never liked having direct contact with the drugs, but I couldn't trust anyone else on the cellblock to accurately report the incoming amounts. By handling the initial package of drugs myself, I was able to see with my own eyes exactly what made its way into the prison.

Once I had the drugs, I divided the product between four guys I ran with to store what I had—and yes, by "store," I mean, if necessary, shoving the packages of contraband up their asses for safekeeping. *Putting it in the vault.* Sometimes they had to walk around all day with it up there. To this day, I shake my head at the thought of these tattooed, street-hardened, and menacing individuals digging Saran-Wrapped and shit-smeared goodies out of their anal cavities like it was nothing. Christ, if I had to acknowledge an employee of the month, I could have wallpapered six cells with their mug shots. As payment, some took contraband for personal use, but most were cut in on a piece of the profits, which they'd send home through inmate accounts to provide for their families. For the most part, these operations ran smoothly. It was an unwritten law, the convict's code, that any theft was dealt with immediately and harshly. This was the only way to maintain control and order and keep the respect of the other animals in the jungle.

I am in no way saying that I solely controlled the market in any institution I served time in. I wasn't Pablo Escobar. I wasn't John Gotti. I wasn't even close. I was a guy with influence, connections, means, and the aptitude for earning money like a Rockefeller—and who, at the same time, would bury a piece of steel in you to protect his investment.

The distribution process took place as follows: I generally got along with everyone, all races. To do otherwise would be bad for business, professional suicide. The reality is there are only so many whites in any institution. Therefore, I dealt with the Blacks, the Hispanics, and the Asians alike. Every group has their own chain of command.

I sold wholesale, directly to the top, whether it was a group of leaders or an individual shot-caller. Doing this allowed these individuals to move product amongst their own ranks and earn money at their own discretion, but most importantly, maintain their own circles. This insulated me from any of their problems, should they arise, as I was paid up front for what I supplied. If they sold it, stomped on it, used it themselves, or gave it the fuck away, it was none of my business. All I was concerned with was my piece of the pie.

In regard to the Blacks, I dealt with a man who went by the name of X. For better or worse, X was the de facto spokesman for the different gangs of Blacks. His gift was being able to deal with all factions of his race. He went around spewing some bullshit story about how he got his nickname because he was a distant relative of Malcom X. In truth, it was more likely the nickname stemmed from his striking resemblance to the revolutionary minister. Standing a head taller than me, he was lanky, light-skinned, smart as a banker, and charismatic as Sammy Davis Jr. I genuinely liked and respected X.

Regardless of whatever the fuck he called himself, I supplied him with quality product. It was common knowledge he got his supply from me, and he got it with the same purity as I did. It allowed him to cut it as he saw fit and control his own earnings. Stomping on it beforehand could have led to either conflict or him seeking another source. Point-blank, I wanted to make money and so did he. X and I had a deal, and we both honored it. Only one thing overrides racial allegiance in prison: fuckin' money. It's just as green in white hands as it is in Black ones.

For the most part, our ships sailed on a smooth ocean, but no sea is ever without a storm. A rogue wave came in the form of Izaiah.

Izaiah, who was affiliated with a certain gang, was buying product from X, then stepping on it too hard and blaming me for the poor quality. I was also made aware that he had been trying to get the ear of the other Black gangs with racially toned rants about taking over my market. X, of course, cautioned against this call to action. He made it clear I had the corrupted guards in my pocket and that without me it was impossible to meet the institutional supply and demand.

Over the course of several months, there were several sit-downs on the topic, and tensions ran high. Izaiah, a young unschooled hothead, kept stoking the fire. This was his first time in state prison, and he had no clue how to keep the peace. Nor did he understand the economics of business. Unfortunately for him, he was soon to learn his place.

In one final attempt to avoid an all-out war, I brought the issue of Izaiah's transgressions to X: a modern-day parley.

"And you got proof?" X asked in an uncharacteristically soft tone, knowing the answer to his question before he even asked it.

"Yeah," I assured him. "You're not the only Black I break bread with."

He knew this to be true and let out a deep sigh to show his anger, frustration, and disappointment. "Izaiah's daddy asked me to look out for him in here, but the young nigga's been nothin' but trouble for me. I got somethin' like three months in the hole because I was lookin' out for his ass. Zay acts like he's hot shit, then gets in way over his head, drags us into his mess to clean it up after. It's bad business all around."

"You promised his father somethin', not me," I said. "Kid's outta line, X. I gave you the chance you asked for, time's up. Now it's a respect issue. Nothin' left to talk about."

"I knew this was coming. Fuck . . . Do what you gotta do, Ghost. You got my blessing. I spoke to his people, little nigga's on his own. Don't no one want a race war," X said, extending his giant hand.

I took it. In that moment, my respect was replaced with a deep admiration for this man's principles. If X knew anything, and he knew a lot, it was the true meaning of honor.

I had to act fast. The downside of consulting X was losing the element of surprise. Our sit-down was no secret; Izaiah would have caught wind of it. I couldn't give him the time to gather support and strike first. Knowing my intentions before the meeting, I had been preparing for over a week. I had also made it a point to supply X with additional contraband and instructions to distribute it amongst his people to make what was about to happen easier to stomach.

Moving on someone in prison cannot be done haphazardly. Emotions need to be carefully checked. It requires careful planning, and even then, a lot can go sideways. To minimize the risk of getting hemmed up and catching another charge, I had to figure out when, where, and how I was going to squash this bug. He had at least a hundred pounds on me (following a common trend, which I have noticed only since writing this book, in regard to the physical stature of many people I fought in my youth). I needed the right weapon. This wasn't going to be fisticuffs—that shit's for schoolyards. In a prison yard, you play for keeps.

Similar to the ancient tradition of Japanese sword smithing, in certain circles the process of making a shank is a respected art form. Lives can be decided on the integrity of a prison shank. It has to be strong enough not to break apart and capable of inflicting sufficient damage. I shy away from toothbrushes sharpened into a point. Hollywood depicts this method in nine out of ten prison stabbings, but it's complete bullshit. The plastic is rigid and prone to snapping off if it hits bone when it's plunged into flesh. Not saying I never used one, but when I did, it broke. Not to say that I'd advocate the shanking of anyone, but a metal shank—affectionately known as a "bone crusher"—is far superior.

For the shank I planned to use on Izaiah, I sourced a heavy-duty spring from my bed frame, straightened out the coil, and folded the thick metal wire into a makeshift, double-pronged ice pick. I gave it a handle by sheathing it with two pieces of a hardcover book and wrapping it with a strip of bedsheet. It was ready. I had a friend stash the weapon in his cell until I needed it in accordance with my "not keeping contraband on hand" philosophy. That was how I safeguarded myself from any raids by guards not on the take.

With the task of acquiring a weapon out of the way, I turned my attention to where I would make my move. Studying and plotting Izaiah's schedule was mandatory as his routine wasn't identical to mine. Unbeknownst to him, due to his mouth, attitude, and brewing conflict with me, he had ostracized himself from his own ranks. I was receiving periodic updates of his daily comings and goings from multiple sources. I knew where he sat in the chow hall, what time he hung out in the library, when he shot hoops on the basketball court, lifted weights in the gym, and when he walked the track around the yard smoking weed. I practically knew when he took his morning shit. He was predictable. And I counted on that predictability.

There were a good number of blind spots in the prison's camera surveillance system. Of the ones I knew about, I liked three in particular. And of the three, only one fit my needs like a tailored suit: the handball court. It was a regular gladiator school at MCI–Concord. The blood of every race had been spilled on that blacktop.

The court was in the northwest corner of the yard, placing a good distance between us and the guards, who generally shadowed the outdoor weight pit located under the pavilion by the yard's main gate and softball field. Truth was, they posted up under there because the rooftop shielded them from the sun. Should they choose to interfere, the time it took to cover the extra ground would allow us to finish our business and dispose of the shank over the wall.

The handball court was a monolithic concrete wall that divided two playing areas. What was unique and appealing about the court was that it was a three-wall setup. On each side of the towering concrete slab, two angled walls shot out of the structure, then tapered off down the court. This created a perfect blind spot up against the main wall. As far as I was concerned, that was the *only* place to handle my business.

A one-third-mile gravel track ran around the perimeter of the yard, used by convicts for walking and running. The handball court was located in the back right elbow of the track and was flanked by the inner perimeter fence. Beyond the fence was a paved road known as the "kill zone." Meeting the pavement was the prison's Gothic twenty-foot-high outer wall.

I was an avid handball player, as were most of the guys I hung with. So, seeing us congregated around the court wasn't unusual. This meant no red flags for the guards on the yard or gun towers.

Hurley was the yard sergeant on the day I made my move. He was a decent guy who worked hard to provide a respectable lifestyle for his wife and teenage daughter. He was also well acquainted with my lawyer, who helped him out in the months when money was tight and occasionally padded his wallet with a little extra cash. As far as prison guards go, I liked Hurley. I knew he wouldn't break things up until backup arrived because, at my request, Milton had paid him not to. Hurley had a talent for following directions to a T.

Izaiah spent his yard time walking laps around the track, smoking marijuana and cigarettes, as was common practice among the prison population. He walked by the courts every seven minutes, shouting derogatory slurs at me. I'd been letting it go unchecked for the better part of a week while I planned my attack. My lack of response only emboldened him, which was all part of my plan. By not engaging him, with each day and each lap, he ventured closer and closer to the courts. This is known as "rocking someone to sleep."

I was validated by the Commonwealth of Massachusetts's Office of Public Safety and Department of Corrections as a member of a security threat group (STG). Being identified this way means you are deemed a possible risk to the orderly running of an institution's operations, the administration and staff, and other prisoners. As such, STG members are subject to greater scrutiny in regard to movement throughout an institution. Before entering the yard, I was regularly patted down and wanded with a handheld metal detector. To get around the increased security measures associated with my STG status, I had enlisted the help of one individual on the prison workforce who was assigned to the grounds crew and had access to the yard when it was closed. He brought in the shank, buried it in the soft sand next to the court, and marked the location with an empty coffee bag under a stone.

The time had come.

In the yard, I was playing a singles handball match. Players and on-lookers lined the outer perimeter of the court's pavement. To further conceal what was about to happen, I had spread the word that the games were being played for money, a hundred bucks a match. This ensured a massive wall of flesh would encircle the court.

I was halfway through my second game, and Izaiah was on his fourth lap. I discreetly gave the nod to an associate, who then left courtside, making his way into the middle of the field and an ongoing soccer game. He briefly spoke with two individuals who, in short order, would stage an argument that would escalate into a shoving match to further draw attention away from the handball court. Another associate sitting on the ground beside the coffee bag began unearthing the shank. Once his task was complete, he passed the weapon off to the next player up. Timing was everything.

As Izaiah closed in on the corner, I had just dispatched my opponent, and the guy holding the shank shouted out, "Next!" I was handed the shank in a sportsman's handshake. Izaiah was rounding the corner, eyes fixed on me. I finally broke my silence.

"Zay," I shouted, "you got somethin' ta say? Seems every time I turn around, you're runnin' your cocksucker."

"Fuck you, white boy," he said, coming near the court.

"Bring your fat ass over here," I said. "We'll shoot a fair one."*

Izaiah had no choice but to answer the challenge. Not doing so

---

* To have a clean, weapon-free fight in prison.

would have greatly diminished any respect he'd garnered and subjected him to persecution. X and other Blacks in the know quickly stepped forward to ensure no one else from their race would interfere. Likewise with the whites.

Izaiah made his way onto the court and toward the main wall where I was waiting. Squaring up, I stepped backward, luring him into the blind spot. At that moment, shouting erupted from the soccer game. Two players began shoving each other.

Izaiah charged forward like a bull, using his weight to slam me against the wall. He was eighteen, overweight, naturally unbalanced, and unskilled with his hands. While he was busy pressing my shoulders into the concrete, my right hand was touching his side in rapid succession. He abruptly threw up his hands, stepped back, and bellowed, "You hit like a bitch, I ain't even feel that."

He was right. The shank's prongs had slid into his flesh with ease. He didn't feel a fucking thing. He charged again, meeting my hand. This happened two more times. I was careful to keep my body turned sideways to him, concealing the shank behind my right leg. Izaiah was clueless, had no idea he'd been stabbed a total of thirteen times, a baker's dozen. Blood flowed from the holes in his chest, stomach, and side like a spigot dispensing red wine. It was then that he was alerted by a voice from the crowd.

"*Oh, shit*, little nigga's leakin' all crazy!"

Up to this point, adrenaline and bravado had kept Izaiah on his feet. Looking down, he took note of his blood-soaked shirt and the reality of what had just happened. He fell to his knees, clutching his midsection, groaning, and gasping. The thick layer of fat hugging his torso may have dulled the initial pain of my shank, but it didn't stop the damage it caused.

Izaiah looked up at me, a bewildered expression on his grimacing face. "You said a fair one."

"No such thing in prison, you stupid fuck," I said.

I had been so caught up in the altercation I hadn't realized the guards had already snuffed out the smoke-screen altercation on the soccer field and were pushing through the crowd of spectators around the handball court. Before the stockade was breached, I handed my shank off to an associate, who I had recruited to dispose of the weapon by tossing it over the outer wall. He broke away from the crowd with just enough time to complete his task.

Hurley got through first. Upon seeing the zeppelin-sized man kneeling in a pool of his own blood, Hurley reached for the radio clipped to his belt and pressed a red panic button.

"Get the fuck down!" Hurley screamed at everyone on the court. "Everyone get on the fucking ground."

A loud voice soon erupted over the loudspeaker: "*Everyone lay face down!*" The command echoed throughout the yard, and like well-trained, Westminster-winning cocker spaniels, every convict dropped to his stomach and spread his arms wide, palms flat against the ground. A blaring alarm propagated throughout the prison. Code Red. Lockdown.

A blitzkrieg of staff members burst into the yard to control the situation. Hurley frantically waved over the two-man medical response team to attend to Izaiah. They ran over, carrying a large red med kit and pushing a wheelchair with an oxygen tank mounted to the back. One of the med techs briefly assessed the bleeding man's vitals.

Satisfied that the convict likely wouldn't die right there on the blacktop, he called over the other tech to help lift Izaiah into the wheelchair. They evacuated Izaiah from the yard and rushed him to the infirmary. With the critical patient removed, the rest of us were attended to.

One by one, we were marched to the gate. Under the pavilion, we were stripped naked and searched. No hole off-limits. They checked for any marks that would indicate involvement in the altercation: scuffs, scrapes, and scratches. They examined our knuckles for bruising or blood. If you passed their inspection, you were allowed to get dressed and were led back to your cell.

I did not, for obvious reasons. My uniform was covered in dark red stains, and I had bruised ribs from where Izaiah had hit me. One way or another, it was clear I had some involvement, so they threw me into the hole while they gathered and examined the evidence against me. For the time being, I'd remain indefinitely removed from the general population.

I wasn't too banged up—a few bruises here and there but no worse for wear. Izaiah, on the other hand, had suffered a few nicked arteries and puncture wounds in his spleen, small intestine, and left lung. I never wanted nor intended to kill him; it was about teaching him a lesson. A week later, I learned he never ratted me out, claiming and maintaining ignorance of his assailant's identity. I respected him for that and was glad to learn he'd make a full recovery. Who knows? Maybe there was hope for the kid after all.

Even without Izaiah's confession, video evidence, the shank, or any hard information unequivocally linking me to the stabbing, I still got six months in solitary confinement. I thought it was bullshit, but when you're an inmate, no one gives two fucks about your thoughts and opinions.

That is, except for Hurley. He looked concerned when he told me I'd stay locked up in the hole for six months. I assured him I would be okay, and that put him at ease. Like I said, he was a solid guy.

I never hated solitary, really. Sure, the cell was more cramped and you were on lockdown for twenty-three out of twenty-four hours a day; but in return, you got the privacy of your own room, and it's a hell of a lot quieter in solitary when compared to general population. Plus, I still got my vodka. *Hell*, I may have even liked solitary better at times.

I lost track of the days in the hole, soaking my liver in eighty-proof "spring water." A six-by-nine-foot cell is among the few places on Earth where six months simultaneously are over in the blink of an eye and last a lifetime. That's how it feels, anyway.

Then, just before I was set to return to my old cell in general population, time stopped altogether. Hurley was the one to deliver the news: the night before, November 2, 1999, my pops had passed away. A heart attack had taken him in his sleep.

*No . . . please . . . fuck, no, no, it can't be true . . .* I collapsed onto my bed and wept for days. The news was painful, far beyond any pain that could be inflicted by hate and evil. No, this was the level of hurt only love can cause. I loved Hank more than anything. The idea that there would come a time when he wouldn't be around had never even crossed my mind. It didn't seem possible. As a kid, I saw Pops as a superhero, the way most kids see their parents—someone who can conquer anything in their path, even death. Watching his health deteriorate with years of worsening diabetes didn't change that much because he always managed to keep his humor and personality and wits about him. So, even with his failing health, he had been indestructible to me.

In a sense, he was what I believed in. The only thing, really. He was what I always looked to when I was lost, a beacon of safety and comfort. I hoped that one day, if I held on to the things he taught me, I could be a fraction of the man he was. That would be more than enough.

It took a while to collect myself and reach the point where I could accept the truth: Henry Simons, born March 15, 1933, my role model, my savior, and above all else, my father, was gone. And to make matters worse, the warden denied my request for a daytime furlough so that I could attend his burial service. Fuck. I was now the son who had to miss his father's funeral. Add that to the résumé.

A lot happened in the time I was in the hole, but not much had changed. The contraband operation carried on without setbacks; Milton had made contact with one of the guys I ran with (or perhaps it was the other way around—*they contacted Milt*), and the supply continued. Race relations were in balance, equilibrium.

It was as if I had never left . . . or maybe I had never been there in the first place. Feeling devastated by my loss and more alone than ever, I started to question if I had been important to the operation at all. *What was the use of being involved if I wasn't needed?* A risk-reward conundrum. A simple answer: it was time to move on. This was one of the few choices I made during this era of my life that Hank would have approved of.

Coming to this realization, I shifted my focus to getting an early release. There are a handful of ways an inmate can influence the commutation of their sentence. For me, in Massachusetts, I had the option of accumulating "good time" and "earned time."

Good time can be summarized as time off in exchange for following prison rules and being on one's best behavior, a model inmate. Earned time is different in that it is granted for participation in extracurricular programs. For all of MCI–Concord's faults, it offered a lengthy catalog of classes and rewarded participants with gratuitous time off. These programs were designed with one of two goals in mind: rehabilitation and reintegration. My lawyer suggested that it would look better in the judge's eyes if I enrolled in classes aimed at both objectives.

I didn't have to be told twice; I greedily loaded my days with every course possible. I sat through lectures on anger management and understanding addiction. I went to trade workshops to learn the inner workings of small engines and HVAC systems. I even took a barber class and learned to cut hair. I was stubborn and immature, and I only viewed the opportunity as a quicker way to get back to my criminal life on the outside. And to my credit, that's exactly what I did.

Two and a half years into my seven-and-a-half-year sentence, Hurley came to my cell and excitedly reported I was getting released. There was a new statewide initiative to combat the overcrowding problem in Massachusetts prisons. Inmates in good standing who had served a certain fraction of their sentences were beginning to be let out—I was one of them. The combination of my good time and earned time qualified me as a candidate for early parole. *Who woulda guessed I was considered a perfect model inmate?*

However, being a model inmate did not translate to me being a model citizen. Far from it. I was out for less than four months before I was indicted as the architect of a stolen traveler's check scam that netted over one million dollars by using a network of corrupt check-cashing stores. And to add insult to injury, they tacked on another charge for my association with an incident that had resulted in the stabbing of a professional athlete.

When the judge's gavel struck the block, I was given another five-year state vacation. *Fuck.* This time I was slated to serve out my time in Walpole State Prison. It didn't matter much where they put me; having just served a third of my initial sentence, my plan was to exploit the same programs, loopholes, and fear of overcrowding. I could do that any-where. It was clear to me that the government was far more afraid of harmful statistics than they were of harmful people. Because of it, I even bet money on my release date.

Again, I loaded up on classes and masqueraded myself as an exem-plary inmate. But there was one major difference this time around: a writing workshop that greatly (though gradually) affected the trajectory of my existence. Sadly, I cannot recall the instructor's name, although he wasn't particularly inspirational. At no point were we ripping pages out of textbooks and jumping up on desks to chant, "O Captain! My Captain!"*

Instead, my writing instructor influenced my life through a simple assignment in the first week. He gave us two weeks to do a standard book report on our favorite book. Most of us had no idea what he was talking about with the words *standard book report*. He must have no-ticed the look of confusion on our faces and described how to pinpoint a theme and support it with different plot points. He tried to set us at ease by saying there were no wrong answers and how the exercise was in-tended to get us to think like a writer and learn to carry a theme through a story arc. It didn't work. I was hung up on the phrase *favorite book*.

*Favorite book?* Fuck. My favorite book up until then was *Green Eggs and Ham* by Dr. Seuss. I didn't read fucking books. After learning to read using children's books, I turned to daily newspapers and leftover magazines to hone my literacy. I couldn't write a report on the story of Sam-I-Am—I have nothing against the book, it is a classic—but it would undo all the progress I had made working toward my goal of never feel-ing dumb again. I should've been reading books the whole time. Why hadn't I been? Fuckin' idiot.

I went looking for something to write the report on.

The prison's library was limited. Many of the shelves were empty, and

---

* This line refers to a Walt Whitman quote in the popular 1989 movie *Dead Poets Society* in which an English professor inspires his students to challenge norms, stand up for personal beliefs, and "seize the day."

the rest held a couple dozen neglected books each. I paced up and down the rows of fraying cloth spines, leafing through unfamiliar titles written by equally unfamiliar authors. I ended up selecting a forgettable book and handing in a meaningless report. But somehow, that meaningless paper had a profound impact . . . because it drew me into the library.

I went back. And kept going back. I checked out books that were too challenging and others that were uninteresting. I wasn't sure what kept bringing me back, but I eventually found whatever it was I was looking for.

I was in front of the bookshelf marked "nonfiction" when I came across a book called *Education of a Felon* by Edward Bunker. I tipped the book off the shelf to skim through the summary on the dust jacket. The front cover was a mug shot of a young white man, seventeen at the time of the photo. He had handsome, neatly combed dark hair and prominent eyebrows. The look on his pimpled face captured my attention; it was the same haunting thousand-yard stare I saw in the mirror every morning. I recognized the remorseless expression, hardened by a messy upbringing. On the back cover was a second mug shot. A few decades separated the photographs. The time was visible in the receding and thinning hair. The man's expression had changed as well. His eyes had softened, and his lips were pressed together in a smug quasi smile. I knew that look too: the smile of a man familiar enough with the justice system to laugh in its face.

I devoured the book the same day, and then again the day after. I connected with his unapologetic delivery, his "This is who I am, this is what I did, and you can fuck off if you got a problem" mentality. It was a masterpiece. Bunker was my god. I wrote to my old friend Quinny and asked him to send me more of Bunker's books.

I worshipped all five of Bunker's books (making a point to acquire the two posthumous works in later years). I studied his style and swagger and how he was able to channel his past into his words. By looking deeper into his influences, I learned of other authors who wrote from the discomfort of their prison cells, authors like Dostoevsky and Caryl Chessman. And from there, I branched out to other works by authors with criminal pasts. I found a particular comfort in the writings of Iceberg Slim and Donald Goines, the so-called "godfathers of urban literature." They wrote with visceral authenticity, shining light on the felonious underbelly of Afro-American society in the mid-twentieth century. As I read, I recognized a common thread—similar themes were present across the works I had read before, from Bunker in California to Slim in Chicago, and all the way to Dostoevsky in Russia. There was a universal criminal experience, regardless of race, upbringing, education, culture, location, et cetera. Granted, these things changed aspects of each story, but at the core of every story was one thing: humanity, imperfect and ugly at times, while still beautiful and redeeming at others. After finishing a book Quinn sent, I would donate it to the library.

I read close to twenty books the month after finding Bunker's memoir. Not long after, I began writing for myself, page after page beyond the assignments from the creative writing program. There were times when I'd go through a whole pen's worth of ink within twenty-four hours. I substituted my addiction to alcohol for an equal addiction to reading and writing.

Reading the few surviving documents I've held on to all these years, I must say that nothing I wrote back then was any good, but I do recall being slightly angry when I got the news of my upcoming release from prison because I was in the middle of a short novel. Getting out meant returning to my old life, and writing wasn't an option there.

# THIRTEEN

## QUINN

The discharge gate at Walpole State Prison banged open, parting like a hooker's legs, as I was dumped back into "civilized" society. I'd "flatlined" another stretch, two years ahead of schedule—thanks again to the miracle of earned and good time.

Outside the prison Scott Quinn and the boys, the usual suspects, were there to greet me with a bottle of Jameson, a case of Heineken, and a ride. It's commonplace for a release to be drowned in celebratory booze, so Quinn drove the lot of us over to the Irish Pub in North Quincy to get the job done. We made our way to the back of the pub, next to the jukebox, and settled around a table pressed up against a built-in booth bench. The table was situated so that whoever was sitting at the bench could see who came through the front door and whoever sat at the chairs across the table kept an eye on the back door. This particular table was generally reserved for a select few and private conversations.

We finished a few bottles as the boys brought me up to speed. There wasn't much to report, mostly routine stuff until Quinn got to the news about Grace O'Connor and how she was strung out on heroin and was being pimped out for the last year or so.

Before going away, I used to fuck Grace on a semiconsistent basis. She was the younger sister of Shane, one of the neighborhood guys who was a friend of ours but wasn't caught up in organized crime like the rest of us. He was the kind of guy that, growing up, the only thing he ever beat was his prick. So, when he caught wind of my imminent release from prison, he reached out to Quinn for help, knowing he'd turn to me. Quinn said he'd found out what he could about Grace's slimy pimp.

"The cocksucker's name is Carlos somethin'-or-other," Quinn said. "He's outta New York. His father was somebody back in the day, but the kid's just a bottom-feeder living off the old man's name. He's got a few whores and moves some coke, nothin' major. Six, eight keys max."

*Six, eight keys max?*

The Grace I knew was definitely wild and could suck a golf ball through a fifty-foot garden hose. Sure, she was from the neighborhood, came from a good family, but like my mother, no one forced her to spread her legs. At the end of the day, she was just another piece of ass. And I sure as fuck wasn't interested in being her white knight. What got my dick hard was the possibility of sticking this clown Carlos for a couple kilos, which I could sell wholesale.

"Look," I said, "the O'Connors are a good family, but they're broke as fuck, can barely pay the mortgage. So, no way can they swing a piece of work. But we can still look good, strengthen our ties in the neighborhood, and get paid at the same time. Works for me. Set this prick up for as much weight as you can . . . let him pay for his own funeral."

Quinn worked his magic. It took him a few days, but he got Carlos on the hook for six keys. The size of the deal didn't set off any alarms once he put our name and reputation behind it. Carlos would have the six bricks from his supplier in New York by the end of the week, which gave us time to prepare.

Quinn was banging this crack whore, so it only cost us an eight-ball of coke and the price of a hotel room to secure the use of her apartment to take care of business. I think he told her that we needed her place for a private meeting, but she probably stopped listening after she heard "free eight-ball." I had presold the coke we were going to take off the prick before we even did him. The going rate back then was $30K to $32K a kilo, but I was unloading all six for $100K—basically half price.

I would never make a habit of sitting on weight like that, nor would I break it down into smaller amounts; I wasn't a drug dealer. I just wanted it off our hands as quickly as possible, and six figures for a simple "oil change" was more than enough.

On the day of the arranged meeting, I joined Quinn at the apartment an hour before Carlos was scheduled to arrive with the product. The place was a complete shithole. The kitchen trash can was overflowing, the sink was full of dirty dishes, and drug paraphernalia covered the countertop: glass cigar tubes and bent spoons with burnt bottoms (synonymous with cooking small amounts of cocaine), bottles of rubbing alcohol, overflowing ashtrays, aluminum foil, nip bottles, the tubes of gutted ballpoint pens, razor blades, baking soda, and film-covered plates from dirty, resinating pipes. A textbook crack shack.

Quinn and I went into the back bedroom, which was just as nasty as the kitchen, and spread the blue tarp we'd brought with us out on the floor.

"You fuckin' get naked and touch shit in here?" I said as I eyed the ratty, stained mattress with no sheets.

"Fuck no, it's just my prick in this bitch's mouth, strictly standing up," Quinn replied with a chuckle.

I checked my watch. We still had about five minutes until this Carlos guy was supposed to arrive. Since Quinn had made all the arrangements, he'd meet him in the parking lot and bring him in to meet me. The plan was simple: Quinn would walk him into the back bedroom; I would grab him; we'd shoot him, roll him up in the tarp, then put him in the trunk of his own car, and take him to a designated location to finish the job. Quinn and I had flipped a coin to see who was going to shoot him and who was going to cut him up after.

*Heads* . . . looks like I was carving the turkey.

"You good to go?" I asked.

Quinn nodded and pulled a .44 Bulldog out of his waistband. "I'm good," he replied.

"No, the fuck you're not," I said, shaking my head in disbelief at the sight of the hand cannon. "Can't let that off in here, it'll wake up the whole fuckin' neighborhood. Why didn't you get a fucking .22 or .25?"

"It's all I had laying around," he said and shrugged his shoulders, giving me the goofy smile he always did when he knew he'd fucked up.

"So now I gotta do 'em *and* bag 'em," I said. "You owe me fuckin' big time."

I told Quinn to go to the kitchen and find a butcher knife. He returned with a flimsy steak knife in one hand and a blunt-tipped bread knife in the other.

"Fuck I'm gonna do with those?" I said.

Quinn shrugged his shoulders, flashed his trademark smirk. "Fuck you want me to say?" he said. "Bitch who lives here is a crackhead. Unless you'd rather a fork or wooden spoon, the fuckin' drawers are empty."

I grabbed the useless utensils from him and tossed them on the floor in the corner.

"We need somethin', this is bullshit," I said and scanned the room, hoping to find at least a baseball bat or something else heavy. Not a fucking thing.

Quinn's cell phone rang. He fished the flip phone out of his pocket, spoke into it, and then snapped it closed.

"He's pullin' in the parking lot," he said.

"Fuck, just go down and get him," I said. "I'll find something to use."

"Right," he said as he exited the room, pulling the door closed behind him.

Quinn would be bringing the pimp through the back door and into the kitchen, so I wouldn't have time to search that end of the apartment. The plan was for Quinn to lead him into the back bedroom, where I would be allegedly waiting with the money. The bedroom was sparsely furnished: a bed, a milk crate topped with a chessboard that served as a nightstand, and a dresser with a broken mirror.

I searched the top drawer of the dresser: more bent spoons and paraphernalia. The face of the second drawer came off in my hands as I opened it. Empty. Nothing under the bed either. The room was tiny, and the only place left to search was the closet.

I opened the door, praying to find anything I could use as a weapon. I rifled through the miscellaneous clothing on the top shelf, scanned the shoes on the floor, and pushed aside some blouses and hoodies hanging on misshapen hangers, and then staring me in the face from the back corner, for some fucked-up reason, was a croquet mallet.

Why this bitch had a croquet mallet was beyond me, but I'm glad she did.

I heard the back door open and close and the sound of footsteps coming through the apartment. Quinn opened the bedroom door and was followed by a small Hispanic man.

Carlos froze the instant his foot hit the tarp, realizing he'd been set up.

Quinn slammed the door shut to keep him from escaping.

Carlos lunged at me, knocking the wooden mallet out of my hand before I could swing it. We wrestled to the floor, where I got on top of him, grabbed a handful of hair with my left, and began pounding his face with my right.

"*Hit this fuck!*" I yelled at Quinn, who, at this point, had done fuck all.

Quinn stepped in, drew his leg back like he was going for the game-winning field goal, and kicked the guy square in the balls, which caused Carlos to scream. I covered his mouth with my right hand. The struggle was already making too much noise, and the sonofabitch started biting.

"Aghh," I grunted, "just hit him with the fuckin' mallet!"

Quinn snatched up the croquet mallet and swung it at Carlos's head. Instead, he hit my left hand.

*Fuck!*

I jerked my hand back in agony. Quinn swung for the fences a second time and connected. The blow took off half the pimp's ear.

He quit moving, and I climbed off him. This whole thing had gone to hell, completely off script. We needed to get the fuck out of Dodge and finish this up at the secluded location.

I told Quinn to fish through the unconscious guy's pockets for his keys, go get the coke out of his car, and throw it in mine. I'd roll up Carlos in the tarp and carry him out. I was going to transport him in the trunk of his own car, and Quinn would trail us in mine. Quinn nodded and went out to the parking lot.

I wrapped up the pimp and threw him over my shoulder. As soon as I stepped out onto the back landing, I heard a car alarm cutting through the dead silence of the night. Quinn's dumb ass hit the alarm button on the fob instead of popping the trunk. I scrambled down the stairs with an unconscious guy over my shoulder as fast as I could.

We *needed* to get out of there. *Shit!*

By the time I crossed the parking lot, Quinn had silenced the car's alarm, gotten the trunk open, and was rummaging around inside the car's interior for the coke. He still hadn't found anything by the time I dumped Carlos off my shoulder to the ground with a thud. I was standing near the open trunk compartment when Quinn approached me with a puzzled look on his face.

"There ain't nothin'," he said.

"Bullshit! He didn't drive here for the hell of it," I said as I leaned into the trunk, lifting the hatch covering the spare tire. Peeking out from under the donut was a nylon duffel bag. "Fuckin' told ya."

Quinn smiled and laughed.

"Ya fuckin' told me," he said. "Sure as shit."

Quinn ducked in and spun the locknut off the donut tire and re-trieved the bag. He quickly unzipped the duffel, peeked inside, rezipped it, and nodded. *Bingo!*

Our moment of triumph was interrupted by the sound of a window slamming home against the top of its casing.

"Scott Quinn, is that you down there?" a woman's voice called out angrily. It was the third-floor tenant, who was now leaning out into the night. "What the hell's going on? And who's that with you?"

Quinn and I had both ratcheted our necks skyward toward the irate woman and hadn't noticed that Carlos had regained consciousness, half escaped the tarp, and was now on his knees, swaying back and forth like a snake before a charmer.

"Please don't kill me! Please . . . take the shit, don't kill me!" pleaded Carlos, pressing his hand against what remained of his ear.

His head was bleeding profusely, turning his face into a crimson mask.

The woman on the third floor retreated back from the window, but not before saying, "I'm calling the cops!"

Quinn kicked Carlos in the chest, toppling him backward. His head hit the pavement with a sickening crack, leaving him dazed. Hurriedly, in an attempt to salvage the situation, we each grabbed an end and tossed the bloodied pimp into the trunk. But before we could close the lid, a symphony of sirens and blue flashing lights was approaching from both ends of the street.

"We gotta get the fuck outta here," I said. "Leave the cars, there's no time. Let's go!"

"I got an idea," Quinn said. "I know a guy, lives one street over."

"I'm followin' you," I said.

Quinn slung the duffel bag's strap over his shoulder, and we made a run for it, jumping over fences and sprinting through backyards, avoiding the main road at all costs. The echoing of sirens grew louder with each step. By now, the cops had blocked off the neighborhood with their cars, and teams of K-9 units were on the hunt.

The guy whose house Quinn led us to was called Gordo. He weighed about four hundred pounds and worked at the tire shop located in Ashmont Square. He sold a little weed here and there, loan-sharked small amounts of money, but for the most part was nothing more than a low-level associate. Gordo knew who I was, but I had never dealt directly with him.

We made our way up the steps to his back door, and Quinn pounded on it with the flat of his hand.

"Gordo, it's Quinn. Open the fuck up!" he said.

The door cracked open, and Gordo's basketball-sized head appeared. Simultaneously, a siren sounded, and his face was washed blue from the glow of a flashing light going down a backstreet. He took one look at us, covered in blood, out of breath, and carrying a duffel bag, and slammed the door in our faces without even saying a word.

"Fuck this piece of shit," I said. "I know where to go."

The O'Connors' home was less than a block away, and whether they knew it or not, they were getting involved. Before departing from Gordo's, I stashed the bag of coke in a trash can on the side of the bastard's house. My plan was to evade the police and retrieve it later. The last thing I wanted was to get caught with six bricks of booger sugar, especially when each one carried a life sentence.

We kept to the shadows, skirting over to the O'Connors'. I scaled the front steps and, with my good hand, started pounding on the door. Quinn ran around back to do the same. The police perimeter was closing in on us, and this was our last hope. No one was answering . . . *Sonofabitch!*

Moments later, a light reluctantly flipped on in the front room, and Mrs. O'Connor, a widow, came to the door and pulled the curtain aside. A look of severe consternation flashed across her face as she recognized me. She opened the door, saw my bloodstained clothing, registered the police presence in the neighborhood, and ushered me in.

"Sean, what's happening?" she asked. "Are you okay?" She reached out, running her hands over my torso, inspecting my person.

"I'm good, it's not my blood," I said. Her head jerked toward the rear of the apartment as the pounding at the back door grew louder. Her mouth opened to form a word, but before she could say anything, I cut her off.

"It's Quinn, *quick*, let him in."

She set off in such a flash that it caused the tails of her bathrobe to fly open and chase after her. She let Quinn in the back door, taking note of his bloodied clothes as she hastily secured three dead bolts.

"What the hell's goin' on?" she said. "What've you two done?"

"Handled that situation with Grace," Quinn said, shrugging.

Mrs. O'Connor nodded silently in understanding. She knew *exactly* the situation with her daughter.

"Did Shane leave any clothes when he moved out?" I asked.

She nodded and hurried down the hallway, disappearing into a room. I went over to the thermostat on the wall and cranked the dial up as high as it would go. The old furnace in the basement growled to life, shaking the entire first floor of the home. Quinn and I hurriedly stripped out of our bloodstained clothing and stood butt-ass naked in the hall until Mrs. O'Connor returned with some jeans and T-shirts.

"Burn these in the fuckin' furnace," I said, shoving an armful of blood-soaked clothing at her. I winced as she bumped my swollen hand. *Aghh!*

"Okay," she said without hesitation and retreated to the basement, leaving us to get dressed.

By the time Mrs. O'Connor returned, Quinn and I had dressed and set up shop at the dining room table, staging it with beer bottles and a deck of playing cards.

"If the fuckin' cops show up, we've been here all night playing cards, got it?" I said. Mrs. O'Connor nodded in understanding.

The three of us then sat around the table, waiting for the inevitable, which came in less than ten minutes. We saw the flashlights and heard the dogs running up the driveway at the same time as the hammering started on the front door.

"Police! We know they're in there, open the door!" a man's voice commanded.

I shook my head and looked down at the table. I already knew how this was going to play out. *Guilty, until proven innocent.*

"Fuck it, we been here drinkin' and playin' cards," Quinn said. "Mrs. O'Connor's got us." He looked down at his borrowed clothes. "I don't see no fuckin' blood. You see any fuckin' blood?"

"Not a fuckin' drop," I said, "but I see a six-foot-four guy wearin' a pair of pants made for someone who's five-ten." The bottom cuffs of the jeans Quinn was wearing cut across the middle of his shins. "At least hide your legs under the fuckin' table."

The pounding at the front door grew louder. We could hear the police surrounding the house. This wasn't how tonight was supposed to go; I was still on fucking parole. As soon they ran my name, my parole officer would be notified.

"Police! Open the door now!"

Mrs. O'Connor got up and cautiously made her way toward the

front of the apartment. The exchange was within earshot, allowing us to hear every word. This woman was Irish through and through: *deny until you die.*

"What do you want?" she said, refusing to open the door.

"We know they're in there, open the door," the voice repeated.

"Who? I've been alone all night," she lied, instantly forgetting the cover story. "I mean . . . it's just me and my daughter's ex-boyfriend and his friend. We've been playing cards and having a few beers."

"If you don't wanna go to jail with them, open the door now," the voice barked.

Mrs. O'Connor turned back to look at me. I exhaled deeply, leaned back in my chair, and laced my fingers behind my head. I indicated with my chin for Quinn to do the same. I didn't want Quinn or me getting our asses shot off by a trigger-happy cop to be added to this clusterfuck of an evening.

"Just open the fuckin' door," I said.

It took the detectives less than twenty minutes to transport us to the county hospital, where we were brought before Carlos for identification. He was being prepped for emergency surgery to relieve the swelling on his brain. We stood handcuffed at his bedside as he laid his eyes upon us and gave a nod.

That's all it took. Quinn and I were formally booked and charged with carjacking, kidnapping, and attempted murder. *At least they didn't find the fuckin' coke.*

The following morning, we were brought from the police station to the courthouse to be charged. Due to the serious nature of the charges, the DA requested that we be held without bail. The judge agreed without hesitation. We were both remanded to the custody of the Department of Corrections and transported to MCI–Concord to be held on pretrial status. Since I was on parole, the new arrest would automatically result in a parole revocation hearing being scheduled. So even if bail had been set at our arraignment, my ass wasn't going anywhere. And now, with a no-bail order in place, neither was Quinn. What the hell, at least we'd be together and would have plenty of time on our hands awaiting trial to finish the card game we had started at the O'Connors'.

Two months later, at our first pretrial conference, we learned that the victim and only witness in the case, Carlos, had apparently been shot and killed at a stoplight during an attempted carjacking incident in New York City. The district attorney added that the New York homicide remained unsolved and stopped one breath short of flat-out accusing Quinn and me of having had a hand in the star witness's demise.

Had he done so, our lawyers would have eaten him alive, and he knew it. In the eyes of the law, it's not what you know but what you can prove. *No face, no case.*

Quinn was released from the courthouse that afternoon following the hearing. Due to the parole violation, I, of course, was returned to prison in order to finish serving the time I owed on my original sentence.

Six months later, I was visited by my lawyer. He informed me that Quinn had been shot and killed while exiting a barbershop. It was an ambush. Subsequently, no one has ever been arrested for his murder.

Years later, while sitting alone in my prison cell and reminiscing about my old friend Quinn, I wrote this:

*I had a friend who, when I'm not in prison, I like to remember on a certain day each year in a certain town in a certain pub. I'm not big on vigils, where many walk away from the altar with lit candles and forced looks of strength and even of pride, feelings they'd lost when their loved one was murdered, or overdosed, or killed themself, or was taken away from this hellhole by whatever unspeakable cause.*

*So, on this particular day, the scarred and sticky mahogany bar serves as my altar and the cigarette-scented barman my priest. I remember my last visit to this Guinness cathedral. I was standing at the bar. Through the archway that led to the lounge, I could see that the lounge was almost empty. Two elderly men with oft-broken noses sat in a cheap red vinyl booth, quietly sipping pints, nodding to each other's remarks. The bar wasn't much busier. Besides a prostitute and myself, there were two men who were studying sports on a television, a young man who looked distant enough to be into transcendental meditation, and a vociferously unemployed painter who was wearing painter's overalls, as if the call to paint something might come at any moment.*

*I nodded to the barman for what had to have been the twelfth time since I'd arrived. His name was Paddy, and he looked as happy as a death-row inmate ordering his last meal. But he was a good clergyman and delivered my eighty-proof sermon without delay. It was that time—just after opening when a pub begins to come awake—a new day starts inside the old one, as if the morning had a stutter. Ice was brimming the bucket. The wood floor was devoid of debris. The moted sunlight coming in the window was clean enough to see through.*

*But remembering the times spent with my friend here, I populated the emptiness. It had been one of his places, and some small part of his spirit had been left here.*

*Holding a brief séance for my friend, I conjured vivid faces and loud nights. I saw that smile of his, sudden as a sunray, when he loved what you were saying. I saw that strained expression when he felt you must agree with him and couldn't get you to see that. I caught the way the laughter would light up his eyes when he was trying, but failing miserably, to suppress it. I heard the laughing when it broke. We had good times here. He had lived with such intensity.*

*The thought was my personal funeral for him. Who needed possessions and careers and official achievements? Life was in the living of it. How you act and what you are and what you do were the only substance. They didn't last either. But while you were here, they made what light there was—the wick that threads the candle wax of time. His light was out, but here I felt I could almost smell the smoke still drifting from its snuffing.*

Rest in peace, my friend.

# FOURTEEN

## SEED MONEY

Shane McKelvey was a talented pilot and an integral part of our drug operation, and he had also become a close personal friend. Once or twice a month, he flew shipments of marijuana up to Massachusetts from suppliers down in Florida. Sometime in 2004, Shane introduced me to the owner of a small South Shore airport where he regularly landed his plane full of illicit cargo.

Shane told me the guy was a fellow smuggler but a total dickhead. The guy had recently raised the rates on Shane for using his runways to import the pot, and he did it without rhyme, reason, or notice. He made the introduction to me because the guy was looking to have a chimney put on his three-story house, and I could overcharge the shit out of him. It was a solid contract with an uncapped budget and unprecedented profit margins. My kind of job.

Years back, I had been taught how to build chimneys from the best steeplejack (a brick mason who specializes in chimneys) in Boston, and I knew the ins and outs of the process. The structure of a chimney is significantly more complex than it appears on the outside; a functional chimney's anatomy has many unique features, chambers, and moving parts.

But on top of it being fully functional, this guy wanted his new fireplace to be the centerpiece of the room, which meant it had to look good—and by "good," he meant that it should look very expensive. He decided on a grand stone hearth and an equally impressive mantel that was too big for the space, and he insisted I build it out of imported Venetian marble. His demands were pretentious and ornate and over the top. And there was no way in hell I was using *imported Venetian marble*. I told him I would check on which materials were available and what I could get my hands on, while still promising to make the least number of compromises to his "vision." He seemed happy with that lie and hired me right away. *When could I start?*

I reached out to my architectural stone supplier, who said the client sounded as if he wouldn't know the difference if I installed cast stone. Cast stone is a cheap alternative to natural stone, made by pouring a mixture into a mold and allowing it to harden. In no way, shape, or form is cast stone a sufficient alternative to real Venetian marble.

Within the next few days, I ordered four pallets of reclaimed bricks and two dozen bags of mortar, enough to get the project started. I placed an order for the elaborate "Venetian marble" fireplace the client wanted: *poured and manufactured in Texas.*

To help me with the job, I called up Eddy Johnson.

When he was younger, before I knew him, Eddy was in a barbaric fight that left him with a hatchet blade wedged into his face like a stump used for chopping wood. The wound closed but had left a menacing scar spanning from his forehead to his chin. The scar, combined with the backstory, led everyone to call him "Hatchy."

Technically, Hatchy was my ex-brother-in-law or something—his common-law wife was my first wife's older sister. But for all intents and purposes, he was a real brother. For years, Hatchy had been my pop's driver after it became too dangerous for Hank to drive because his eyesight was shot. In addition, when I was locked up, Hatchy had gone out of his way and moved in with Hank to look after him. Hatchy's significant other, Nancy, had not been thrilled about it when he did that, but Hatchy had stood his ground.

Even after I divorced Juanita, Hatchy and I saw each other as family, and over time we worked countless construction jobs, rackets, and rob-beries together. He happily accepted the chimney job.

The first day on the jobsite, when I was down on the lawn taking inventory of the delivery, Hatchy was walking through the house and going over the architectural plans. On the third floor, he came across a hidden scuttle attic: a pull-down ladder in the ceiling was disguised under a large air-conditioning vent. The attic was small and messy—it would have made tunnel rats of the Vietnam War feel cramped. To make way for the chimney, the boxes and clutter and cobwebs had to be moved. And when Hatchy was shuffling all the things around, he found a four-foot-tall safe tucked behind the mess. He called me up right away.

The safe had a simple combination lock and was not secured to the floor. The safe's security revolved around never being found rather than it being impenetrable. It would be easy to crack knowing it was there. Hatchy could hardly control his excitement, looking like a fat kid in a candy store. I could practically hear his thoughts.

"Whaddya think's inside?" he said to me in a rush. "Who is this guy anyway? You think he got money?" I filled him in on what Shane, my pilot, had told me about the client: that he was a smuggler and how the guy's wife didn't know anything about her husband's criminal activities.

That only made Hatchy more excited. "C'mon, Ghost, we gotta crack it open . . . just ta see what's inside. If it's a bunch o' worthless shit, we'll just close her back up and act like we ain't seen nothin'. But all I'm sayin' is a guy like that don't keep a safe hidden in the attic for no reason. Plus, it's not like the guy'll get the cops involved. He don't want any cops sniffin' 'round here anymore'n we do. We ain't got nothin' to lose."

Hatchy had a good point—a few of them, actually. And who was I to turn down a job this easy? At the very least, it piqued my curiosity. I convinced Hatchy to wait until the chimney was built; that way we got the payday from the client before we robbed him.

All the while, as my crew worked, I wondered what the client thought was worth hiding in the attic.

He didn't disappoint. A week after the paycheck was signed and cashed, we went back into the attic when the homeowner was out and cracked the safe in no time flat. There were stacks of hundred-dollar bills, a few Rolex watches, and three boxes of foreign coins. We cleaned out the safe and never returned to the property again. The whole thing took less than fifteen minutes.

As Hatchy drove the two of us away in his Lincoln town car, I decided to take a closer look at the coins.

"Holy fuck," Hatchy exclaimed as I slid the lid off the first box. His attention was drawn away from the road. "Those things are solid gold? Tell me they're fuckin' real."

*I think they're real . . . Holy fuck, I think they're actually real.*

"How 'bout you just get us back to the club without killing us? And we'll count everything there," I said, realizing we had drifted halfway into the other lane. I put the lid back on the box.

I learned later that the coins were uncirculated South African Krugerrands—one ounce of 22-karat gold apiece. And each box held around three hundred coins—nine hundred Krugerrands in total. Nine hundred ounces (56.25 pounds) of gold, the equivalent of roughly two gold bars. But that was seeing the coins at face value, quantifying only their raw weight. In reality, the coins were worth twice their weight in gold. We were sitting on over a half-million dollars before factoring in the rest of the money and watches.

We didn't get the full value for the coins, of course. We needed to find someone who would purchase the coins in bulk, as well as not ask questions about their provenance. *And would that same person be in the market for a Rolex?* Why, yes, as it just so happens, they were looking for a new wristwatch . . . or three.

When all was said and done, we made a clean $285,000.

And that's when things became dangerous because Hatchy got an idea, and he always saw opportunities on the wrong side of the caution tape.

"I got an idea," he said. "It's a, uh, a business opportunity, actually. I been lookin' into for some time now . . . Don't worry, I'm not askin' you for a kidney or nothin'. It's a good moneymaker for both of us. Just hear me out . . .

"So, there's these twin brothers down in Apopka, Florida—real cutthroat sonsabitches—and they's runnin' a big company that does orchids . . . grows 'em and whateva. Anyways, these guys grow more orchids than anyone else. No joke, they're the fuckin' orchid kings of America. But in reality, the whole thing's really just a front for the biggest fuckin' pot farm you eva seen. I'm talkin' rows of plants stretchin' a thousand feet long. It's premium shit too. I can vouch for that shit myself." He smiled mischievously. "They make decent money on the orchids too."

"I know where you're goin' and it's a bad idea, Hatchy," I said. "The DEA's gotta be up their fuckin' asses with a farm that size."

"Just lemme finish, Christ . . . then ya can decide for yourself. I seen the place myself, the DEA won't neva find shit. The guys got these official permaculture nursery hoop houses with poly sheathing over the top, the ones that look like giant plastic caterpillars. They even painted the plastic so those fuckin' alphabet boys can't see shit if they're flyin' over."

"So what? Good for them, they sure as shit aren't gonna cut us in . . . Unless you're tellin' me they wanna sell? Why the fuck would they wanna sell?"

"Not exactly what I'm sayin' . . . I've worked it all out—I been lookin' into this a long time, it ain't just pullin' this idea outta my asshole. It all started 'cause I heard they was lookin' for investors . . . So, what we's gonna do is give 'em a small buy-in, just to get our foot in the door, ya know? And once we're in, we fuckin' take it from 'em . . . cut out the middleman. You always lookin' for ways to increase profit margins—this is our chance. It might get a little messy, but that's why I need you in on this with me. We'd run it together, fifty-fifty partners. C'mon, with you in, it's a sure thing."

"How much money you think it'll take?" I asked, not sold on the endeavor yet, although it was starting to look better.

"To get us in the door? Two hundred fifty Gs each oughta do it. But that's fuckin' chump change compared ta after we own the joint. We'll be makin' that every two or three months. I can't do it without you, Ghost; I'm askin' as your friend if you'll do this with me."

"*Fuck it* . . . it's just money, right? Let's do it."

If it were anyone else, I would have known better. But fuck it, it was only money.

It turned out to be a lot more complicated than Hatchy led on. And a lot messier. Those scumbags were violent, ruthless, and paranoid. It got ugly. But it ended when the two of them drowned in a freak duck-hunting accident—unrelated to our feud.

Anyway, that's how I became the proud co-owner of a sizable pot farm.

# FIFTEEN

## THE BANK JOB

After taking over the grow operation, I didn't have much liquid capital. We were making money hand over fist, but the demand was outpacing our supply. Every dime we earned went back into the business. We were buying more seeds, soil, grow lights, nutrients, humidifiers, multiple reverse osmosis water filtration systems, more caterpillar-tunnel greenhouses and hiring more staff. More of everything just to keep up.

Clearly, things were going well. Until they weren't. Shane McKelvey, our pilot, was arrested in connection to a recent wire fraud bust, and the judge slapped him with an unreasonable $150,000 bail. We were fucked.

With all my money tied up in the farm, and without his shipments, there would be no money coming in. To make matters worse, taking Shane out of the airways put our whole distribution chain in jeopardy; this was an open invitation to steal our customers. Dealers who relied on the regular availability of our product would have to turn elsewhere. And it wasn't just our customer base at stake; it was our reputation. So, if I wanted to maintain our foothold in the marijuana market, I needed to scrape together the full amount for Shane's bail and come up with a solution—fast.

The only chance I had to get that kind of money in that short a time frame was through the help of Alan Schliemann, my "rainy day fund."

Alan Schliemann was a good family man and a faithful husband. He was also a terrible sports bettor, a die-hard New England fan who never had the heart to bet against his team. He said it was bad juju. Unfortunately for him and his biased strategy, not a single New England team did particularly well that year. By the time the bookies stopped taking his bets, Alan was close to twenty-four thousand bucks in the hole. For standard customers, credit limits were capped between five and ten thousand dollars, depending on the bettor's payback history and seizable assets.

I'd suggested to the bookies that Alan's limit be increased for three reasons: (1) he worked at a local Citizens Bank, (2) he was a degenerate gambler, and (3) I'd make the collection myself when the time was right. It was a win-win situation, though not for Alan. We gave him enough rope to hang himself, and once the noose was tied, I would be there to extend him one last lifeline.

Thankfully, my plan for Alan had been cooking on the back burner for months now, simmering until the time was right. Twenty-four thousand dollars later, Alan was ready to be served.

I intercepted him at the Dunkin' Donuts he went to every morning before work. Our conversation was brief and to the point. I informed him that he was going to help me rob a bank—his bank. And if he did, all his debts would be forgiven. And if he didn't, he'd be fucked—simple as that. There wasn't much of a choice here: twenty-four thousand is a dangerous figure to owe a bookie, who, in turn, generally owed the mob.

*Time to pay up, Alan. Don't make me ask again.*

With the addition of Alan to the team, there was one spot left to fill. Unfortunately, I couldn't take Hatchy away from the pot farm; there were too many supply-chain snafus that required attention. But I had someone else in mind already.

William "Billy" Smith was a professional bank robber. Born in 1943, Billy had a handful of jobs under his belt and had only been caught twice. Strike one had happened after an old girlfriend tipped the cops off about a bag of money in Billy's closet. He got a seven-to-ten-year stretch for that. The second time it went wrong was nothing more than a stroke of bad luck: a flat tire as he was driving away from the armored car his crew had just hit. They gifted him an eighteen-to-thirty-year state-paid vacation in the penitentiary for that one.

Billy had recently been released when I approached him with the new job. He was excited; he'd be able to retire more comfortably with his cut of the take. But at the age of sixty-two, Billy said the years had started to catch up and that time had slowed his joints, and knowing that the margin of error is slim in a bank job, he thought it best for him to drive the getaway vehicle. I agreed, and we started preparing.

*Two heists in back-to-back chapters. Well, aren't you lucky?*

I sat in my attorney's wife's car, a white Lexus I sometimes borrowed when the need arose to stay inconspicuous. A yellow legal pad with time stamps and observations written in my shorthand sat on the passenger seat, and a large gas-station soda cup half-full of warm vodka and Coke was in the cup holder. The ashtray needed emptying.

I was on a stakeout, monitoring the staff's movements and the police cruisers that routinely drove by the bank. Over the week leading up to the heist, I arrived an hour before the bank opened and stayed an hour after it closed.

Billy came by here and there to relieve my post, so I could shit and whatnot. We were given a surprisingly thorough scouting report from Alan, our inside man, but we had to be extra careful because it was our necks that were on the line if anything went wrong. I fucking hated reconnaissance, but prison was worse, so I saw being overprepared as the lesser of two evils.

The day arrived, and everything was set. I wore a black tear-away track-suit, the kind preferred by both professional basketball players and exhibitionists, and a matching plain ball cap. Underneath the top layer of removable clothing, I had on an oversized white T-shirt and blue jeans. I dressed to have no discernible features: a faceless man.

We drove over in Billy's Caprice Classic. For whatever reason, he had forgone swapping the plates, and to make matters worse, the car's rear windscreen was plastered with a giant "Yankees Suck!" sticker.

The Citizens Bank was located inside a busy Stop-n-Shop super-market. To avoid bystanders identifying the car, we parked in a vacant loading dock roughly an eighth of a mile away. I got out and walked to the bank entrance; Billy kept the car running.

I was going in alone and unarmed; a gun was unnecessary when a note would have the same effect. If the bitch went tits up, I would get a lot more time carrying a firearm versus a square of paper. Armed robbery is best saved for the larger banks; they have more tellers and bystanders to control and are also staffed with armed guards, who require overpowering. Not all bank robberies are glamorous. Most aren't, like this one. John Dillinger was probably turning over in his grave.

I approached the automatic doors at the supermarket and triggered the motion sensor. The doors slid open, and I walked in, pulling my plain black ball cap down over my brow to shield my face from any cameras.

Apart from the automatic doors, there was nothing special about the inside of the branch. It had cold AC and those black stanchions with retractable nylon belts indicating where to form a line—a typical bank.

To my left, I noticed a customer (one of three in the bank) helping themself to a complementary cup of coffee and a donut. To my right was an office with a glass wall front. Inside the office were two potted plants, a few filing cabinets, a big desk, and a panic-stricken Alan Schliemann. The realization that this was actually happening was painted across his face; he looked like he was shitting his pants. His eyes followed me as I casually walked to the counter; I felt them burning a hole in my back.

A female teller was politely covering her mouth and yawning. I was her first customer of the day. She was young, blonde, and attractive.

"Good morning, how can I help you today?" she said. I pulled my hand out of my tracksuit jacket and placed the note on the counter, sliding it over to the blonde. Her eyes widened and her mouth gaped open, a look of pure terror, as she read the simple note:

*This is a robbery*
*It's not your money*

*Don't be a hero*
*NO ALARMS*
*NO DYE PACKS*
*Make it quick*

She didn't move a muscle. Right on cue, Alan came over to check on her and the situation. There was already a quiver in his voice, but I don't think she noticed.

"How're you doing today, sir? Is Rachel here taking good care of you?" He faked a courteous laugh and placed a calming hand on the teller's shoulder.

She picked up the yellow note and handed it to him.

He read it slowly, and I snatched it back when he was done.

"I'll, uh . . . I'll take it from here," Alan said, swiveling his head to see if any of the other customers had noticed what was happening yet. "Please, uh . . . follow me, sir, right this way." *Fuckin' moron was forgetting the plan. I couldn't leave the teller unattended.*

"I'm staying right fuckin' here," I said so only the two of them could hear, "and the girl stays too. You got two minutes to bring me everything you got, you hear? Don't fuck this up."

Alan scurried off in a brisk walk toward the bank's vault, where he had left two blue money transport bags. The bags had been delivered by an armored car earlier that morning. And Alan, knowing I was coming, hadn't put the money away in the vault yet.

A bank is required to keep enough money on hand to satisfy all foreseeable daily transactions. This was usually a surprisingly small number, less than $50,000, but fuck that: we needed more. Thankfully, Alan was a genius when it came to taking advantage of banking loopholes. With the power his job title granted him, he had taken the month to accumulate quite a bit more in cash reserves. I wasn't sure how he had managed to pull it off, but it didn't matter—the money bags were heavy. Now as long as he kept his mouth shut, I would consider his debts paid in full.

Alan walked around the front of the counter and placed the two bags on the floor.

"No fuckin' cops for five minutes—and don't think about tryin' anything, no fuckin' games. We know things, we know your name's Alan Schliemann, you live at 65 Upland Terrace. We know where your wife, Ayla, gets her hair done, and we know where your two kids go to school," I said, making shit up and using the phrase "we" to further throw off the teller. "Five fuckin' minutes, ya hear? Don't fuckin' try me."

"Ye . . . Yeah," he stammered. "Five minutes, yeah."

I picked up the two bags and headed for the door. I knew I had less than five minutes; at most I'd have half that. Alan wouldn't call right away, but the blonde would. Nothing Alan or I could do about that. I just hoped he'd slow her down, give me as much time as possible.

*The sliding doors open to the outside . . . a rush of warm air . . . I scan the street . . . empty . . . Do I run for it? . . . No, don't want to draw attention . . . a brisk walk . . . I turn the corner . . . put the bags down . . . rip off the snap pants and zip-up hoodie . . . stuff them under my oversized T-shirt . . . big belly . . . I look ridiculous, but different . . . one more block . . . pick up the pace . . . a slight jog now . . . skip in my step . . . I listen . . . birds chirping, a car door shuts, welcome bells on a bakery door jingle . . . no sirens . . . yet . . . but there are more people on this street . . . pedestrians, eyewitnesses . . . keep moving . . . close now . . . I turn down the alley into the loading dock . . . see the car . . . engine's running . . . I yank the rear passenger door open . . . "Get in, get in! Shut the door," Billy yells. "Cops a minute out. Been listenin' to 'em on the scanner. Get in!" . . . I toss the first blue bag on the floor, then the second . . . Billy backs the car out of the bay, and eases it onto the street . . . careful . . . slow . . . obey traffic laws . . . mind the speed limit . . . I hear the sirens now . . . much too late . . . and heading away from suspects . . . and the money . . .*

Billy pulled the car into a Revere Beach hotel and killed the engine.

"Ha ha!" Billy exclaimed, rubbing his hands together like an old-fashioned, greedy villain. "I missed that fuckin' rush. Nothin' better'n the world than a good bank job."

"Let's get this shit to the room 'n' count it," I said, grabbing a box cutter off the rear floor and slipping it into my pocket.

We placed the money transport bags into black trash bags from the trunk, and each carried one up to the room Billy was staying in. He excitedly jostled the keys into the lock and let us inside. He threw his bag on the bed and started talking. "Motherfuckers are heavy," he said. "How much you think we got in total?"

The two bags looked fat with money.

"Dunno, feels like a good take. Your cut's still thirty Gs, though . . . like we agreed."

I took out the box cutter and started slicing the blue nylon bags open. *Good God, there was a lot of fuckin' money inside.*

I counted out Billy's cut, threw him an extra $5,000 for a rolling suitcase he had in the room, which I commandeered, emptied out the contents, and stuffed the remainder of the money into. I wished him a good retirement and all the best, then left, but not before telling him to destroy the blue money bags.

Later that night, when I got home, I put the bail money into an aluminum-sided briefcase I would hand over to my lawyer, Milt, the next day. I started to recount what was left over.

Even with the $209,000 ($35K going to Billy, $150K to Shane, and $24K to Alan's bookie) off the top, it was a big fucking haul. There was $370,000 left. The following day, I did what I always do following a successful heist: I boarded a jet plane and got the fuck out of Dodge. I had business to attend to in Florida.

Things were looking good after the heist. Milton and I talked on the phone every day when I was in Florida; he kept his ear to the ground, listening for whispers about any breaks in the case. For the first few days, there was nothing, hardly even a mention in the papers. Nothing about it on the nightly news either. Besides a vague police sketch, the police didn't have shit to work with. When there isn't immediate progress on a bank job, the chances of solving it practically vanish.

We were in clear—or so it seemed.

Alan held up under the interrogation, kept to the story, and provided sufficient answers to explain away his actions. He was exonerated from the suspect list and able to keep his job, his family, and his life, as well as start fresh with the bookie. He could place all the ill-advised sports bets his heart desired, although now he was held to a significantly lower credit limit.

Billy was getting his assets in order in preparation for his full-fledged retirement. "To hell with the goddamn snow!" he had said to me a thousand times over the years. He was planning a migration, equator bound.

Hatchy was happy to see me, and he looked relieved when I told him that we'd get our pilot, Shane, back soon. When I mentioned the remaining $370K from the bank job, Hatchy shit himself, figuratively. With that kind of money, we'd finally be able to get ahead of the voracious demand. On my first day there, we got to work. If we budgeted accordingly, there would be a whopping three hundred grand left over—the only question was what to do with it. Again, Hatchy had the answer, another investment opportunity. He set up a meeting for me later in the week.

That's when shit hit the fan.

I got a call from my lawyer. Bad news: Billy Smith had been arrested. The police had been canvassing the area around the bank and asking local businesses for any security footage they might have. It was a long shot, but it paid off for them. It took four days of looking for them to find the smoking gun. A security camera in the loading bay had caught everything: the car pulling in, me throwing the bags inside, and the car pulling out. It didn't capture our faces, but it didn't have to. Billy had never changed the car's license plate, and the camera caught that, clear as day. They traced the plate and had Billy in cuffs less than two hours later.

Worse yet, when searching the vehicle, the cops found a disposable camera in the glove box. After developing the film, they found a photo of Billy and me drinking together. When they presented it to the eyewitnesses (Alan Schliemann and the teller), the teller identified me immediately. Alan reportedly said that he couldn't be sure if it was me or not, but the teller stood her ground. Apparently, that was all they needed to put out an all-points bulletin broadcasting my description and information, then obtaining a warrant for my arrest. The hunt was on. *Fuck.*

The line went silent for a moment, the sound of bad news sinking in.

Milton apologized for having to be the bearer of bad news, and he asked me what I wanted to do next. It wasn't an easy question to answer, and silence descended again as I weighed my options. I could stay in Florida until the case ran cold; they'd never find me down here and Billy would *never* rat me out.

But that wasn't a viable option; the consequences were too severe. A man's life was at stake. What was left of it anyway. As I mentioned earlier, Billy had already racked up two strikes for past robberies, and if convicted again, under the three-strikes rule, he'd go away for life.

He was sixty-two, I wasn't about to let him wither to a pile of dust behind bars. He had earned the right to die booze-soaked and sunburnt, banging hookers on a beach somewhere in the tropics. Plus, by this point, prison had become my second home.

I told Milt I'd take the fall, claim full accountability.

If I turned myself in, could he promise immunity for Billy? *Immunity?* No, but a damn good plea deal, most likely no prison.

And how much time could he buy me before I had to turn myself in? I still had the meeting Hatchy had set up for me—the prospective outlet for my remaining three hundred grand, a deal that would require time. Milt said he would bring the offer to the state prosecutor, and it would take a day to get an answer.

"Hang in there, Sean," he said and then hung up.

*Silence.*

The next day he got back to me. Six months, he said. The deal was good for six months. During which time, they'd hold on to Billy as collateral.

Milton had more good news: the Honorable Judge Moriarty would "somehow" preside over my case. Milton and Judge Moriarty had a long history together, a long-proven track record resulting in lower sentences for Milton's clients. Coincidentally, this would be the judge's last case before retiring. And seeing how this would be His Honor's final court ruling, the verdict would be Judge Moriarty's legacy. But with a generous retirement gift and Milton cashing in a final favor, the sentencing would be tilted in my direction.

I told Milt to accept on my behalf and to get in touch with Billy, inform him of my decision and that he would be back on the street in six months' time. With the rest of our conversation, we ironed out the details of my surrender. With everything finalized, we ended the call, and the countdown began.

The clock ticked.

Knowledge of the inevitable has a tendency to enslave its bearer. But just as knowledge can be a poison, acceptance can be the antidote. Many people view a doomsday clock as a burden. They only see the outcome when the timer hits zero, but I don't. For me, it has the opposite effect. I see the stretch of time where, no matter what I do, the outcome is predetermined. That's fuckin' freedom if you ask me, and I had six months of it.

So, the next day, I went to the prearranged meeting and bought a strip club.

Time passed quickly while I got the Booby Trap up and running. With Shane McKelvey bailed out of lockup and back to work, our marijuana supply chain was back on track and more lucrative than ever.

Under his pretrial supervision, Shane would, of course, be breaking his probation if he just hopped in his airplane and left the state. To get around this, he had to obtain a travel permit, which meant supplying detailed flight plans, a daily itinerary, and verifiable employment information each time he flew. Luckily, his probation officer was an old friend of my pops who became even more friendly with the extra $10,000 a month, assuming he approved the travel permits and forwent double-checking any work details.

With my surrender date approaching, I made arrangements for the club to be self-sufficient in my absence. I hired a reliable manager, replaced problematic staff, and paid my liquor distributor in advance for the monthly shipments. Everything was set, so I migrated north and turned myself in as planned. Six months to the day.

I pled guilty to unarmed robbery and was handsomely rewarded with two and a half years. Not bad, if you ask me.

For how callous the Massachusetts Department of Corrections may have been, not even they had the heart to deny us Sunday football. To do such a thing to a New England sports fan would be completely inhumane, a blatant violation of the Eighth Amendment, which bans "cruel and unusual punishment." And with two Super Bowl rings in back-to-back seasons, it was a good time to be a Patriots fan.

Every Sunday (and the few Thursday night and Monday morning games), me and four other inmates would get together for the game. I had the biggest television, so we all crammed into my cell. One of the other guys, who had sanitation duties most days, always brought one of those yellow mop buckets along. We would empty out the dirty water, stretch a trash-bag liner around the lip of the bucket, and fill it with prison-made moonshine and packets of instant Kool-Aid powder. The fruit punch flavor was my favorite.

The five of us sat around the bucket with our Styrofoam cups, dipping them into the juice when we needed a refill, and cheered rambunctiously for the Pats. Of all my time spent in prison, this stint was one of the best.

The rest of the time I spent reading or playing cards. I had gotten good at whist, a strategic card game built around tricks and trumps. It is played in two teams of two. (The game has many variants and differing sets of rules, which, for the purpose of this story, are completely unimportant to explain further.) My pops had taught me the basics of how to play years ago in Uncle Toby's basement, but I learned the game's intricacies in prison by playing thousands of hands. However, there were some guys in there with tens of thousands of hands under their belts, so I was still considered a novice.

My partner was no better; I had taught him two months back. Even though we were comparatively inexperienced, we had a respectable win rate and recorded wins against almost every opponent. (You can't help but chronicle statistics in prison; it adds another layer to the mundane and makes things slightly more interesting.) In fact, we had beaten every team except one: two older guys who were in on multiple life sentences— real card sharks. They beat us every time . . . that is, except once.

It was 2005. Winter. Very cold. The holes in our jackets and cheap beanies we were given did little to combat the frigid chill. The four of us were playing first to fifty points, which would take between ten and twenty-five rounds. We were three hours in, maybe three and a half, and by this time we were up 44–41. If we outscored them in one of the next two games, we would likely win the whole match. Fifty Cadillac cigarettes, two one-liter bottles of vodka, and two seventy-five-dollar canteen bags from the losing team were on the line . . . high stakes. Higher tensions.

My deal. Thirteen cards apiece. Last card decides the trump suit. Diamonds. I check my hand: two diamonds and an assortment of low-value off-suits. *Fuck.* (Yes, I do actually remember this.) We were halfway through the round, and we were losing. My partner was of little to no help, and one of the old card sharks was dealt a ringer of a hand. We were getting crushed, but there was still a chance to pull it off. As my turn to lay down a card approached, I felt a soft tapping on my right shoulder.

"Sean Scott Hicks?" said a soft voice.

"Who the fuck—?" I said, pissed that someone was not only interrupting our game but hadn't addressed me as "Ghost." (I have stabbed people over that level of disrespect.)

I spun my head around to see the kindly face of the prison chaplain. He was accompanied by the serious faces of two serious guards. I coughed and readjusted my tone, words, and demeanor. He was a supposed man of God, after all.

"What can I do for you, Father? Kinda in the middla somethin' right now." I nodded toward our teetering game.

"Well, son, maybe we better talk somewhere a little more . . . private," the chaplain said, eyeing the others at the table.

"We can't talk here?" I asked. "What's it about?"

"Your mother."

"Don't give a fuck then," I said, spinning back around to the game at hand. I played a card and lost the trick. The guy who won didn't scoop up the cards, he didn't move. Instead, the three other players stared at the chaplain; apparently, he had more to say.

"Sean, she um . . . well, she passed away two days ago. We only just got notified by a . . ." He trailed off and looked at a pocket notepad he'd brought with him. "Valentina, your . . . uh, your sister, it says here. She said you oughta know. She also said that the funeral—"

"Look, Father," I interrupted, "with all due respect, I don't give a flying fuck about that whore. Maybe we're better off with her gone. Now if you don't mind. I'm in the middle of a fucking game that I'm about to fucking lose. Tony, you fuckin' won that one, now take the fucking cards. It's my turn to go first." I slouched down in my chair and fumed over another shitty hand. *Fuck . . .*

Constance Elaine Hicks was gone. My mother was dead. The two sentences are interchangeable, yet only one feels true. My "mother" was dead? Maybe. I guess, it depends on your definition of "mother." Did I have one to begin with? Is the person that beats you unconscious a mother? How about the woman who points a gun at her son and pulls the trigger only to realize the safety was on—is she a mother? Maybe it's the woman who gets fucked by eight strangers in front of her six-year-old son? No, no. It must be the woman who forces her starving child to hit a crack pipe so she doesn't have to feed him for a fourth day in a row; surely, that woman fits the definition of a "mother"? Or is it just whoever owns the vagina you came spewing out of? If that last one is the only criterion, then fuck it, yeah—Constance was my mother.

However terrible a mother she was, I feel as if I owe the reader one happy memory with Constance. If I can think of one . . .

Years back, not long after that hurricane hit Florida and flooded our neighborhood, I recall a moment, the only moment in fact, where I felt loved by my mother. We had made a deal that if I wanted to go play in the flood, I had to choke down a tablespoon of cod-liver oil to protect myself from the bacteria growing in the three inches of standing water.

I was around eight years old at the time, meaning my understanding of danger was all but nonexistent. I was a hellion of pent-up chaotic energy and negligence, running through the streets completely unsupervised. Without fear and without shoes—which is a problem if you know anything about Florida.

For whatever reason, the Sunshine State is fucking *covered* in broken glass. Just walking the streets is hazardous; running without shoes is a recipe for disaster. And in less than a half hour, my foot was a pincushion for shards of glass, the sole resembling Caesar on the Ides of March.* I sat down and howled in throbbing pain. I felt my heartbeat in my foot. The water around me turning redder with every second. I tried standing up, but it was no use. The slightest pressure was a shot of pure agony.

Not knowing what else to do, I cried for help.

Constance burst out of the house wearing a bathrobe and pink house slippers with large fuzzy pom-poms glued on the top; the curlers stuck in her hair were bouncing as she came high-stepping through the water. She panicked at the sight of my bloody foot. Then, with strength I didn't know she had, she picked me up in her arms, quickly carried me to her car, and put me in the front seat. My pops must have been at work because we sped off without him.

Constance must have broken every traffic law imaginable getting me to the hospital. When we arrived, my mother left the car in the emergency drop-off zone with the doors wide open and told an employee to shove the car up their ass when they informed her that she couldn't park it there. She caused a bigger scene inside at the intake desk; the term *waiting room* wasn't going to apply to her. Irate and hysterical, my mother got us an audience with a doctor in a private room within sixty seconds.

The doctor put on blue gloves with some difficulty, lowered the side railing on the gurney I was lying on, and took me by the ankle to inspect the injury. By this point the bleeding had stopped, but the rhythmic throbbing persisted. The doctor brought his face in close, then laid my leg carefully back onto the bed.

"Everything's gonna be all right, ma'am. No clear cause for concern. The glass doesn't appear to have nicked anything major. I mean, it's in there good 'n' deep, but it shouldn't warrant surgery. I can take care of it right here. I'll numb the area, remove the glass, and clean it up a bit. But we'll stitch and bandage everything and get ya outta here today. He'll have to stay off it for a couple days but give it a week and

---

* The Ides of March—March 15, 44 BCE—was the infamous date on which Julius Caesar, dictator of the Roman Empire, was stabbed to death by sixty political rivals.

he'll make a full recovery. How does that sound to you, son?" he said, addressing me for the first time. I nodded.

"You barely looked at it. How do you know he'll make a 'full recovery'? Shouldn't we get the foot doctor in here for a second look?" my mother asked, squeezing my hand as she said it.

"There's no need, ma'am, I've seen this a million times before. Half of the patients we get in here come in with a similar injury. I'll send ya along with a prescription for some antibiotics to err on the safe side, but at most there might be some minor scarring once it heals, but there won't be any impact to his mobility. Think of it as a rite of passage." He turned back to me again, smiling. "Every young man earns a few scars growin' up. I got one myself, right here," he said, patting his upper thigh with the gloved hand that wasn't bloody.

"Fine," my mother said curtly.

"Good, we'll get started right away," he said and stood up, going over to the cabinets against the wall to retrieve the things he needed.

I looked to my mother. She was half-sitting on the bed with me, rubbing my hand; the bed was rocking from her anxiously shaking her leg. For a moment, the pain vanished. I didn't feel a thing. No anesthesia. The pain was just gone.

The doctor returned to his bedside stool and pulled over a tray on wheels that had an assortment of gauze, tweezers, picks, prods, and a shiny kidney-shaped bowl. The shot of anesthesia was hidden behind the silver bowl. It was a cheap doctor's trick to hide the needle like that.

He slipped on a clean pair of gloves, grabbed the concealed syringe, and took up my ankle again.

"You'll just feel a little pinch, son."

I turned my head into my mother's chest. Her arms wrapped around me and pulled me in tight.

"Three . . . two . . . and . . . there we go, all done." A sharp prick . . . but nothing compared to the glass. I let out a sigh. I thought the worst was over. The doctor took a piece of gauze and dabbed where the needle had entered. "And now we wait," he said, looking at the clock on the wall. "I'll come check back in ten minutes or so." He got up and left to go check on other patients or fill out paperwork or whatever.

For the entire ten minutes he was gone, my mother and I didn't speak a word to one another. She just held me tight, rubbing my hair in silence.

"All right, how we doin' in here?" the doctor asked, whizzing back into the room. "How's the foot feelin', champ? Fully numb yet?"

"Uh-huh," I said, upset that he had come back.

"Good, good," he said, checking his handiwork with a newly gloved hand. (*They go through an awful lot of those gloves*, I remember thinking.) "I think we can begin," he said, this time to a nurse who had accompanied him into the room. Looking back to me, he said, "This time, you'll only feel some pressure, it's nothing to worry about. You doin' great."

Except the motherfucking anesthesia hadn't kicked in at all. The moment he pulled at one of the larger shards, a bolt of searing pain shot through my body. The shock made my leg spasm, which in turn caused the doctor to push the glass further into my flesh. I screamed.

That's when my mother lost it. She jumped at the doctor and began pounding on his chest. Tears of genuine worry streamed down her face as she yelled, "YOU'RE HURTING HIM! STOP HURTING MY SON!"

And that's where the memory stops. I assume she was eventually restrained, and the doctor was allowed to proceed; at some point, the glass got taken out of my foot.

It may seem strange how my happiest memory regarding my mother began with blood and pain and left scars (minor ones, as the doctor had promised), but in some ways that makes sense. It's almost poetic. As a mother, Constance never kissed my scrapes, scratches, bumps, or bruises to make them better, the way other people's mothers did. But I never expected her to. However, that afternoon in the hospital was as close as we ever got. It was the only time I felt compassion from my mother, like maybe she didn't hate me after all.

So how did I feel when Constance died? *Indifferent* isn't the right word. But neither is *emotional*. I don't know if I have yet come across a word

188 SEAN SCOTT HICKS

or phrase that fully encapsulates my feelings toward my mother being in the ground. I still struggle to define how I felt about her in general. I was hard on her in this book, I know that. But she was not a very nice woman (at least, to me). It's also my belief that children have the right to be critical of their parents; perhaps it is their duty to do so. A child should not only learn from their parents but strive to improve upon them. The only way to achieve this is to be critical—to observe, critique, learn, analyze, and ultimately implement what's learned.

However, she was not the monster I painted her out to be. She was a deeply flawed and disturbed individual who found comfort in the wrong place. Drugs. And she gave up everything for them: her body, her family, her life. She caused a lot of pain to a lot of people, but perhaps that was what she was put here to do. Not to cause pain, but to teach us about it. It just so happens that the only way to learn of it is to experience it. That can't be helped; that part is not her fault. For better or worse, I learned more from my mother than almost anyone I've ever met. It has taken me a long time to get to this point where I can truly say that I have forgiven Constance, my mother.

Anyway, that's about all I have to say on that.


*Getting back to the game of whist I was in the middle of . . .*

Through some sort of demented divinity, we won that match. My partner gave me his condolences and his half of the winnings. I told him to go fuck himself and gave it all back, all except the vodka.

Later that week in the chow hall, someone cut me in line, so I stabbed him in the stomach. It was the last time I'd ever be able to blame my fucked-up actions on my fucked-up mother. From there on out, it was all me.

# SIXTEEN

## SOUTH BOSTON SHOOT-OUT

They finally caught that sonofabitch Whitey Bulger on Wednesday, June 22, 2011. It was the top story on every news station: *Fugitive Boston Mobster Whitey Bulger Arrested in Santa Monica*. His mug shot was plastered on every television screen in New England, but it wasn't the same Uncle Jim that I remembered. The picture was of an old man, eighty-one-years tired. He was bald and had spots of discoloration from aging poorly in the sun. He had grown out a snowy-white beard. For over sixteen years, he had been on the run, twelve of which he'd spent on the FBI's Ten Most Wanted Fugitives list, second only to Osama bin Laden. Time had changed him. It was as if I were looking at a stranger.

The only thing that hadn't changed were his eyes. Cold and blue, they still contained the evil and malice I recognized. It was Uncle Jim all right. They had found him out west in California of all places, as far away from Boston as he could get. Two days later, the front page of the *Boston Globe* read: *Bulger Ordered Home*. Underneath the boldface title was the header *Justice, finally, for Boston*.

I winced at the header. There was no justice to be found here. How does passing judgment on inhumane crimes according to a legal system rooted in humanity and righteousness lead to justice? It doesn't make sense. Any systemic consequences simply cannot fit Whitey's heinous crimes. What the headline should have read was *Closure, finally, for Boston*. Before this, the unknown nature of Whitey's fate had left an air of uncertainty lingering in the minds and the streets of the city. Now at least we all knew where the bastard was.

I read the article. As it turns out, he wasn't even hiding anymore. Police officers had picked him up in broad daylight, acting on a credible tip from a neighbor, an Icelandic woman named Anna Björnsdóttir. It seemed to be a lackluster affair: he put up no resistance. When searching his rent-controlled apartment, they found $800,000 in cash, thirty firearms, fake identification documents, and his long-term girlfriend, Catherine Greig.

Authorities were shipping Whitey back home to Boston, the city he'd terrorized for decades, to be tried in our courts. He was facing forty-eight charges, nineteen of which were counts of murder. But the truth was he had left untold numbers of victims in his wake, a lot more than those directly involved in the counts he was now facing.

Unsurprisingly, two weeks later, on July 6, he pleaded not guilty to all of it. That spineless fuck wouldn't even own up to a fraction of the damage he had caused.

Staying true to his disloyal nature, the moment his feet touched New England soil, Whitey started talking to authorities. Nothing was off-limits, and little to none of it was credible—nothing pertaining to me at least . . . and he said a lot.

He knew the game was up, that he'd never see the outside of a prison cell again, and he probably figured he could trade his bullshit for a favorable sentence—if not for himself, then for his girlfriend. The delusional fuck was throwing everyone under the bus for the hell of it, fucking over as many people as he could. He was determined to be a goddamn rat to his dying breath.

My lawyers started sweating on my behalf, but I wasn't worried. There was nothing he could definitively tie me to because the evidence either never existed or was lost to the perils of time. *Let Whitey run his mouth about me, I don't give a fuck.*

The *Globe* ran Whitey's story on its front page for what seemed like a month, providing updates on any trial proceedings. If I am being honest, the news didn't matter much to me. After Whitey went on the run, and the subsequent downfall of the Winter Hill Gang, came the deaths of my other uncles, leaving me on my own. By the time of his capture, Whitey hadn't been around in over a decade, during which time I had made my own contacts and business opportunities and fortified my reputation. As far as I was concerned, the capture of some eighty-one-year-old relic of even worse times meant fuck all.

Since going underground, no single person, race, gang, mob, et cetera had assumed the level of power and territory in Boston that Whitey had obtained. Instead, opportunities were evenly spread among those strong enough to seize them. Having lost Quinny the previous year, my usual crew was smaller than it had been in a long time—he wasn't the type of person who could ever be replaced. And with a smaller crew, I was taking on smaller jobs—a few robberies here, a fraudulent check-cashing operation there—but there was no big scheme in the works.

Mostly, I stuck to honest, aboveboard construction work. When Hank passed, he left me H&S Custom Home Improvements, and I wasn't going to let this part of his legacy be buried with him. I always thought he left me the construction company because he felt a sense of guilt for my introduction to a life of crime, and that by leaving the company to me, I'd have a lifeline to grab hold of and leave that underworld behind should I choose to do so. In the meantime, the legit job helped pass the monotony of everyday life. Eventually something illegal would turn up. And, naturally, it did.

I got a tip from a lobster fisherman of a possible opportunity. Though I didn't have my hands directly in the commercial fishing business anymore, I still had my contacts and would meet with them time and again. The tip was actually a nonchalant comment the lobsterman made during a conversation we were having at a bar one afternoon. The guy offered to buy me a drink, which was completely unlike him; usually he was cheap and tight with his money, most of all with me. While the offer would make most people gracious, it made me suspicious.

The lobsterman was in a good mood, and he didn't take offense to my apprehension. Instead he explained that he was making good money at the docks. There was a new Chinese player in town that had started paying over market value for lobsters right off the boat, and better still, they paid in cash.

*How could they turn a profit if they were overpaying per pound? And they paid in cash?* It made no sense.

But sure enough, it was true. My contact had seen the buyer shell out thirty grand to a line of other lobster potters for what should have cost no more than twenty. When I asked him for the name of the company buying the catch, he said, "Seven Seas, Incorporated."

I was intrigued. So, later that week, an associate and I began staking out and following a few Seven Seas box trucks as they pulled out of a warehouse on the Southie coast and made deliveries. We noted how the drivers were always by themselves and without protection in the vehicles, making them easy targets. The process was always similar: when the driver arrived at their destination, they parked by the back door, hopped out of the cab, removed four or five boxes of lobsters from the back of the truck, and went inside.

Less than ten minutes later, they would reappear carrying a duffel bag (or analogous bag of equal capacity) with the strap slung across their body. *A few cases of lobster in exchange for a heavy bag of money?* Either the Seven Seas, Inc. was dealing in fucking pure-gold crustaceans, or there was something else in those boxes.

I don't claim to be a criminal genius, but it doesn't take a genius to realize something criminal was going on. Regardless of what it was, they carried large sums of cash on hand, and that was enough for me to know. I'd learn the rest later. For now, taking down one of their trucks would be a good place to start.

I started asking around for more information on Seven Seas, Inc. It's always a good idea to know who you're about to steal from. And surely somebody had to know who the fuck they were and what they were moving. Or so I thought. To my surprise, almost nobody even recognized the name. Only one person, David Ho, my contact in Chinatown, knew anything about them, and his info was vague at best. He said they were two brothers who came from San Francisco and pushed massive amounts of pure heroin through the lobster industry. He didn't know anything else, but at least now we knew that the bulk of their organization was on the other coast.

After ten days of watching the repetitive nature of the trucks, we felt comfortable enough to make a move. We were careful to stay a few car lengths behind as the truck took an off-ramp after a few miles of highway. The truck took a few more turns, then pulled into the parking lot of a Chinese restaurant. We parked across the street and watched. Waited. The delivery driver followed the same timeline he had in the past. Ten minutes later, we were in pursuit as he retraced his route back to the warehouse. We hit the truck on a back road.

The job took all of two minutes: my associate pulled the car in front of the truck and slowed down to a dead stop. I hopped out of the car, ran to the truck's cab, and pulled the driver out onto the ground. My associate restrained the driver while I went into the cab and retrieved the black duffel bag. While in there, I noticed a checkbook perched on the dashboard and scooped it into my pocket before leaving the truck. We jumped back into our car and sped away.

Back at my house, we counted the money—only a few grand shy of $200K. However, what looked more promising was the checkbook. They weren't personal checks linked to an individual's bank account—it was much better. In custom-printed font in the top right corner of the pad was the corporation's name, Seven Seas, Inc. As one might assume, the corporate account checkbook is essentially the holy grail for anyone who operates a check-cashing operation—which, as it just so happens, I had an associate who still did. The question now became, *How far could we reach into their pockets before being caught?*

The answer? Somewhere around $400,000, but they never caught me. I ran out of fucking checks.

Months went by without so much as a whisper of the name Seven Seas, Inc. I would have forgotten about them had it not been for a small group of concerned Southie parents. I got a knock on my door one day and was greeted by three sets of grieving eyes: two mothers and a father. I recognized them: hardworking blue-collar people from good, respectable families.

They were openly grieving on my doorstep. I invited them in and offered everyone a drink; the man accepted, the two mothers politely declined. The younger of the two women, who was about a decade older than me, asked if it was all right if she smoked inside. I didn't mind. The other woman sat in Hank's old chair and quietly sobbed. I still didn't know why they were there.

Finally, we all settled down into seats, and they filled me in on the purpose of their visit. Their children had overdosed the past week. They knew of others too—names of other dead children, of more grieving parents. Names of good kids who started down the wrong path but died before they got a second chance to turn their lives around. Half a dozen names spit into the air: some teenagers, some older, but all at the age where mistakes are meant to be made. The time when you discover life's a royal bitch who'll either destroy you or teach you something of value. Whether I knew the person directly or through a relative, they were familiar. Southie was like that in those days. That was part of what made it so special: everyone had each other's back. Which is why these folks were in my living room, crying onto my carpet. They needed my help and didn't know who else to turn to.

They had done their due diligence, collecting evidence that linked their children's deaths to the others. Heroin. For the past few months, dealers around the area had been receiving increasingly stronger product. Less cut, purer . . . deadlier.

It is important to note that cutting agents back then were fundamentally different than they are today, at the time I'm writing this book. Back then, as product trickled down the supply chain, it got diluted by a benign compound designed to pad the weight and increase profit. But essentially you would still know what was getting you high. Heroin was still heroin and coke was still coke; there may have just been a little extra "filler." Nothing necessarily harmful. Certainly, nothing *intentionally* harmful. This epidemic of new dealers lacing their product with harmful shit hadn't caught on yet—or at least, it was uncommon.

In their quest for answers, my name had come up. Someone had suggested that I might be able to help. My visitors weren't looking for retaliation or revenge for their loss; they were looking for help preventing anything like this from happening again to another family. After a half hour of dialogue, the parents rested their case in my hands and left. They had done all they could do, and now I would do the same.

Following a hunch, I asked around some of my less-than-scrupulous contacts. The uncut heroin was coming from Seven Seas, Inc. However, my brief inquest uncovered more information than I had expected: a big shipment of heroin was being delivered later that month. It would quickly be turned around and sold direct-to-customer out of the warehouse, meaning the drugs and a large sum of cash would be in the same location at the same time.

The kicker was that I got the information from the guy who sold the drugs wholesale to Seven Seas, Inc. If I retrieved the product, he agreed to buy it all back from me—at a heavily discounted price. He'd resell it elsewhere, double his money, and I'd get to keep whatever I took down at the warehouse plus a guarantee to off-load the drugs at $200,000.

I needed to get a good look inside the warehouse before the shipment arrived. Going in blind would be stupid. I didn't know the extent of the operation's security measures. *Cameras? Armed guards?*

Conveniently, I now had a reason to enter: to have a talk and get them to stop selling such strong shit. I arrived outside around noon. It was a large white building with no identifying features. There was no retail storefront and no sign to draw in customers. Three generic metal numbers were displayed above a windowless front entrance. Fifty feet to the left were two bay doors; it was a sunny day, and one of the garage doors had been cracked open to let in some fresh air. A pungent sea odor wafted out of the gap and onto the street, letting me know I was in the right place.

Not wanting to give away my presence right away by entering the front, I ducked under the garage door and found myself inside and alone—the employees must have been taking their lunch break. The warehouse was large and divided into three sections. To the far right were basic clerical rooms and bathrooms, presumably a lounge area to eat in as well. A galvanized staircase had been installed, leading up to a second level, where a single office was built.

The wall of the office facing the work floor was primarily occupied by a large reflective mirror: a one-way window. There was an overwhelming "Big Brother is always watching" aura about it. In the middle of the room were four long rows of blue open-top holding tanks rigged to a network of pipes and hoses, and to my left were stainless steel tables equipped with stacks of shipping boxes. Between the shipping tables, six-by-six containers stood waist-high and were filled with a mountain of damp seaweed used to package the lobsters for delivery.

Looking around, what caught my attention was how the live holding tanks were empty: no water, no lobsters. But before I could investigate, a small Asian man wearing a hairnet ran out of the bathroom and began yelling his head off at me in Mandarin (if I had to take a guess), accompanied by frantic hand gestures pointing toward the exit. Two more Asian men popped out of the lounge door and mirrored the first in confusion and agitation.

Conceding to the obvious language barrier, I decided not to waste my time and muscled my way through them to the staircase. As I reached the bottom step, the office door above flew open, and a man in a clean suit emerged. The clamor must have alerted him.

He began shouting down at me, showering me in the word *fuck*. He spoke English peppered with more profanity than I do, creatively using expletives in ways I hadn't thought of. But essentially, he wanted to know who I was and what I was doing there. Fair questions.

I gave him my name and told him that I knew what went on in this place and that we needed to have a talk in his office. The request resonated. He nodded curtly, then turned to his employees, held up the palm of his hand in a commanding gesture, and ordered them back to work (or something to that effect).

"Let's go," he said to me and walked back into his office. As he turned his back to me, I noticed a lump in his suit coat: the imprint of a handgun grip sticking out of his belt.

A second man was in the Seven Seas, Inc. office, a clone of the first. Identical twins. Equal in appearance and vocabulary. One of the men instructed me to take a seat, but I refused. I preferred to stand. Sitting put me at a further disadvantage against the man with the gun. I could only assume the brother was armed too.

They appeared to be the only security for the building. I hadn't seen any other guards. No cameras either. And the two of them certainly appeared vain enough to believe they could provide all the protection the operation needed.

When we got down to it, our conversation was anything but friendly. They knew of me and made it clear that was the only reason I was standing where I was. It was a courtesy out of professional respect, but it would be the last time I was allowed in. If I showed up again, they would put a bullet in me. That was a promise.

When I finally got the chance to speak, I laid out the situation for them. *Cut your shit, it's killing people. End of fucking story.* They were new in town so I'd let it slide this time, but I'd check back in a month, and if they didn't change anything, I would put a bullet in each of them. Between the goddamn eyes. *That was a fucking promise.*

I didn't wait for an invitation to leave, I took it upon myself and walked out, using the front door this time.

The Seven Seas shipment was coming in two weeks. Time to plan. I put together a strategy and three-person team: Mikey, Casino, and me. Me and Mikey would go in. One of us would grab the money; the other would grab the heroin, whoever was closest in the moment—we couldn't plan out everything. Casino would wait on the curb and keep the van running. We'd be in and out in under two minutes, three minutes max.

I don't like using guns, but they were necessary for this. I had a .40-caliber, striker-fired Smith & Wesson—a compact handgun. Mikey's gun of choice was a pump-action, pistol-grip shotgun, the sight of which usually garners compliance to the demands of its holder. Casino got us a van, and we were good to go.

As a precaution, I put extra loaded clips in my pocket on the day when the shipment arrived. Casino picked me up from my house. Mikey was already sitting in the car. I got in and shut the sliding door.

Mikey turned around in the front seat and said, "Take your pick," as he held up two Halloween masks. Wearing a mask was his idea, but it wasn't a bad one. I got away with robbing Seven Seas, Inc. once and had not hidden my identity, but now they knew my face; it would be like waving a red cape in front of a bull, except the bull was two arrogant Asian motherfuckers with guns.

My two options for disguise were a silicone Michael Myers mask or a simple Jason hockey mask. I grabbed the bloody goalie mask; it had better visibility and wouldn't be as hot—not that it mattered, but the cheap Michael Myers mask didn't look right. It was closer to a pale Chucky doll with alopecia.

I got a call from my contact; he just delivered the sixty kilos of high-grade heroin to the Seven Seas twins. We were parked a block down from the warehouse on the opposite side of the street, waiting and watching for the brothers to return and for the buyer to arrive.

The brothers pulled up to the front ten minutes after the call. Not long after, a blacked-out Cadillac Escalade drove up and parked. Two men got out.

*One would have been better, but two were still manageable.* I checked the time. They would take no more than three minutes from the time they entered to get down to business. The deal wouldn't take more than an additional five, giving us just a small window of opportunity. I checked the clock again: the pleasantries would be over by now. *Time to go.*

I looked to Casino and nodded. Mikey double-checked his shotgun was loaded and pulled his mask down. I flipped the safety off on my pistol and slipped on my disguise as Casino drove us over.

I had the sliding door wide open and hopped out of the van before it stopped moving. Mikey followed in my shadow. We were in sync.

He knew what he was doing without me having to tell him, and I liked working with him because of it.

We went in the front door. The hallway was empty. Nobody was in any of the rooms either. We passed a few more doors and stopped at the one with a placard that read "Floor."

I could hear muffled chatter from the other side. I grabbed the handle with my left hand, pistol drawn in my right. I took a deep breath and held it, praying it wouldn't be my last. My heart beat twice, and I ripped open the door. Mikey rushed in like a madman, just as we had done on more than one occasion.

We were on them before they knew what was happening. The four men had been standing around one of the packaging tables; a bag full of money and two bags filled with heroin bricks sat in the middle.

I got up behind one of the brothers, keeping my gun pressed into the center of his back; I didn't trust him for a second. Mikey had his shotgun held up in front of him, fully extended, and was rapidly shifting it from target to target—not like that bullshit you see in movies where it's held down by the waist.

"*Nobody fuckin' move!*" Mikey shouted into the now silent warehouse. We had decided in advance he would do the talking so the brothers couldn't identify my voice.

*Bang!* The first shot went off, flying six inches over my left shoulder—an explosion of cataclysmic volume, amplified by the tall ceilings.

*No time to think.* I grabbed the brother around the neck and used him as a shield while dumping clips in the general direction of anything that moved. A choir of lead echoed in response.

There was a grey cloud of cordite smoke in the air stinging my eyes and burning my nostrils. I felt the thud of bullets enter my shield as my hostage's twin brother shot at us without regard. I dropped him and dove behind cover, slamming a fresh clip into my gun.

I looked over at Mikey. He got hit twice, real quick: one in the arm, the other in the chest. It didn't stop him, though. He reloaded and stood up, letting off another blast.

I left cover in unison with my partner and let my remaining ten bullets provide the cover we needed to snatch the three bags and run for our fucking lives.

*Twenty-one seconds. Fifty-seven rounds.*

"*What the fuck?*" Casino yelled from the van through an open window at the sight of us as we fled from the building.

"Get Mikey fuckin' outta here. Take him and go. *Go!*" I yelled back, pointing off to the distance with my empty gun.

"What about you?"

"*Just go!*"

Mikey jumped into the van, and Casino drove off.

I ran up the block and turned a corner.

A fraction of a second later, a blacked-out Lincoln came screeching up onto the sidewalk. I threw the bags into the back seat and dove in on top of them. The car jerked into motion and sped off in the opposite direction.

Okay, so I lied: it had been a four-man team.

The worst part about getting shot in the ass isn't the getting shot part. The worst part is when your friend is taking the bullet out in your kitchen with needle-nose pliers. That part hurts like a motherfucker. But at least I got away.

Mikey and Casino didn't. The cops got to them, quick. Pulled them over before they got home. Mikey got eighteen months, and Casino got "time served." They never gave me up.

However, law enforcement knew of a third person's involvement. They also knew Mikey and Casino were a part of my usual crew, so it didn't take a genius to connect the dots. A warrant was issued for my arrest.

I was already out of town, so I stayed out for as long as I could. I had to come back at some point, obviously. What I didn't account for was that someone would tip the cops off when I returned. I still haven't figured out who did it either.

Within an hour of me getting back into town, the staties were outside. Half a dozen cars. I was inside my house having a drink when my phone rang; it was the captain. He wanted me to come out the front door with my hands up. *Don't resist.* I knew they had me. *I wasn't going to give them any trouble . . . just let me finish my drink, I'll be out in a minute.* The captain obliged.

I went to my closet and grabbed a paper bag I kept stashed in the ceiling tile. It had $9,999 in it. For emergencies. I'd put it in my commissary account. Anything under $10,000 they can't seize.

It had taken a fair amount of practice, but by this point, I was quite good at going to jail.

I slipped on a good pair of shoes, laced them tight, and went outside to face the music.

A lot of shit came to light during the trial, much more than the prosecution wanted. But once the genie was out of the bottle, he was raising a lot of questions. Nobody was safe. The details that came out were equally damning to both sides of the room. First off, the whole thing was caught on camera. We watched it all: two men in cheap Halloween masks, the money, the drugs, the shoot-out . . . everything.

The tape was twenty-one seconds long, but where did it come from? A gypsy cam. A covert recording device, except this one hadn't been installed by Seven Seas, Inc. No one owned up to who put it in or where it had come from.

The problems with the prosecution's case were only just beginning. A question regarding the police response time arose next. How had they been fast enough to catch the getaway vehicle immediately after the incident?

The police officer's testimony came under heavy scrutiny. According to him, he was off duty and happened to be walking by close enough to hear gunfire. A squad car was in the vicinity too. Very lucky, he said.

Although, why was he walking by? Someone asked it, cutting the legs out from under the officer. He stammered for a second, then said he was getting takeout from his favorite restaurant.

Judge Ball stepped in with a few questions of his own. "Are you sure about that? I've been going to that restaurant for over twenty years and never once have they served takeout. They're also closed at the time you claimed to be walking by. Is there something I am missing here, Officer?"

The truth was on the hook. Judge Ball just didn't know what he was reeling in.

To clear up any confusion you might have had in court that day, all you had to do was to look into the gallery . . . see who was there.

*Ah!* The faces of several DEA agents. Now, why would they be in the room? What did my case matter to them? Put them on the stand, ask them! Screw that cop, he doesn't know anything. He's an idiot, a patsy. Those DEA agents, they're the ones you want to talk to. They could enlighten us on the true events of that day in the lobster warehouse. But they weren't going to say shit. They'd rather hold their tongues and watch the squirming cop squirm.

If there was an honest one in the bunch (which there wasn't), I think I know what they would say. So let me, with a degree of accuracy, speak on their behalf.

This is my best interpretation supported by the evidence presented by the prosecution.

The agents would say, I believe, that I had found myself in the midst of an undercover operation. Not only that, but I completely ruined it. I had fucked up months, if not years, of their hard work. *Oops.* It explained the camera, though. If it was installed without a warrant, no one would come forth and claim that they were the ones who had put it there.

It also explained why a cop was the only one to come forward about being on the scene. No one else had any reason to be there, but at least a local cop might be able to explain his presence—that is, if he wasn't a bumbling idiot.

I understood their silence too. They were protecting their own: their informant, their inside man. It made perfect sense, but it didn't get them their $660,000 back—if it was theirs to begin with. That was gone, along with the sixty kilos of heroin. All in the hands of a masked man. Unfortunately for the prosecution, the surveillance tape was deemed inadmissible. The missing money and drugs couldn't be pinned on me.

But even without the tape, some evidence was allowed, and some charges stuck: two counts of attempted murder with a firearm.

The whole case had pissed off Judge Ball. You could see it on his face. Uncovering the truth has its drawbacks at times, and this was one of them. Laws had been broken on both sides of the aisle, and he wanted to rid himself of the whole thing. When it came to my sentencing—an unavoidable conclusion to the trial—he went easy. He reminded me that I already owed three years for a parole violation. But would I take five years total, serving the sentences concurrently?

Yes. Yes, I would.

Case closed.

# SEVENTEEN
## ROCK BOTTOM

Finding honest work is one of the most difficult hurdles to overcome as an ex-convict. In my opinion, it is the main reason a convict reoffends. Recidivism rates would benefit greatly from increased funding for programs that employ ex-convicts, or at the very least, allocating more of the budget for training programs that increase the hireability and desirability of us ex-convicts. If an ex-con isn't a self-employed entrepreneur, then their résumé isn't worth the paper it's printed on. To even have a chance at being hired, you have to call in every favor you've got, and even then, a job is not guaranteed.

I was lucky when I got out of prison in 2016 and an old foreman of mine, Fat Paulie, hired me right away. I had to accept a lower wage than I was used to, but few things pay as well as crime. Don't get me wrong, I wasn't complaining at the pay cut. For the time being, I wanted to go straight, be on my best behavior—or at the very least, avoid prison.

It was a general contractor gig as a foreman. I still owned H&S Custom Home Improvements, but I didn't have the up-front capital necessary to take on my own jobs, let alone pay employees. Fat Paulie was throwing me a bone, and I was grateful.

He set me up with a crew of first-timers up in Burlington, Mass. Mostly young kids, virgins in more ways than one, but a couple of extra

THE DEVIL TO PAY

hands to expedite the build never hurts. I was twenty years their elder, minimum. When I got there, hardly anything had been done. I forget the specifics of the project, but it was something on the exterior of a big house, three or four stories up. A young kid, eighteen, had spent the previous week assembling the scaffolding against the house, so when I arrived, we could get to work.

I always arrived at jobsites in the early morning when the dew has yet to be burned away and the cool air lingers from the previous night. I didn't work in the darkness, but I commuted in it. This way, the work-day could end earlier and make way for the drinking to begin. I never drank on the job; power tools and liquor don't mix too well.

I was the first one on-site and started to gather the tools from my truck bed that I'd need for the job. Five minutes later, the young kid pulled up in an old Chevy. It was a beater with a rusted chassis and a cracked windshield. The kid looked no better: dirty clothes, unwashed hair, sunken cheeks.

He introduced himself as Barry and said that the other guys always showed up an hour later; he heard a new foreman was taking over and wanted to make a good first impression. I made a mental note to talk to the others later about getting to work on time.

I asked Barry if he had his own tools; he didn't. He could borrow mine. I had an extra toolbelt in my truck. I told him to go grab it and bring an extra box of nails. While he was suiting up, I climbed a ladder to the top of the scaffolding and started scoping out the job. That's when shit went sideways.

Never having assembled scaffolding before, Barry had built it on top of soft, muddy soil. The whole structure shifted and collapsed under my weight. I plummeted thirty feet and blacked out.

*Shit . . . what the fuck was this?* I woke up with a tube shoved up my cock—in the hospital, if you didn't catch that information from my "tube" comment.

I was told by the doctor that I had landed on my back and decimated my spine. "Severe damage to intervertebral discs and to the vertebrae themselves," is what he said. It sounded like bullshit to me because I didn't feel a goddamn thing . . . not even the tube. Must be the morphine drip. He left the room without a word. *What the fuck was going on?*

The doc returned ten minutes later and clarified that I was at Rhode Island Hospital. They were a Level I Trauma Center and well equipped for my operation, having the best surgeons on staff.

*Operation?* Before I could question anything, I was transferred to a gurney and wheeled down to an operating room. No time to lose. Four people were waiting in blue scrubs. A needle was pushed into my arm, and I slid into a vast unconsciousness.

When I woke up, there was a dull, hollow numbness all over my body. A nurse noticed I was awake and paged a doctor, who arrived seconds later. I recognized him from before. Tall, dark-skinned, handsome, with peppery-grey hair. Midfifties, if I had to guess. Before he spoke, the doc consulted a clipboard, lifted my bed covers, poked and prodded around for a minute, and finally took a deep, serious breath. Then he gave me the bad news: I might not walk again.

*Excuse me. What the fuck did you just say?*

It was only a possibility, he tried to assure me. He went on a tangent of smart but meaningless medical lingo and ended his rant by saying he remained optimistic, so I should too. It was going to take a lot of time, a tremendous amount of rehab, and a blessing from God.

I was terrified because of how fucked that meant I was. I could do the time and complete the rehab, but the God thing . . . *Fuck.*

I was kept at the hospital under observation until the doc signed off for my transfer to a rehab clinic. And by "under observation," they meant under lock and key. In all my experience, I have never met a person stricter than a good hospital nurse. It's like they've been trained by the gestapo. They were completely incorruptible too. All my usual tactics, which worked wonders in prison, didn't so much as get me a smile here. The justice system could learn a thing or two from them.

I was immobile, and my nurse refused to let me smoke. And she wouldn't get me alcohol, which was even worse. I had to go through withdrawals on top of everything else. But no matter how much money I offered her, she wouldn't budge. The night nurse was a little friendlier, but she too remained steadfast to the militant nurses' code.

A few days later, a stranger visited. She walked into my room without knocking, a young girl no older than twenty.

"You know who I am?" she asked in a Boston accent. She was rude, but in a familiar way; I couldn't help but play along. I looked at her closely. She was skinny and short, and what was exposed of her body was covered in tattoos. Her face was beautiful, like a young Drew Barrymore with long brown hair. She held a baby on her hip, swaddled in a blue blanket.

I smiled, recognizing her: Asia, my daughter. I had not seen her in over fifteen years.

"You must be my daughter," I said. *What was I supposed to say?* I had no fucking clue. "Now that you're all grown up, you look just like your mother."

Asia was clearly nervous, unsure of her next move. I assume she had prepared a long speech detailing her resentment toward me, but instead she just said, "You look like shit."

*Yup, she was definitely my daughter.*

"I fell," I said, sticking to the facts. I didn't want to scare her off with an apology or inundate her with unearned fatherly bullshit.

"Thought you were dead," she said.

"They were able to fix me up, I gotta relearn to—"

"No," she interrupted. "Years ago. You were supposed to be dead." She went on to tell me how her adoptive parents had told her that I had died when she was an infant and that she had just found out that I was alive and she had made her adoptive mother bring her to the hospital. We talked awkwardly for a few minutes until she broke the ice.

"You're a grandfather, by the way," Asia said, finally addressing the tiny human on her hip. She paused for a second, then conceded and brought my granddaughter closer. To my surprise Asia was kind enough to allow me to hold her.

"And who do we have here?" I said, accepting the innocent bundle into my hands.

"This is Evelyn," Asia said. "Evelyn, this is . . . Sean," she said, introducing me reservedly.

"Hi, Evelyn," I said. The infant turned and pressed her puffy face into my shoulder. Moments later, a soft snoring emanated from my armpit.

Asia and I talked as the baby slept. The hours went by in seconds—for me anyway.

Our conversation was cut short by the nurse kicking her out. Visiting hours were over.

"Time to go, Evelyn," Asia said, scooping my granddaughter off my chest.

More than anything, I wanted her to stay. I wanted time to apologize, to make up for everything. I wanted to tell her how much I loved her and wanted her in my life. *Just give me one more minute with my daughter, goddamnit, please, I beg you!*

Instead, as Asia was almost out the door, I managed to say, "Thank you"—they were the only meaningful words I could get out. She stopped and turned back around to look at me.

"Yeah," she said, hurrying out before either one of us had the chance to get emotional.

"That your daughter?" the nurse said after the sound of Asia's footsteps faded away down the hall.

"Yeah," I said.

"She's beautiful."

"Yeah," I said again.

Walking is not "just like riding a bike" in the sense that it's the type of skill you are able to quickly pick back up. Instead, relearning the fundamentals of walking is more like pulling your own teeth out with a fork.

The process turned out exactly like the doctor had said it would be: long and painful. I was moved from the hospital to a decent rehab clinic in Worcester, Massachusetts, to finish the recovery program. The building was old and smelled like geriatric decay, but I liked it better than a hospital. Hospitals are depressing; death haunts their bleak halls. Physical rehab centers are better because, for the most part, nobody dies in them. That, and the staff is a touch more lenient.

While I was there, I met a woman named Jasmine Lee Sully. She stopped by my room one afternoon on her way out after visiting with her uncle. She wanted to say thank you, having learned from the staff that I'd befriended her uncle and would take my wheelchair to his room and keep him company a couple hours each day. On occasion I had food brought in from the street, and we would have lunch together.

Her uncle was in worse shape than me. He had the most severe case of diabetes I had ever seen, a hundred times worse than my pops. The disease didn't stop at taking away his eyesight completely; it went after his limbs too. He'd lost two digits on one hand and three on the other. The necrosis was more drastic in his legs, what was left of them. His left leg was amputated from the knee down. Bad luck. I was grateful that I didn't have to see Hank go through the same shit; it was pretty awful to watch.

Regardless, Jasmine made it a point to take time twice a week to visit with her uncle. And after our first introduction, she also made a habit to come to my room when he dozed off—which was often early into her biweekly visits.

She and I would talk for hours until it was time for her to go.

Jasmine was a breath of fresh air. She was the only person I had seen in the past few months who was less than a century old, and if I was forced to have another conversation about AARP benefits, bingo, Judge Judy, or green Jell-O, I was going to go fucking postal. We got along well. Our conversations flowed effortlessly. She was smart and friendly and had a good sense of humor. And she had a good job too: a therapist. *Dr. Jasmine Lee Sully.* What I told her of my past didn't seem to bother her either.

It took six months of extensive rehab and many sleepless nights, lying in excruciating pain, before it was finally over. When all was said and done, I was able to walk again, just in time to walk down the aisle and marry Jasmine—or rather, stand before a justice of the peace.

They gave me a cane and advised me to exercise a minimum of sixty minutes daily. I promised my physical therapist that I'd walk to the package store at least once a day instead of driving. I was glad to be done with the rehab. The one thing I learned from the whole ordeal was that the freedom of mobility should never be underappreciated.

But recovering the ability to walk led me down a path to the worst state of health I had ever been in. I healed one ailment while another one worsened. I was drinking heavier than ever before.

By the end of the year, I put on forty-five pounds from the booze alone. I was a middle-aged, overweight, mentally fucked-up former mobster who could barely walk and couldn't work. I didn't know what else to do other than to dive deeper into the bottle. Maybe I was afraid for the old saying "you can't teach an old dog new tricks" to have some merit. What else was there for me besides drinking? Fuck if I know. So, I drank. Bottle after bottle. Day in and day out. Morning to night. *Another bottle?* Yes, please. *One more?* Fuck it, make it two. *What was the difference?* There was nothing out there for me anymore . . . *another fucking bottle . . .*

Everything went black, peace at last.

The coma lasted three days. Jasmine had found me seizing violently on the kitchen floor and called an ambulance. The seizures didn't stop. All my organs began shutting down, and my body wasn't responding to any medication, so I was put into a medically induced coma. When the brain swelling was under control, I was slowly brought out of the coma and thrown back into my shitty existence.

I woke up furious, like when a dope fiend gets hit with Narcan: *you motherfuckers!*

I was forced to have a psychological evaluation to determine if my drinking was a suicide attempt, to see if I was at risk of harming myself or others. The psych eval was inconclusive, and I was allowed to leave. However, the shrink mentioned how some patients who experience bouts of severe depression and feelings of emptiness find direction and purpose in the companionship of a pet. The reliance of a pet on its human caretaker can have a therapeutic effect or some bullshit like that.

I told Jasmine about it, and we adopted a white pit bull mutt named Dallas. The dog and I did everything together, and he followed me wherever I went. He slept next to me in bed, sat with me on the couch watching Sunday football, and liked to lick my feet when I sat at the kitchen table for meals.

I thought my coma was the lowest I could go—what I believed to be my rock bottom. But I was wrong. Just as I was getting my footing back with the help of Dallas, the floor dropped out from under me, and I kept falling. There was still plenty of room left to descend.

I began spiraling out of control a year later when Dallas was killed.

I don't know who did it, but eyewitnesses saw Dallas being thrown out of a moving car on the highway and being hit by an oncoming vehicle. *Sick motherfuckers.* Whoever it was had staked out my house and broke in minutes after Jasmine and I had gone out to dinner.

We were gone less than two hours. When we returned, our place had been turned over. Nothing but the dog was missing. When I learned of what had happened to him, I was devastated. I loved that dog. Whatever love and affection I had left died with him.

Jasmine and my marriage soured after that. I started to pull away. The relationship felt empty because that's how I was inside. I crawled back into the bottle. Now my drinking became more than a problem; it was dangerous. The liquor was no longer shutting out the bad thoughts; it was ushering them in, twisting and amplifying the torture. Like a bellicose activist for anarchy, the voice in my head refused to be silenced.

And I began listening to what it had to say.

It was a Wednesday around this time when I got a phone call from another one of my attorneys, Kevin Salvaggio.

There was urgency in his voice. "Please tell me you haven't had any fuckin' contact with Freddy, no fuckin' phone calls, letters . . . no fucking *nothin'*," he said. He was referring to Fotios Geas—Freddy. Freddy was a hitman for the Genovese family—one of the Five Families of the American Mafia out of New York City. We had met somewhere along the way a decade ago. We hadn't talked in a while, but I knew he was locked up somewhere in West Virginia.

"Nah, haven't talked to him. Why, what's goin' on? He all right?"

"There's a rumor goin' around that Freddy killed Whitey in his cell this morning. The story's all over the news. It doesn't look like they got Freddy's name yet, though. I was just calling to make sure you didn't have anything to do with it . . . Neither of us wants to deal with that fucking headache in court, am I right?" he said, relaxing into his usual, jovial tone. "But how's everything else going? I mean, I haven't heard from you in a while. Staying out of trouble?"

"Yeah. Look, Kev, I can't talk right now. I gotta go."

"All right, give me a—"

I hung up before he finished. I had to see it for myself. When Freddy Geas gets involved, you call the mortician, not a doctor. He hates rats as much as I do.

I grabbed the TV remote and turned on the news. Kevin was right; Jim's name dominated every headline across the country.

"WHITEY" BULGER KILLED IN PRISON.

I was surprised that he'd survived this long, eight years since his capture. Considering half of the inmate population wanted him dead, I would have thought he'd have been taken out sooner. It wasn't for lack of trying, though. This wasn't the first attempt on his life. Two years back, someone almost got to Whitey before Freddy did. The old bastard was stabbed in the neck, but the shank sent him to the infirmary for a month instead of the grave.

Jim's problems spanned more than just a few guys inside prison wanting him dead; he had made countless enemies outside the walls too. And it was the ones on the outside who were more dangerous. They were the people Whitey could fuck over if he said the wrong thing—assuming anyone would listen. Unfortunately for Jim, those were the same people who were powerful enough to get to him first. Seeing how Whitey was in for two terms of life imprisonment plus five years, he was in no position to exploit whatever leverage he might've thought he had.

Ultimately, it required a collaboration between enemies on both sides of the wall.* Questionable transfer papers took Bulger out of Coleman II—a prison in Florida known for being a safe haven for many high-profile members of organized crime and police informants—and dropped him into the general population of the United States Penitentiary Hazleton, in West Virginia.

USP Hazleton was a goddamn war zone. The penitentiary was experiencing a severe staffing shortage, a brutal reality easily observed in two separate inmate homicides in the previous forty days. Whitey was number three.

There were more red flags with that transfer order than in the Imperial City of Beijing, China. First off, the order lacked clear and concise reasoning behind knowingly moving a high-profile rat into the general population of one of the most violent prisons in America. Reports indicate that Whitey was cleared for transfer because of a recently lowered "care level" requirement—meaning that he had completed medical treatment, despite suffering from frequent chest pains, high blood pressure, aortic stenosis, prostate and bladder problems, and confinement to a wheelchair. When asked directly, the Bureau of Prisons contradicted the physical evidence and stated Whitey had been moved because he had made a direct threat on a staff member. Furthermore, there is evidence that an entire cellblock at Hazelton, including the three assailants who killed him, received information of Jim's impending transfer five hours before his arrival.

The Federal Bureau of Investigation declined to comment when asked if they had any involvement in Jim's transfer—or should I say, *Jim's execution.*

It is unclear who initiated Whitey's transfer request and if anyone influenced the destination it stipulated, but somehow it went through. At 8:30 p.m. on October 29, 2018, Whitey rolled his wheelchair into USP Hazelton.

At 8:20 a.m. the following morning, he was found bludgeoned to death. Three inmates had entered Jim's cell, armed with a shank and a

---

* Despite explaining all known evidence and accounting for the strange "coincidences," this statement is technically unproven and only my theory.

heavy padlock dropped into the toe-cup of a tube sock. The lock-in-a-sock was responsible for the blunt force trauma, the ultimate cause of Jim's death. But the shank was used to gouge out his eyes, nearly cut his tongue out, and slash his flesh. The slaughter took only seven minutes, a swift and thorough job by professionals with nothing to lose.

It took a while for reporters to catch up and learn the names of the assailants—Fotios Geas, Paul J. DeCologero, and Sean McKinnon—but the three men were eventually named and indicted four years later.

Hearing the news about Whitey bothered me. Not because he was gone—*fuck no, good riddance*—but rather, I was upset thinking of how I was unlucky enough to have known him and, in some ways, been molded by him. I'd venture to say that he was a worse influence on me than my mother. Over the years, I had come to despise the constant reminders of his existence from the excessive media exposure.

Even though Whitey was dead and gone, nothing changed. I was still spiraling downward, still drinking to die. It was only a matter of time before I succeeded in killing myself . . . or worse.

And it didn't take long at all. In November 2019, I hit rock fucking bottom and pled guilty with no contest.

What else could I do? More than thirty eyewitnesses saw everything. There is an upper limit to legal corruptibility, and I would venture to say that thirty corroborating eyewitness accounts is far over the threshold. No argument I could present would hold under the weight of such crushing evidence. But I didn't care. This time was different. This time I had gone too far. *This time*, I had hurt innocent people.

I was at the pub with my wife and some friends. Gregg, Adam, Jasmine, and me. I was shit-faced. Wasted. The usual. We were sitting at the table furthest from the door. The other tables were full, and a handful of barstools were occupied. It was loud in there, with each group talking over one another.

I was annoyed; I preferred drinking in silence and alone. And it was taking an eternity to get another drink.

I looked around for the waitress to flag her down so I could preemptively order a new round. I spotted her by the front. She was cleaning off a table for a small group of customers who had just walked in. When she was finished removing dishes and cups and wiping down the tabletop, the group took their seats.

Two of them had their backs to me; the other was facing my direction. I watched as menus were passed around. For whatever reason, I was fixated on the man who faced me. Something seemed familiar. It took a moment for my eyes to adjust, but when they did, I recognized the man instantly: Miguel. He'd worked a few construction jobs for me.

He was also the goddamn fucking maggot that had raped his niece— an innocent twelve-year-old girl—so violently that they had to remove her uterus. The family never pressed charges, claiming they were protecting the girl from being further traumatized at a trial. But I knew the truth: Miguel had paid off the parents and sent the girl away to live with her aunt in Puerto Rico so she couldn't testify.

What he didn't realize was that sort of thing doesn't just go away: not here, not with me. In my inebriated mind, Miguel was a rabid dog that needed to be put down.

There was no stopping what was about to happen, but unfortunately, four or five people tried to. What happens when an unstoppable force meets a *movable* object? It wasn't good. Among a frenzy of lacerations and contusions, Jasmine got hit with a glass candleholder, Gregg lost an eye, and Adam lost a few teeth.

But I didn't stop there.

When I got to Miguel, I stomped his testicles so violently that he went on to lose both of them, and his ability to walk.

Finally, the dust settled. The damage was done. It wasn't supposed to happen that way, but I was drunk, and people got in the way. That isn't much of a defense in the courtroom or much of an excuse in general, but at least now that paraplegic eunuch can't molest another child.

The trial was nothing more than a formality, an unnecessary waste of time. By the time the gavel struck, we hadn't learned anything new. I was guilty. The judge gave me five years. It was prearranged to have me thrown in the hole twenty-three hours a day to protect the other inmates; they thought I would incite violence. And in all likelihood, they weren't wrong. I was at the lowest point of my life, incapable of control.

Adding to the rubble, the whole thing proved to be the last straw for Jasmine. She left, escaping while she still could. Divorce papers were sent to my lawyer.

I didn't care about her leaving because I had given up caring about anything . . .

There have been a few moments where I can pinpoint exactly when the projection of my life took a hairpin turn in the right direction. One of those moments occurred on my second day in the hole when I ran into Walter Rafferty, or rather, when he came to visit.

I knew Walter from his past life as a bookie. I had never dealt with him directly back then, but he had a reputation for being careful and fair with whomever he took on as a customer. He was smart enough to only take bets from people who could afford to pay up, but he wasn't entirely averse to the darker requirements of the job should they arise.

But Walter had left all that behind a long time ago. He was a rein-vented man that day he came to visit me. He had found a new purpose in life as the assistant director of substance abuse treatment, helping hundreds of people find their way out of the darkness.

The first words out of his mouth to me were: "You're a fucking mess. I mean . . . look at you, Sean, you're about to explode." *Hadn't I already?*

Coming from anyone else, those words wouldn't have meaning, but I respected Walter. Having been a former criminal, he understood some of what I had been through. So, when he called me out on my bullshit, I listened.

Walter's visits became daily occurrences. We talked a lot about the past—Walter had known my pops and some of my uncles—but our conversations always found their way to the topic of sobriety. My so-briety. He told me his story and said that he'd read my file; there were similarities.

I tried explaining how I was different. I used alcohol as a numbing agent; it was never my main problem.

"Cut the shit, Sean. You're not foolin' anyone besides yourself. And we both know how this ends if you don't get your head outta your own ass. You not makin' it another six months like this. It don't matter if you're in prison or not, someone'll fuckin' kill ya the way you've been acting . . . I mean, if ya don't kill yaself first . . . Look, I get it, all right? I've been there. I know it's not easy to look at yourself in the mirror and live with the face you see. But the alcohol isn't doing you no good. You can't just drink the past away. It don't work like that."

Walter gave me a similar message every day for two weeks, at which time he put his foot down. "All right, Sean. You gotta make a decision. You either accept my help today, and together we give you one last shot to make a serious change, or . . . you don't. And I get to use you as an example for the next guy to show him what wasted potential looks like: a fuckup who never made anything of himself."

The thought of absolute sobriety had never crossed my mind until those talks with Walt. I finally agreed. *Let's give this sobriety thing a try.*

I'm not going to go through and describe what each of those twelve steps in the program entailed. Just know that it sucked and that it worked.

It was fucking hard, though. I had to fundamentally revise my attitude toward alcohol. And as I quickly found out, the center of my problem was the relationship I had with myself. Once I realized that, I was able to start rebuilding from the ground up. It might sound lame and cliché, but who the fuck cares? The result was final: I quit drinking. Holy shit.

Walter went above and beyond his word. He followed through and supported my request to return to the general population. But what I didn't know was that Walter kept going with it, advocating to a judge on my behalf for early parole.

Next thing I knew, I was changing into my street clothes, signing my name on the dotted line, and being buzzed out into a brand-new world.

# EIGHTEEN

## BACK FROM THE DEAD

I walked out of prison for the last time on August 17, 2020. My release was different this time. I wasn't picking up where I left off; I wasn't diving back into the criminality I'd temporarily put on pause for my lockup.

This release was also different because my pops wouldn't be waiting outside to give me a ride. There would be no Quinny and the boys with celebratory liquor and a job; no uncles, wives, brothers, or sisters in a car with the AC on full blast waiting for me. There was nothing outside . . . and I couldn't have been happier. Not because those people weren't there, but because this time was different, that's what excited me. *Change.*

I had been released a total of nine times before, but this was the first time I walked out as a free man. Free to make a decision for myself about my future. In fact, it wasn't "nothing" waiting outside; there was everything: endless possibilities. The only question I had was, *What the fuck do I do now?*

But before we continue, let me clarify a central concept that took me a lifetime to comprehend: freedom. Even now, I am not sure I get the full meaning of the word, but I understand its value.

It is not a simple word to define. The dictionary offers a flaccid clarity that barely scratches the surface. It is such a complex concept that there are entire schools of philosophical thought devoted to its definition, and many cannot find common ground. Because of this, I'm only attempting to define it as it pertains to me in my life.

As far as I am concerned, freedom has little to do with the ability to do whatever one wants, whenever one wants. I did this for years to no avail. I drank, hurt others, and stole to my heart's content, but the more I acted this way, the less free I became. I was a slave to my impulses.

Acting this way, without accountability, places a person at the mercy of fate. Submitting to fate strips you of free will. If every decision is predetermined by destiny, then free choice cannot exist. So, for free will to exist, self-accountability must also exist.

However, relying solely on free will to interpret the meaning of freedom leads to an incomplete definition. I've bought my way out of prison numerous times, but I've never bought freedom. You can't buy it—it's not for sale.

When I returned to my life outside a cell, I was instantly sucked back into a world built by others. Sure, I had carved out my own space, but I was still living in someone else's world, a world that cultivates thoughts and belief systems I wouldn't have given the time of day had I known freedom.

Therefore, there must be an inward component as well when attempting to establish a complete definition. Beliefs must come at one's own discretion, without ultimate influence from others. That's not to say ideologies cannot be learned and adopted from others, only that they cannot be thrust upon you. Similar to the act of strapping blinders to a racehorse so it sees only what the jockey wishes it to see, if an individual is only introduced to certain ideas, they do not have the resources to challenge them. While in pursuit of freedom, skepticism is a vital combatant for blind faith. To achieve freedom, you must, as they say, "Think for yourself."

Combining these elements, we find my definition of freedom at the intersection of inward and outward liberation, where free will, self-accountability, and free thinking are achieved.

My release in 2020 was the first time I found real freedom, and it had taken me forty-nine years. I was finally sober—a necessary place to start.

My work with Walter was the only reason I was allowed back outside. And I wasn't about to forget what he had done for me. I had spent over three decades using alcohol as a crutch, dampening any guilty feelings. But with my new clarity of thought, I was able to face the feelings head on. That didn't free me from the guilt, but I was free from punishing myself over it.

The other difference I encountered upon reentering society this go-around was my lack of clear direction. Like treading water without a strong undercurrent, I had a moment to look around, swim in any direction I pleased. For once, there was time to question if I wanted to return to the same hellish lifestyle. And without inertia forcing me, the decision was easy: fuck no.

By leaving my past behind, I reclaimed my independence for the future.

With this newfound freedom, it might be the part of the book where you expect me to detail my redemption, go off on a diatribe of how great a person I have become—it's not. You can't redeem an irredeemable character in a single story—which is to say, in a single lifetime. It's not believable and it's not true. These things take time, especially with the scorecard of atrocities that I have.

If you expected some fairy-tale happily-ever-after—something to make you go, *Gosh, what a nice and pleasant resolution*—you are reading the wrong book. That's not going to happen here, not yet anyway.

But I have made progress. Plenty of rehabilitation has occurred. So, to answer my previous question, *What the fuck do I do now?* I did exactly what some of you would expect. I adopted another dog.

Loki had been through some trauma as a puppy that really fucked him up. No one at the pound knew what to do with him. He was going after anyone that came within ten feet, snapping at the hands and heels of those who fed him. More than a few potential parents had left the shelter with his teeth marks on their flesh. I was told they were one incident away from putting him down when I arrived. *Sound familiar?*

The staff couldn't understand why it had to be him: the deaf, partially blind, albino American bulldog who bites everyone. He's a fucking lunatic, and I loved him right away.

It took me a couple days to convince the shelter that I was serious about adopting him. But they were easy. It took me a whole month to convince the dog. I had to spend two hours at the pound with him every day so he'd get comfortable with me. I got bit several hundred times, but I didn't care. We understood one another, I think. Eventually it got to the point where I was ready to take him home. I had moved into an apartment in downtown Worcester, right off the main street. The whole apartment was around eight hundred square feet, but when Loki walked in, every inch belonged to him.

When I wasn't down at the shelter, I was giving my time to Walter and the program that had saved my life, however he saw fit. I wanted to give back for once. Go figure.

My first assignment was helping acquire placement in a sober-living house for one of the guys I had just done time with.

Prior to my parole, Brian and I were on the same cellblock—Little Dublin, Walter called it. We had been friendly with one another, but that didn't make us friends. From time to time, he would ask to borrow my hair gel or sneakers or whatever, and I am sure he offered me something of his in return, I just don't remember what it was. We had been on good terms when I left, so of course I agreed to help.

I started the process, calling several people who could do a background check for me on Brian. I would need it to convince whoever was in charge that Brian would be a good tenant.

An hour later, I got a call back. The background check turned up some pretty evil shit. Brian was a fucking wife-beater—an exceptionally awful one at that. Every wife he had had, he beat. His latest outburst landed him in prison and his wife, Charlene, in the hospital with a broken neck from being choked.

After hearing that, the thought of helping this prick disgusted me. I couldn't justify finding him a place and facilitating his bullshit. And I wasn't going to put that woman back into harm's way.

But before I relayed the message to Brian that he could go fuck himself, I wanted to talk to his wife, Charlene. I wanted to verify the accusation, but more importantly, I wanted to make sure that if I refused to help, Charlene wouldn't become a victim.

Through Walter, I was able to find the address where she was staying. It was the only contact information on file, so I wrote a short letter asking her to give me a call. I included my phone number at the bottom, stuffed it into an envelope, and threw it in the outgoing mailbox.

Sometime the next week, shortly after a 6:00 a.m. AA meeting had started, my phone rang. It was Charlene. She had gotten my letter. Instead of talking it out over the phone, I suggested we meet at a coffee shop and talk there. She said that she doesn't drink coffee but agreed to come anyway. *Did Wednesday at ten o'clock work?* She could get tea or something, she said.

Two hours before we were scheduled to meet, my phone rang again. She had to cancel. She had been called into work that morning. I don't remember what I said in response, but somehow I found myself sitting across the dinner table from her later that night.

Now I don't advocate for the pursuit of someone else's wife, but that wasn't the case here. She was quick to tell me how her relationship with Brian had ended. The paperwork wasn't done, but the effect was in place.

We wound up talking long after the restaurant closed. We were finding common ground in every topic that was brought up. She laughed at times; I laughed harder at others. The conversation flowed effortlessly and was the best I had had since talking to my pops. Plus, she was fucking beautiful. *Goddamn!*

Eventually we were kicked out when the last of the kitchen crew was trying to lock up and go home. Before parting ways, we decided to try again and meet at the coffee shop—10:00 a.m. on her next day off. She showed up this time, and the time after that.

This isn't a fucking romance novel, so I'll spare you the rest of the details. But what you need to know is that I got the girl, I had the dog, and I had the apartment; so next on the list was a career.

What did I want to do with my life? I was approaching fifty and didn't have a résumé. I had no intention of building one now. I had other plans; the first of which would focus on taking care of the bills and the second aimed at fulfilling a lifelong dream of mine.

To start, I wanted to reestablish the family business, H&S Custom Home Improvements. Hank always made sure to be there for me, even after his death. I had all the tools, the connections, and the knowledge; it was a no-brainer. And running my own business had the added benefit of providing an employment opportunity for some of the ex-cons Walter was sending me.

But I wasn't born yesterday. I knew I couldn't rely solely on the ex-cons in rehab. I needed a couple other good guys who I could count on. Immediately, Tommy Murphy came to mind. He was an old neighbor of mine who had been a loyal friend for over a decade. He was the type of guy who would bend over backward to help in any way he could. He's also the biggest ballbuster I know. He's quick on the draw to give me shit, but that just makes me like him more.

On top of all that, he's a master carpenter. Needless to say, there wasn't anyone I'd rather work with. He agreed to help without hesitation.

I also decided to reach out to my cousin Eric. He'd been in and out of my life for as long as I could remember. My uncle Howie had kept him out of organized crime, but he still had his own demons from proximity, spillover from association. Although, one positive thing he took from that association was a loyalty to family above all else. He had always been a hard worker too. I was glad when he accepted the job.

With Tommy and Eric on board, I started looking for work: smaller jobs to get the momentum going. A few phone calls led to a few contracts. And those contracts led to more contracts. The ball started rolling . . . and it hasn't stopped.

I need all the help I can get to keep up with it.

*Are you looking for a job, by any chance?*

With the bills being taken care of, I could shift my focus to another passion: music. When I was younger, all I ever wanted was to write and record and perform music. I had even obtained a small degree of success in a rap group along the way, but my other obligations always came first. They had to. I was a criminal after all, not a musician. That wasn't an option for me. There was no time to take it seriously. I was too busy committing crimes or sitting in a cell paying for them.

Now I was out—out of prison and that life. The day finally came to right the wrong I had done to myself by not following my dream. I was ready. Excited. I had a backlog of hundreds of lyrics scratched out in a stack of composition notebooks; I just had to pick one and find a studio. Go from there, one song at a time.

I could have called any of the dozen or so studios I found listed online, but I got lucky. The first call I made was to the Wachusett Recording Company. Owner and founder Mike Harmon answered. I started explaining to him what I was trying to accomplish, the type of sound I was going for, the direction I wanted to take: heavy rock with rap-like lyricism over the top.

Before I finished my pitch, he was sold. He was even giving me ideas of his own, building upon what I had fed to him. The match was perfect. You could tell he was a musical genius, just over the phone. And he backed it up in person when I arrived at his studio. It didn't matter that I wasn't classically educated in the language and terms of music; he understood what I was saying and was able to translate it with instruments. He played all of them.

We finished my first song in under two hours. The second I heard the final product, I knew we were on to something. The sound was raw and visceral: a lethal guitar riff, aggressive drums, and powerful lyrics. It was everything I had been wanting for forty-plus years, exactly as I had imagined.

And just like that, my dream became reality—Test Human, my own band, had their first song, "Genocide." For one of the few times in my life, I had done something I was proud of.

Over the ensuing months, as Mike and I continued working on more songs, something bigger began taking shape, bigger than just me and Test Human. I could start a record company, a company whose vision

THE DEVIL TO PAY

was not to fit into the music industry, but to make room. A company that would create a family of artists with a similar goal: to make real music for real people. As far as I was concerned, the only suitable name for it was Mob Rock Records.

From Mob Rock's conception, I have been extremely fortunate to have talented individuals see its potential and attach themselves to the project, joining the Mob Rock family. Besides Mike Harmon, I was introduced to Rob Schwartz, a music mogul in his own right. His company WHO?MAG Multimedia is a multifaceted pioneer in the industry credited with playing a vital role in bringing hip-hop to the mainstream, public stage. Rob and I became fast friends. He agreed to take on Mob Rock Records as a client and distribute our artists through The Orchard, a subsidiary of Sony Music Entertainment.

Our affiliation with Rob put Mob Rock on the map. Word was getting around. Calls began pouring in, bands wanting me to listen to their music, to sign them. And that's what I did.

With a couple artists and bands on board, in addition to the completion of Test Human's first EP, I started planning a national tour. The only thing missing was the core members of my band. Mike couldn't play every instrument and he had a studio to run, so he was out. I'd have to find talent elsewhere. Big shoes to fill. But as I have said, I have been lucky to attract wildly talented and accomplished people. And through a network of contacts, I met Rotten Rollin.

Roland Banks (his birth name) has been a member of a number of multiplatinum-selling bands. And he's shared the stage with practically everyone at some point, from members of hip-hop's Wu-Tang Clan to the multigenre band Fishbone. You name it, he's probably done it. And the timing of our meeting couldn't have been better for both of us.

His previous band was dealing with a fucking shitstorm. The downfall of any band starts with the frontman every time—without exception. And Roland had been dealing with the asshole of assholes. The frontman of his band had gone off the rails in a ball of fire, completely delusional and deranged from an inflated ego and smoking too much crack.

Roland had put up with it for eight years, and it was time to move on. He was also looking to venture into a solo career; he had his own music he wanted out there. And it just so happened I could offer him both. But it wasn't his drumming ability or his résumé that impressed me most about Roland; it was his character. He has the biggest heart and is the most genuine person I've ever met. To this day, I consider him a brother.

It just made sense for him to become my business partner in Mob Rock Records. I knew he'd always have my back, which is invaluable, and with his decades of experience, knowledge, and connections to the scene, we were able to pull off some pretty cool things.

To date, Test Human has toured around the country twice, headlined at iconic venues, had a song added to the soundtrack of a major motion picture, and collaborated with members of the multiplatinum band Suicidal Tendencies to form a supergroup named Suicidal Human. Mob Rock Records has signed a half-dozen artists, and four of them (Test Human included) have songs being considered for a Grammy Award. Not bad for an old guy trying his hand at something new. We accomplished all that in two years . . . and there's plenty more to come.

Somehow, my life was coming together. I was staying sober. Charlene had moved in—and Loki hadn't eaten her. H&S Custom Home Improvements had steady work, repeat customers. And everything with Mob Rock Records. There was one thing left: my children.

I was finally at a place where I wouldn't be a danger to them. Maybe I'd even be able to help them in some way. It would take a long time to get to that point, though. I knew we're never going to sit around the campfire together and sing kumbaya, but we were never going to be the fucking Brady Bunch anyway. If I wanted a chance to have them back in my life, the first thing I had to address was the fat white elephant in the room. Since they were born, someone else made the decision for them that their father wasn't going to be a part of their lives. That had to change. I wanted to give them the option to tell me to go fuck myself, to fuck off if they didn't want me around. They deserved that much.

I hadn't seen Asia since the hospital, but I got in touch with her first. She made her stance clear: she wasn't going to call me her father right away, but she wasn't opposed to getting a chance to know me. It was all I could ask for, really. And as it turns out, we get along all right. We piss each other off, sure, but that's how it's supposed to be.

About a year and a half after getting out of prison, Charlene and I moved into a big house with a separate live-in apartment attached. We offered the extra space to Asia, who had just informed me she was pregnant again. To my surprise and delight, she took the offer. Moved in the next day. Saara Harper Hill was born nine months later with a full head of bright-orange hair. The cutest, funniest, and happiest baby in the world. And I'm lucky enough to watch her grow up, which she's doing awfully fast.

Rekindling a father-daughter relationship didn't go quite as well with my oldest daughter, Mercedes. She was in trouble when I first contacted her, caught up in the middle of some illegal shit. The conditions of my parole stated that I couldn't legally leave the state, so I had my lawyer Kevin Salvaggio help her out of it. Which he did.

Unfortunately, though, it was the tip of the iceberg. I learned the hard way that there's a lot of my mother in Mercedes. Long story short, a few months later she set me up and got me and some other people close to me into some hot water. Fucking boiling hot water. I don't really want to go into it, it was fucked, I wish I could report otherwise, but we didn't have a relationship after that. There was nothing salvageable.

And that leaves my relationship with my other three children. As it stands, those are yet to be determined. There is still hope there, and I'm hanging on to it. I lost custody of them a long time ago when I went to prison. And unfortunately, while I was locked up, there was an incident between me and their mother's father that resulted in a restraining order. I was barred from having any contact or communication. Nothing whatsoever . . . it was bullshit. And it wasn't their choice.

I fought it tooth and nail for years, trying to get it overturned. I called in every favor I could, offered envelopes of cash to anyone just so I could see them. Nothing worked. The order stands. Fortunately for me, though, my son Chase is turning eighteen soon and will age out of it. He'll be an adult, and I'll give him the same option as my daughters. I wonder what he'll say. More than anything, I'd just like to have lunch, get to know him. I have tried to keep up with him and what is happening in his life, but I know there's a lot to learn. A lot I missed out on.

My two other children will eventually age out too. I'll bide my time, but I won't hold my breath. Besides being told off, I would never expect anything from any of my kids. I don't deserve to do so. I've been lucky enough as it is with Asia and my granddaughter Saara.

So there it is . . . my second attempt at life, and my first attempt at making it my own. It's not perfect, but it beats the hell out of what it used to be.

# AUTHOR'S NOTE

Looking back on everything, it all seems so fucking crazy. It's no wonder I wound up the way I did. A disastrous childhood, a cataclysmic adolescence and young adulthood, an apocalyptic adulthood—not exactly a recipe for success, is it?

This book was one of the most difficult undertakings I have ever attempted. It may seem like an autobiography should be the easiest story to tell. After all, it's just a chronological retelling of the events in one's life. In truth, it's easy to escape into worlds we make up, to find shelter in characters we control inside and out—I envy the novelist's ability to explore truths through fabrication. The process of isolating details of real experiences and weaving them into a made-up tale is an idealistic way to present the author's message. In my experience, it's harder to look in the mirror and write about what you see with brutal honesty, especially when the mirror is telling you things you don't want to hear. *The fucking truth!* For years, I couldn't even look in the mirror. No chance in hell I'd let others look into it.

But in the summer of 2021, everything changed with one of those moments when someone makes a casual, nonchalant comment that completely alters the way you think. My wife, Charlene (we got married on September 11, 2022), said it. She said that nothing I could put in a book would change the man who stood before her, the man she had fallen in love with. That was it: the spark that made me think, made me reconsider the truths I once held.

In one sense we are the complex sum of all our experiences, but in another, who we are is not determined by the actions of our past, but of those in the present. Yes, events of the past can help explain some things, but they need not define anything.

I sat down at my desk and began writing. Immediately I had my first encounter with writer's block. *Ain't that some shit?* The first time I knew all the details was the first time I didn't know how to tell them. For a week, the blank page remained blank. I went through and started analyzing everything I knew about writing, breaking it down to the building blocks of storytelling: plot and character development.

The formula for a plot consists of the setup, rising action, climax, falling action, and resolution. I realize, of course, that there is no hard-and-fast rule, and to say otherwise oversimplifies the complexities of literature. However, there is some value to understanding and dissecting this simple outline.

A good setup allows the reader to immerse themselves into the story, giving them a chance to connect with the main character, or as in the case of a first-person story, the narrator. If this first step is executed exceptionally well, when conflict (rising action) is introduced, the reader is able to experience the struggle alongside the narrator, not just from afar. The key to having a reader walk a mile in the narrator's shoes is to make that character relatable on some level. With luck, the author can get a reader to understand the driving motives behind a character and, subsequently, present an opportunity to feel the same gamut of emotions the character experiences. Essentially, giving the reader firsthand emotions about secondhand experiences.

The trouble with a compelling autobiography is figuring out how to make relatable environments out of foreign settings. What allows every Tom, Dick, and Mary to connect with the shit I went through and the decisions I made? Not an easy question to answer—at ground level, they can't. And it isn't because they are incapable of empathy;

it's because the myriad of bad decisions required to bring them to that point are unfathomable.

So, once again, writer's block took over and the page remained barren. *Fuck.*

It wasn't until, at the recommendation of my agent, I started with an outline. "Start with bullet points," he said. "Take it one true sentence at a time and see where it goes." It was a poor paraphrasing of the classic Hemingway quote, but it carried the same meaning. He was right (so was Hemingway): one sentence led to the next. And an outline provided direction. To start, I gathered tokens of my past (the shit I could find, anyway): photographs, letters, et cetera.

When it comes to writing an autobiography, there is one undeniable advantage to being a lifelong criminal: the state cataloged an accurate timeline of every arrest. My rap sheet would be a good reference, so I went about acquiring it. In Massachusetts, after bypassing a twenty-five-dollar paywall, you can gain access to a digital copy of the arrest record, which I decided to print out.

Twenty-nine pages into the report, my printer ran out of ink . . . twelve pages left in the queue. *Fuck, this was going to be a long process.*

With the outline complete and before it went out to potential publishers, the book needed a title. *Could I summarize the "Sean Scott Hicks story" using only a fragment of one sentence?* No. No single phrase can embody the totality of a life, mine or otherwise. But that's not how fucking books work; they all have fucking titles. Name one that doesn't. You can't.

So, I tried to come up with something, anything, but got nothing.

Then, days later, I came across an old pirate idiom from the 1500s: "The devil to pay and no pitch hot." Looking at the sentence, I realized that at first glance I had misread its meaning. The words *the devil to pay* can easily be used to describe many of the situations I would depict.

If the reader looks at my crimes and sins and takes the lack of legal ramifications into careful consideration, it's easy for them to say, "Oh, well, he must have made a deal with the devil . . . that's what the title is referring to—now he's gotta pay for his end of the bargain." But that misses the whole fuckin' point. Yeah, sure, I have accrued debts no honest man can pay, but I don't owe the devil a fuckin' dime. I didn't take anything from him. I took from my children and my significant others. I took from the people I hurt and their children and their loved ones. I took from my friends who have passed and the few left roaming around above ground. Those are the people I owe, who I am in debt to.

The second half of the saying, ". . . and no pitch hot," refers to the action of sealing the gaps between planks in a ship's hull with cold pitch. Which essentially means fuck all, complete nonsense.

In order to understand the full meaning behind this book's title, you have to take into account the entirety of the old pirate saying.

On long sea voyages, wooden planks of the ship's hull would occasionally separate, and water would leak through the cracks. To plug the leak, an unlucky crew member would go down and pack the opening with tar pitch. The first challenge the crew member would have to overcome was to find where the water was coming in. Going below deck on a pirate ship was to descend into complete darkness, making the task of locating the leak much more difficult. Once the source was located, the crew member filled the gap with melted pitch. Pitch is essentially a solid and unmalleable resin unless it is hot, which it needed to be to plug a leak.

Taking the idiom in its entirety, "The devil to pay and no pitch hot," refers to the descension into darkness, finding the source of a problem before it's too late, fixing it with the limited tools at your disposal, and then somehow returning to the light to face the sun another day. Essentially, it means overcoming a difficult task with the odds stacked against you.

I tailored the phrase only slightly, but the message remains. Most of the content that fills the pages is me wandering around in that darkness, blindly searching for the leak. But I do reemerge. And though the sunlight may be harsh, my eyes are slowly adapting.

So, although it may not be possible to summarize a life with a single phrase, I got damn close.

All that was left to do was write the fuckin' thing. Even with the story laid out for me, it wasn't easy. Because you can't have an autobiography be both thorough and unabashed, I had to choose one. And much to the detriment of my character and legacy, I did my best to stick to the truth.

At no point did I cut corners. I had a responsibility to the truth and to tell it to the best of my ability, which was fucking awful at some moments. Countless times I paused midsentence and thought, *What the fuck am I doing?* But I kept going. I had to.

For obvious reasons, I didn't chronicle every waking moment of my life. That would have dragged down the story and inundated the common reader with monotonous details. For those in the know, I glossed over much of the complexities and intricacies associated with the legal system, among other topics. I tried to strike a fair balance between having a deficit and superfluous amount of detail.

The hard part wasn't the writing aspect but the reopening of closed wounds. Once the scabs were ripped open, words bled onto the page like puddles on the floor of a slaughterhouse.

Then the next issue presented itself: How do you know when to stop writing an autobiography? It is a mildly inconvenient question, to say the least, because you can't just wait for the story to be over—it ends in death . . . my death, at which point I don't think I'll be doing much writing.

Who knows what I'll be doing at that point, and equally unknown is where the fuck I'll end up . . . Your guess is as good as any. Make no mistake, they don't let angels in hell, but they do allow sinners in heaven. I'm just leaving both options open. Someday, I'll find out. It'll be a miracle if I ever get the chance to plead my case to St. Peter—a second O. J. Simpson trial. I know there's at least one person out there who'd pay good money to be a fly on the pearly gate for that conversation.

And all of this is working under the assumption that both or either of these places are real. Maybe I'll be met by forty-two virgins or whatever. That doesn't sound too bad. But more likely I'll be reincarnated as a bug or maybe a raccoon or something. Fuck that, I'd prefer to be dead when I die. As if I get a choice in the matter.

The end of this book isn't the end of the story, but the end of the "background" information—one hell of a setup. I like to think we're somewhere in the "rising action" of the full story and that I still have a few good "climaxes" left in my bones. There's more to come, a lot more. It's just too bad Pops never got a chance to read this and see what I've become—I think he would've got a good kick outta it. At the same time, I wonder what my mother would say, though I doubt she'd bother to pick up a copy. Regardless of their imaginary judgments, it says a lot in and of itself that I finished the fucking thing.

Like it, hate it, use it as kindling to thwart off the chill of winter, I don't give a flying fuck what you do with the book at this point. Completing it was a burden I needed unloading, a shit I needed shat, returning the weight back to Atlas, all twelve steps of recovery wrapped up in a nice bow—take your pick, whatever metaphor suits you best.

For half a century, I walked a well-trodden road to eternal damnation before turning around. It's a long way back to atone for my actions and the harm I caused. I may never get there in this lifetime, I likely won't get all the way, but I'm going to try. I have some time left, so fuck it, I'll give it a go.

# ACKNOWLEDGMENTS

All credit for this book goes to those in my life who contributed to its creation: AJ, my agent, who pushed me to consider the project; Andrew Jones, without whom this project wouldn't be a fraction of what it is today (thank you, brother); and the love of my life, Charlene Margret Hicks. A special thanks goes out to Brendan Deneen of Blackstone Publishing for believing in me and for his guidance and professionalism throughout the writing, editing, and formatting process—you are an absolute gentleman and literary expert in every way.